TWO OWI AIDES RESIGN

**Poulos and Olson Charge Inter-
ference, but Dir...**

WASHIN(
Constantine
Olson of the
mation's For
tion resigned

... the asser-
tion that George W. Healy Jr.,
OWI domestic director, had "hamstrung" the activities of their division. Mr. Healy quickly issued a
statement declaring the claim un-
true.

Mr. Poulos, acting chief of the
section, and Mr. Olson, assistant
chief, contended that what they
termed interference by Mr. Healy
and Dowsley Clark, who is director of the OWI News Bureau, had
prevented them from functioning
to offset Axis propaganda aimed
at creating dissension among
America's 35,000,000 citizens of
foreign ancestry.

Mr. Healy's statement said his
sole "interference" had been to insist that the information dispensed
by Mr. Poulos' section be checked
for accuracy before being distributed to American newspapers
printed in foreign languages. Mr.
Healy announced that Achilles M.
Sakell, an employe of OWI since
its inception, had been appointed
as new chief of the section.

a little history

a little history

Ammiel Alcalay

edited with a preface by Fred Dewey

re: public / UpSet Press

Los Angeles —— New York

re: public is an ongoing project dedicated to fostering and preserving principles of a democratic republic in culture, thought, and the public realm. This book is published and distributed in collaboration with UpSet Press, an independent press based in Brooklyn. The original impetus of UpSet Press was to upset the status quo through literature. The press has expanded its mission to promote new work by new authors; the first works, or complete works, of established authors, including restoring to print new editions of important texts; and first time translations into English. Established in 2000, UpSet Press organized readings and writing workshops until 2005, when it published its first book, Theater of War, by Nicholas Powers. The University of Arkansas Press became UpSet's official distributor in 2011. For more information, visit upsetpress.org.

Graphics consultant, Biotop 3000.

ISBN: 9780976014287
Library of Congress Control Number: 2012940481

Printed in the United States of America

For Luis Villalta, in good memory (1940–2012)

¡Oh, qué anciano soy, Dios santo,
oh, qué anciano soy!...
¿De dónde viene mi canto?
Y yo, ¿adónde voy?

Rubén Darío

And for Peter Anastas, Diane di Prima,
Benjamin Hollander & Duncan McNaughton,
true companions, all

"it's getting late now"

Albert Ayler

CONTENTS

EDITOR'S PREFACE

a little history is a rich work of discovery, recovery, and
response whose purpose is to dig, to find, and to preserve.
The lectures that provided a beginning for the heart of the
book—investigating international politics through the lens
formed by the work and choices of Gloucester poet and
thinker Charles Olson—were delivered at Cornell in 2002
and at Poet's House in New York City in 2004. While the consequence of these talks, delivered by poet, translator, critic,
and scholar Ammiel Alcalay, has percolated out—through
public events, a web site, and Alcalay's crucial *Lost & Found*
chapbook series at CUNY's Graduate Center, recovering lost
works—the original thinking has existed, until now, only in
clandestine form.

The impetus for the talks and the book emerged out
of conversations Alcalay and I had before 9/11, assembling
materials to accompany his book-length poem *from the
warring factions. a little history,* crafted, re-written, spoken,
developed, and researched over a decade, presents a series
of examples that, while they build around Olson's work, seeks
to develop its implications in multiple directions. New materials have been added, edited, and developed from a wildly
divergent, even conflicting set of registers. The final result is
a living, breathing experimental archaeology of our ongoing
present. Alcalay sheds light on, formally explores, and builds
up the historical existence of a poetics serious and powerful
enough to respond to the world, to facts and events, *from*
the world.

In the introduction to his earlier, groundbreaking 1993
work, *After Jews and Arabs: Remaking Levantine Culture,*
Alcalay speaks of "the swamp" where virtually everything

seems to end up, countering this with a quote from the Palestinian poet Mahmoud Darwish: *Make amends with your past, date your wounds and your estrangement.* To do this, it now seems, requires carving stone paths through the propaganda undoing memory, the ability to witness, and the capacity for depth. The response here develops in an entirely new direction the basic method of Alcalay's earlier effort, turning it fully towards life lived in, and born of, "these United States." In the process, Alcalay affirms a principle of scholarship at odds with almost all reigning models. Knowledge is firmly and clearly rooted in an ethics of risk and responsibility. This must begin with a frank confrontation with the exclusions and suppressions that underly much of what we have been taught is legitimate.

Our lives and our knowledge are subject to an ever-burgeoning regime of sanctions and foreclosure, manufacturing an increasingly mental and political form of structural adjustment. Debts, burdens, and wounds are piled on, as if to rob us of experience, facts, and our capacities. The poets featured in Alcalay's work, and the examples of their work that Alcalay focuses on expose this world in its formation, presenting a way of living that answers it and refuses to conform.

What is genuinely surprising, and wonderful, about the material here is not only how Alcalay teases out much needed evidence, but how the poets and works featured show us what an honest, engaged, and experimental response might be and could be. The ability to personally gain traction in the world is crucial to any sense of reality or power. This becomes, again, a question of organization. The poets answer this. They can, if one follows the evidence Alcalay offers, help to reconstruct our experience, and, most importantly, to learn, as if for the first time, how to do this. Much of what these poets combat is born of what President Eisenhower, in his farewell speech—having seen so much war—called "the disastrous rise of misplaced power." This "power," if power it even is, is bound in war and conquest. Since the end of the 19th century, it has more than shaped U.S. society, its so-called "culture," the so-called "popular," and all we are permitted to see, hear, and bring to fruition.

That power is misplaced infuses everything we now do and are. We might call this "injustice," but the problems Alcalay's deep ethics seek to address are structural and not merely moral. Poets deal with the organization of language, thought, and image directly. Those who provide us with courageous examples, both here and abroad, work in a terrain of organization. This is why Alcalay demands we look carefully at notions of authority, the native, the classic, and what we consider to be settled. Can we answer the dispossessions and expropriations making up what Olson first called the "unrelieved"? The beginning step is to ground ourselves in the deeds and words of those who, at great personal risk, seek to speak, in the form of poetry, about the country they are in, its deeds and words, and so help us find and take back a body of experience that has been systematically taken from us.

The book Alcalay has written does not seek answers or formulas, but rather to foster and inspire, through deliberate experiment with form and content, each person's search for what Olson called "the evidence of what is said." This search is realized by those willing to risk. It is the courage of such an exploration—working against all forms of bureaucracy, inertia, violence, and suppression, and relentlessly exposing each—that can provide us with tools to recover what has been waylaid, buried, torn out, or forced into chains. The writer and exile James Baldwin put this challenge best, in a late book brilliantly titled *The Evidence of Things Not Seen*: "I am referring to the movement of the human soul, in crisis, which, then, is forced to reexamine the depths from which it comes in order to strike water from the rock of the inheritance."

Senator Robert LaFollette, Sr., from Wisconsin, gave public shape to the urgency of such matters a century ago, on October 6, 1917. Speaking to the Senate, addressing a wave of suspension of rights, on the eve of entry into a war to consolidate a new, total organization of control over politics in the U.S.A., Senator LaFollette said "now is precisely the time when the country needs the counsel of all its citizens." This profound, courageous, and democratic call is so buried and crushed that we must, as it were, start from scratch, from under the rubble. To do so we need precisely the kind of work done here by Alcalay—to find and preserve those who care enough, are tough enough, to strike water from the rock of the inheritance. Only then can we, and others, recover that body of experience necessary for a political realm that is truly ours.

For me, the beginning of the project, back in the days before 9/11, was a quote Alcalay offered me, now repeated in the book. It was Olson's statement, years earlier, at the start of book three of the *Maximus Poems*, where, addressing Gloucester and the world, the poet announces he has set out "to write a Republic / in gloom on Watch-House point." In this one quote one could feel a whole landscape opening up. Alcalay has attempted to describe this landscape, to preserve its *existing* documentation. With his life drained and near its end, Olson concludes his *Maximus*

Poems with a call that remains as daring and unbowed now as it was then. We must initiate, Olson says, "another kind of nation." Alcalay opens that door, and it is our task to stand up and walk through it.

—Fred Dewey, Berlin and Los Angeles,
September 2012

a little history

"IF ALL THE WORLD WERE PAPER"

—for Jess Collins, in memoriam

I.

Life opens out of a dream of the end
I thought I wrote about but only spoke of
that night in the snow
of Baghdad (the poem in Arabic)
the huge crowd now part of
"the great unraveling"
the generations
turning
almost everyone gone
the mantle
there
to be taken up
like a gauntlet
the dead everywhere
I can hardly remember them

TRUTH IS MARCHING IN illuminated

even a glimpse into your life
as it got darker and the fabric
ripped the idea to find a republic
UNDERGROUND undone now
by a watermelon patch
by a thatched hut
a horse and buggy
a door in time

II.

sick in bed
turning
       I have seen green globes of water
a field of pumpkins grown for seed
a castle spun from yarn
the place of the lion

     "you turn off the light and turn on the dark"
     "you turn off the dark and turn on the light"

      "ON THE WAY TO ROSE MOUNTAIN
      THE TRUTH SHALL BE THY WARRANT"
      "YOUNG PEOPLE
      IN PARTICULAR
      WILL FIND IT"

"WHEN WILL WE,"

  "CROSSING AND RECROSSING THE HEART,"

    "TEMPT THE FRAILTY OF OUR POWERS,"

      "TORTURE THE EAGLE TILL SHE WEEP?"

1

In 1989, I returned to New York from five years in Jerusalem,
the second leg of a circuitous journey that both expanded
my horizons and complicated my relationship to what I had
once grasped as a purely American idiom, as "the pure products of America" themselves, of which I both was and was
not one. I had grasped at this idiom like someone drowning
might grab at a rope. I brought back with me the manuscript
of what would become my *After Jews and Arabs: Remaking
Levantine Culture*, a book destined to make the rounds for
four years before finding a publisher. It would inspire some
of the cultural openings I have come to question. While my
political involvements in Jerusalem informed every sentence
of that book, the form it took—at least on the surface—did
not match the intensity that I felt needed to be conveyed
about my experiences. As I underwent waves of erosion and
sedimentation, resettling in a place that had once been
home, it became clear to me that I would have to put some
messages into bottles or they would break into irretrievable
fragments. I began work on *Understanding Revolution*, a
piece that evolved into *the cairo notebooks*, a text for which, in
many ways, my *After Jews and Arabs* was an elaborate set of
footnotes. It was then I started looking around to see what
kinds of things people were doing, or not doing, and where
such things were either published or not published. Several
journals—purportedly progressive both politically and formally—rejected *Understanding Revolution*, ostensibly on
stylistic grounds. It was then that I re-established contact
with Gil Ott.

I had first come across Gil in the mid-1970s, long before
my trip to Jerusalem, through early issues of his *Paper Air,*

shown to me by a dear and sadly departed friend, the sculptor and musician Brad Graves. Brad had worked with John Taggart on material that Gil published. I had been a reader of Taggart's *Maps*, and even sent John a query of some kind. *Maps*, like *Paper Air* and the dozens of other little magazines that had been passed on to me through my parents (*Black Mountain Review, Origin, Evergreen, Big Table, Kulchur, Yugen, Floating Bear, Neon, Set*, etc.), or that I came to follow (*Caterpillar, Bezoar, Vortex, Fire Exit, Intransit, Intrepid, Io, Living Hand, Text, Sun & Moon, Vital Statistics, Big Sky, Angel Hair*, and so many others), formed a kind of autobiography of association out of which I would eventually be able to reconstruct a sense of myself. I had been living in New York, working at a variety of jobs—construction, building superintendent, auto mechanic/body repair, truck driver, laundromat manager, bookstore manager—and writing. Formally, I took classes with Toby Olson and Gilbert Sorrentino at the New School before going, off and on, to City College. Through Toby Olson and his life in Philadelphia, Gil's presence again manifested itself and, even though we still hadn't met, *Paper Air* remained in my inventory of things to look for and pay attention to.

In Gil, I encountered an interlocutor who had chosen a way of life that could embody his aesthetic and political intentions. As we worked together in editing the piece that would become *the cairo notebooks*, I found Gil knew what he *didn't* know about the particulars of the situation I was describing. He knew exactly what conclusions the addition of missing information might lead to. I was feeling isolated in an everyday existence whose instigating sources I had to uncover, or perhaps rediscover, if I was ever going to translate perceptions into political activities. Gil served as an example. He was someone going about his business in an imperfect realm he would simply rather not add to. The literary and political sources on the Middle East that he was familiar with were just right, allowing him to build on a solid foundation rather than, as is most often the case with people, having to begin by pulling apart a weak foundation of misconceptions and false assumptions. This ability to transpose and apply his political and aesthetic knowledge and intuitions to situations was a source of continual sustenance to me. In his capacity at The Painted Bride, a public art space in Philadelphia, Gil took more than some public risk in producing an evening on Palestine presented by myself and the Palestinian artist Kamal Boullata—at a time when any public manifestation regarding Palestine was rare and embattled.

When writing about the Lebanese writer Etel Adnan, I have referred to the permission her work gave me to explore a sense of historical burden uncommon in American discourse. Gil's suggestion and offer to publish *the cairo notebooks* with his Singing Horse Press was a defining instance of this permission, akin to music that I had absorbed even further back, following the American poet Robert Duncan, "as if it were a scene made up by the mind, / that is not mine, but is a made place." Gil's place was very made and very concrete. We worked out the details of my book together, slowly and with great care, from the photographs to its irregular size and its odd reverse order in which the lines of each fragment end at the bottom of the page, only to scroll back above or below the horizon line, represented by the elegantly side-barred numbers a third of the way up each leaf.

It was this quality of Gil's work and presence that I want to emphasize, his way of being as editor and publisher, in the face of small and large scale conglomeration, exclusion, and erasure. Within *Paper Air*, Gil managed many such meetings between covers that would have been difficult, if not impossible, in "real" time. Gil moved across aesthetic and political lines, his way local, unpatronizing, non-ideological, generous, and fiercely independent. I realize now that he is gone that no matter how time-consuming and difficult his work as an editor, publisher, and activist was for him, he saw such outwardly directed activities as an integral part of his work as a poet. It is out of such a fabric and commitment that the best of our culture, a home-made culture we can claim to be a part of, is woven and preserved.

The ancient Egyptians and Sumerians used stone or parchment; our collective memory is often stored in much more precarious forms—letters, newspapers, and books, acetate, vinyl, photographs, emulsion-coated films, and digital media—requiring labor intensive recuperation, storage, indexing, and care. On a bicoastal itinerary from New York to San Francisco, with major stops in Boston, Boulder, Vancouver, and Los Angeles, you can find thousands of these decaying materials—from countless rare publications and chapbooks to reels of audio, film, and video. Four of the most important collections of such literary materials are those of the Poetry Project in New York City (now at the Library of Congress), the Poetry Archives at San Francisco State University, the Jack Kerouac School of Disembodied Poetics at Naropa University in Boulder, Colorado, and Beyond Baroque in Los Angeles. These materials have mainly to do with what came to be called the New American Poetry, through the publication of Donald Allen's 1960 anthology, and include a wide range of movements and groupings that either named themselves or were given names (the San Francisco, Venice, and New York Beats; the San Francisco Renaissance, Black Mountain, the New York School, Umbra, the Black Arts Movement) as well as many other loosely affiliated clusters and individuals.

Before these materials disappear, you can still listen to Langston Hughes in 1958 praising Kenneth Rexroth and Lawrence Ferlinghetti for initiating poetry-and-jazz performances the year before—an audio moment linking the Harlem Renaissance, the San Francisco Renaissance, and the Beats. You can watch James Baldwin discuss his novel *Giovanni's Room* with Philip Roth in 1960. While the tape and film last, you can watch John Cage persisting in a performance piece about Henry David Thoreau on the night Richard Nixon resigned—as the audience, wanting to celebrate, gets steadily wilder. You can see a San Francisco poetry reading for Gay Liberation in 1971, or Allen Ginsberg in the basement at City Lights bookstore discussing William Carlos Williams, joined by Neal Cassady informing him of a recent arrest. You might see young Alice Walker discussing Zora Neale Hurston when Hurston was still forgotten, and Walker hardly known.

Letters of prominent literary and cultural figures, while preserved, are often housed in disparate institutions, remaining unedited, unlinked, and out of touch with each other. Distortions can be introduced, depending on which letters are seen, and where. The record of work, as well as of the coming together of people in common endeavor and friendship, is atomized, pulled apart, stored in separate containers, making it much harder for us to inhabit coherent stories, to make sense of ourselves, our history, and the times we live in. Properly preserved, these materials offer context that is absolutely essential and provides an invaluable legacy—readings, classes, public discussions, correspondence, and other encounters with many of America's most important writers of the past fifty years. They need to be available to the public in accessible and stable formats, much as the Smithsonian Institute has preserved our musical and technological heritage, or we will lose what the Arab poet Adonis has called "an innate quality." Without this, all we will have is the corporate version of, say, Jack Kerouac, in the name of selling pants—the cropped, airbrushed "Beat" posing in khakis, without then-companion Joyce Johnson in the background. We will not have the dense literary, poetic, and social culture from which that photo was lifted. There are, for example, only two archives I am aware of dedicated exclusively to housing underground newspapers, self-published poetry chapbooks, and other ephemeral materials by veterans of the war in Vietnam. The work of Timothy Clover, killed in Vietnam in 1968, is a remarkable instance of an essential but ephemeral document—it exists, as far as I am aware, in only two copies.

The poem by Clover, below, has been an ever-present inspiration to me since I first encountered it in Jan Barry and W.D. Ehrhart's groundbreaking anthology, *Demilitarized Zones: Veterans After Vietnam*. It stands with the greatest World War I poems, such as those by Wilfred Owen, Siegfried Sassoon, or Charles Hamilton Sorley.

THE GIFT

What can I give you, child of the Asian sun?
Child of the holy rain, what shall it be?
You stand by the road, hopeful-eyed tiny one

Silent your cry though it echoes inside me,
Burns in the hollowness that once was a boy like you
When the future was vague and the whole world was new.

But when you are six you'll have twice the years I've had
Learning that no one cares if you are good or bad
When you're a gook and I'm a white man
Who preaches ideals and takes what he can. Tyranny's only a
fact of your life, my friend.
Do you expect me to help you pretend
That I'll give you your freedom, the better to live?
I've nothing inside me, so here's what I'll give: I'll bury your
father who died by my hand
And build you a desert on your green land.
You'll have soldiers for brothers and if you want more,
For your sister or mother I'll give you a whore.

Why do you stare at me, shining-eyed ageless one?
Am I accused of betraying a trust?
Wheels are turning and leave you I must.
Your home is all burning: I give you the dust.

The implications of our ignorance regarding such a poem's existence—the record of a journey into the depths of our collective national consciousness—are staggering.

While "deconstruction" has been the reigning theoretical rage in academia, driven by fantasies of rendering Western culture powerless through critical discourse, projects characterized by construction, reconstruction, and historical recuperation provide people with real political footing. We can see this in projects as varied as *Sir, No Sir!*, David Zeiger's groundbreaking documentary on the GI movement to end the war in Vietnam, recovering rare footage, documentation of unknown base newspapers, and historical research; in Milliarium Zero, Winterfilm, and the Vietnam Veterans Against the War's reissue of *Winter Soldier*, preserving footage of the soldier-run investigations that took place in Detroit in 1971; in *Polis Is This: Charles Olson and the Persistence of Place*, a film by Henry Ferrini, twelve years in the making, in which Ferrini starts from present day Gloucester to create a broad historical context for the poet and thinker's work; in *A Secret Location on the Lower East Side*, the massive documentation project of the independent post-WWII literary small magazine scene, put together by Steven Clay and Rodney Phillips; and in something like the Albert Ayler *Spirit Box*, with its meticulous, extensive presentation, including reproduction of the extremely rare Black Arts publication *Cricket*.

In the preservation of such a history, it is crucial that we weigh and measure our efforts in light of our relationship to, and reception of, things that take place in other parts of the world. Otherwise, no matter how profound the personal impact of such acts of creation and preservation might be, they can revert to mere markers of identity and ownership. They cease to serve as proof of the refusal to let our histories and experiences be administered.

Following WWII, our most courageous North American poets, artists, and thinkers removed themselves from the restraining orders of Cold War vocabularies and structures, going underground to create their own channels of communication. One of these, the writer Robert Duncan, wrote:

The Symposium of Plato was restricted to a community of Athenians, taking its stand against lower or foreign orders,

not only of men but of nature itself. The intense yearning, the
desire for something else, rises not in our identification in a
hierarchy of higher forms but in our identification with the
universe. To compose such a symposium of the whole, such a
totality, all the old excluded orders must be included. The
female, the proletariat, the foreign; the animal and vegetative;
the unconscious and unknown; the criminal and failure—all
that has been outcast and vagabond must return to be admit-
ted in the creation of what we consider we are.

As part of a planetary consciousness, people all over the
world have come to similar conclusions, and poetry as a
form of knowledge has played a crucial role. The French
philosopher Jean-Paul Sartre wrote: "The crisis of language
which broke out at the beginning of this [20th] century is a
poetic crisis." And the Martiniquan poet Aimé Césaire, in
Discourse on Colonialism, wrote: "Poetic knowledge is born
in the great silence of scientific knowledge."

Adonis, born Ali Ahmed Said in 1930 in Syria, has
expanded this, giving it broader implications: "When there
is no poetry in a period of history, there is no true human
dimension. Poetry, according to this definition, is more
than a means or a tool, like technology: it is, rather, like
language itself, an innate quality. It is not a stage in the history of human consciousness, but a constituent of this consciousness." Spending the bulk of his mature, creative life
between Beirut and Paris, Adonis has sought to redefine a
specific language of poetry and codify the materials from
which language derives itself. He occupies a space in the
history of language as far removed as possible from what
he has referred to as "the poet as manufacturer who trans-
forms words into a product." Even if they are its prisoner or

in exile from it, contemporary Arab poets must speak *outside* the state, and when they speak of Palestine, they must speak of a place that once existed but does not yet exist. Language becomes a dwelling place significantly more tangible and real than the bookish homelands fashioned by current theories. We should remember that Dante leaves his guide Virgil behind and so condemns the pagan world to oblivion. To the Guyanese writer Wilson Harris, such an act is an amputation, creating a phantom limb, invisible but still felt. For Adonis, no part of language can be left behind. It is a wound that must be explored, inhabited, discovered, lost, and rediscovered again and again. As he writes: "This language that suckles me betrays me... I walk along the edge of a time that has not come."

Because of the specificity of language and Adonis's central role in redefining the Arabic language, the concerns of his poetry and poetics are necessarily our concerns. In the 1950s—like American poets—Adonis responded to official versions of the world that bore no relationship to living political, historical, and aesthetic realities. In creating new communities of thought, another form of kinship could base itself on poetic knowledge. Adonis writes: "I call the 'total poem' a poem which ceases to be merely an emotional moment but becomes a global moment in which the intuitions of philosophy, science, and religion embrace each other. The new poem is not only a new form of expression but also a form of existence." The American poet Robert Creeley, in conversation with Allen Ginsberg at the Vancouver Conference in 1963, put this in a larger frame: "All the terms of consciousness are undergoing tremendous change... the change occurring now is more significant than the Second World War by far, because it's the residue of the war in reference to the atom bomb and, equally, the shift in all terms of human relationship that have been habitualized for thousands of years." Charles Olson wrote: "What does not change / is the will to change." Adonis writes: "Man is essentially a will to create and to change."

While there are many ways to read Adonis's poetry of intimacy and his embrace of humanity, his constant use of paradox in relation to what is imaginable remains essential. As in the story of the 8th century poet Abu Nuwas, he has learned everything about poetry only to forget it. An encounter with a word or a concept makes you feel you are seeing it for the first time. In this way, poetry can resist domination, even of its own orders. When Adonis asks: "How did knowledge transform into shackles?" it is not only the petty tyrants who are implicated but ourselves, as readers or writers. Robert Duncan writes: "I have to break up orders, to loosen the bindings of my own conversions, for my art too constantly rationalizes itself, seeking to perpetuate itself as a conventional society. I am trying to keep alive our awareness of the dangers of my own convictions."

We are being asked not to let our own assumptions bind us. When Adonis writes: "Say: mass graves. Do not say: My poetry was a rose and became blood," reader and writer are mutually entangled in a search for meaning that leads into "the abyss of the alphabet." If we are blinded by the darkness of this world, the abyss is also a place of infinite combination, of infinite possibility, in which new meanings, new memories, and new realities can be excavated from all that has come before us. Zora Neale Hurston once wrote that "the group mind uses up a great part of its life span trying to ask of infinity some questions about what is going on around its doorsteps." No matter how far Adonis journeys into the infinite realms of time and space, history, or the cosmos, he remains acutely aware of these doorsteps, just like the one he stepped out of long ago in his native village of Qassabin.

Until recently, the dominance of Zionist points of view has tainted the reception of the Middle East in the United States, especially concerning Arabic, the Middle East's dominant literary tradition. For years, Adonis, perhaps the Arab literary world's single most important figure, was ignored here. We find ourselves in a position where, while Arabic writing in translation has become somewhat more available, as in all such energy transfers, the movement is contradictory. The sudden appearance of major poets like an Adonis or Mahmoud Darwish in places like the *New Yorker* or on major publisher lists can, in its way, be attributed to the U.S. occupation of Iraq, even as pressure for such work to appear in mainstream venues must be attributed to the tireless work of translators and advocates working for decades outside the mainstream.

The work of Palestinian poet Samih al-Qasim is a case in point. His book *Sadder Than Water,* published in 2006, provides access to poems of international and historical significance and resonance. The most important of these, "Kafr Qasem," is dedicated to the victims of the infamous 1956 Israeli massacre of Palestinian villagers in the Galilee. But as we are drawn to the power and terrible beauty of these and other poems, we can be prevented from thinking about the role translation from conflicted zones plays in our imperial landscape and the enforcement and coercion that determine this landscape.

The predominance of single collections of poetry and novels devoid of context can contribute to a larger erasure nearly as destructive as overt loss and decay of materials. This restriction has the paradoxical effect of legitimizing generic categories and new critical receptions of "works of art" as "aesthetic" objects. Even if these works provide an opportunity for individuals, and especially other writers, to face challenging encounters, the public learns little about why things are written and the vast tradition of which they are a part. What we are now most in need of is the extra-literary: the poetics and polemics; letters and newspaper exchanges; biographies and gossip; all the barnacles and detritus that go into situating a culture densely within its time and place. As Adina Hoffman tells us in her introduction to *Sadder Than Water*, al-Qasim's

ample journalistic and critical writings over the years have revealed an especially engaged and open sensibility... he has mused on a wide variety of political, literary, and cultural subjects—from Ho Chi Minh's prison diaries to Israel's bombardment of Beirut to Meir Kahane's racism to the artistry of Egyptian story writer Yusuf Idris.

As one of the primary Palestinian poets of resistance, al-Qasim forms part of the international decolonization movement, one whose significance "post-colonial" theories, the rhetoric of globalization, neo-liberal economics, and aesthetic "appreciation" of "global" poetry often dispense with. Culture in much of the world outside the United States finds anchor in just such bedrock political, economic, historical, and aesthetic assumptions, and it is out of these that al-Qasim's poetry emerges. Material and class references make up the inspiration that brings us humanly close to the poet's world:

You die and remember.
Armies have passed,
and coffins... And you ask:
Was that the peace of wars?
Were those the wars of peace?
And you ask how you die and recall
an aged child,
an old man whose childhood hasn't departed,
the torture of domes and silence of graves,
and you are patient with patience—
alone and sad.
Sadder than water.

This "aged child" is also the "child of the holy rain" in
Vietnam that Timothy Clover's poem addresses, but the
reigning fiction about the place of poetry in American society makes such connections almost impossible to understand. These connections and allegiances are not self-evident
but need to be forged through personal initiatives made visible and available as challenges to what is allowed to pass for
cultural and political history. The key, then, is not to treat
someone like al-Qasim as simply a window into another
world but as a means of finding our own. Having the
courage to take up the historical burden also means knowing how precarious and open to manipulation cultural
materials are, how necessary it is not just to preserve them
but to reanimate the contexts in which they were created.

2

Following the events of 9/11, I was having a difficult time finding an outlet for my writing in the United States. As a result, I began contributing regularly to *Dani* and *Feral Tribune,* two papers in Bosnia and Croatia open to me because of my work with certain journalists and writers during the war in ex-Yugoslavia. We had a true sense of mutual understanding and reciprocity. In one of a series of columns called "Politics & Imagination," I wrote that 9/11 did not, contrary to cliché, represent a failure of intelligence gathering and security institutions. Rather, it represented a systemic failure permeating all that Americans have allowed into, and pursued through, the imagination. Contrary to the way Paul Wolfowitz and other officials of the time used the word "imagination"—as in acts "we" could or couldn't "imagine terrorists perpetrating"—the real failure revealed itself in the restrictions put on "imagining" what our own government might or might not be capable of doing to others and to its own citizens.

Restrictions like this have long obscured the reciprocal relationship between cause and effect, between what our government does, purportedly in our name, and the steady blowback that follows. This blowback reaches far, surfacing in the way intellectuals, writers, poets, and artists respond and act. The systemic failure is hardly limited to government institutions; it permeates imagination, erecting restrictive forms of behavior to short-circuit and curtail the kinds of knowledge that might lead to changes in political and cultural consciousness.

As the media bombards us with ignorance, misinformation, and disinformation, as the United States government continues to try to violently rearrange the political, economic and cultural allegiances around the world, it becomes almost impossible to imagine the cultural space of other times. From the late 1950s to the late '60s, for example, texts, documents, imaginative works, and popular actions sympathetic to, and emerging from the cauldron of decolonization struggles made the relationships between cause and effect, repression and resistance, colonizer and colonized, visible. Henri Alleg's *The Question*, Pierre Bourdieu's *The Algerians*, Pierre Vidal Naquet's *Torture: Cancer of Democracy*, Simone de Beauvoir and Gisele Halimi's *Djamila Boupacha*, Albert Memmi's *The Colonizer and the Colonized*, the writings of Frantz Fanon, Gillo Pontecorvo's film *The Battle of Algiers*—these and many other resources were easily available in the United States, depicting a contentious political reality that was neither ignored, trivialized, nor theorized out of existence.

Organizationally, the time was remarkable. The Black Panther Party, following in the footsteps of Malcolm X and generations of black thinkers and activists, made efforts to establish diplomatic and cultural ties with newly independent states in Africa, reaching outside usual categories in an attentive and active way. There was tremendous risk involved in trying to bring home the vocabulary of decolonization. There was even greater risk in seeking the intellectual and communal support necessary to achieve this. On the one hand, the Panthers were a deliberately localized organization, responding to local conditions in particular neighborhoods, organizing to protect and enhance their communities on the ground. On the other hand, they needed protection, and that came through global recognition and solidarity. Moving into an international arena, however, exposed the

Panthers and other radical movements, already vulnerable to infiltration and disinformation, to great danger. Internationalization provided the perfect excuse to represent these home-grown movements as anti-American, and to separate them from local and popular bases of support.

It is ironic that, while COINTELPRO, the FBI's covert operation to subvert political activities, worked tirelessly at home to force a wedge between Jews and African-Americans and between African-Americans themselves, fabricating and fomenting irreconcilable differences, the Moroccan intellectual and future political prisoner Abraham Serfaty, a Jew, delivered a "salute to the African-Americans." This was at the 1969 Pan-African Cultural Festival in Algeria, a festival featuring Archie Shepp performing with North African Tuareg musicians, long before "world music" had become a fashionable commodity. It was a time when American soldiers in Vietnam were fighting amongst themselves almost as fiercely as they fought the Vietnamese. Domestic alliances were splintering, as the country divided bitterly over the ever more pointless last years of the war. Veterans were returning home, in some cases, to the charred ruins of de-industrialized cities and towns, drifting into drugs, drink, and homelessness. Adding insult to injury, representations of the brave struggles of many of these veterans in the anti-war movement would be distorted, manipulated, and, finally, turned against vets themselves.

This was the time when United States policy shifted completely towards Israel, following the June War of 1967. From that point on, almost everything coming into the United States from the Middle East was filtered through a mainstream Zionist narrative, from political history and cinematic representations to the structure of novels and poetry. At the same time, the model of self-defense and community control was attacked by the state. The Panthers followed in a long line of self-defense and local control movements, from the Revolutionary War to returning African-American veterans of the Civil War, from Reconstruction up through the struggles of the 20th century—one notable example being activist Robert F. Williams, author of *Negroes With Guns*, who armed against vigilante terrorism. These were part of a tradition that would enable the most dramatic achievements of the Civil Rights movement, only to be deemed, like veterans against war, "un-American."

In the shift from the local, the model of self-defense was neatly displaced onto the defense of something else. A new model, Israel, fit retroactively into standard accounts of cultural retention and the pioneering movement of westward expansion. Black-Jewish relations became a battleground, as a globally unpopular foreign policy was made domestically bulletproof. Identity politics and nationalisms of all stripes began to spread through North American discourse, eventually settling into a "multiculturalism" that was in some ways, in terms of the world at large, cut off from access to examples of common political power at the local, country-wide, and international levels. The matter of Palestine would become the litmus test, saturating countless aspects of American intellectual and political life with collusion and collaboration. Very few public voices rose to face the realities and consequences of Israel's expanding occupation and influence. Lobbying power and policy interests parlayed into a broad policing of imaginative boundaries. Certain things became unimaginable and unsayable. At the same time, other things, always off-stage or under the cloak of the covert, became publicly imaginable, sayable, and real for the first time.

It is no accident that the prime mover of the first Gulf War was the only U.S. president after the fall of Saigon to openly mention Vietnam in an inaugural address—George Bush Sr.: "The final lesson of Vietnam is that no great nation can long afford to be sundered by a memory." Bush Sr. left to the imagination what these sundering memories might be, and what exactly this implied. As a former director of the CIA, Bush could not have uttered a phrase like this without a clear understanding of its effect or consciousness of his part in Cold War political and economic interests. Vietnam had given way to covert backyard wars of the 1980s, with things like the Phoenix Program expanded globally, followed by Bush Sr.'s first made-for-television, prime time global bonanza, the Gulf War. From 1990 until 9/11 and the assault on Afghanistan—through bureaucratic stereotyping, slander, and suppression of the effects of U.S. policies in Palestine—reality was reshaped to create the narrative of a relentless and unyielding enemy, a binary formula whose default position could only be a "victimized Muslim," as in Bosnia, or an "evil-doer" Muslim all over the world as a threat to "our freedom."

To retrieve the cultural and political complexities of the Arab, Middle Eastern, or Islamic world, and to try to think about their meaning for daily life in America is a formidable task. While conventional wisdom has it that culture and writing are too marginalized to matter, the opposite holds true—it is through poetry that new relations, disruptions, and interventions can occur, that assumptions can be challenged and the imagination opened up. The American poet Muriel Rukeyser outlined this in the 1940s, in *The Life of Poetry*:

Everywhere we are told that our human resources are all to be used, *that our civilization itself means the uses of everything it has—the inventions, the histories, every scrap of fact. But there is one* kind *of knowledge—infinitely precious, time-resistant more than monuments, here to be passed between the generations in any way it may be: never to be used. And that is poetry.*

As our cultural borders are ever more heavily policed, as mop-up operations to consolidate official versions of history move into high-gear—from new affirmations of the lone gunman theory in the Kennedy assassination to the reductive stereotyping and marketing of Beat and hippy culture, promoting them as usable tools of American cultural domination—the objective of such explicit and implicit campaigns, as Martin Schotz so cogently put it in *History Will Not Absolve Us: Orwellian Control, Public Denial, & the Murder of President Kennedy*, is to "make everything believable and nothing knowable." In every way, the United States is living out the aftermath of a kind of occupation. In this, foreign and domestic, cultural and political are inextricably enmeshed.

The actions and inactions of the U.S. and British military forces in Iraq, Afghanistan, and beyond confront us with what has been, in no uncertain terms, all along, a culture war, a clash of civilizations, not in the sense proposed by American think tanks and journalists, but rather as new motivation for military and cultural preparedness. Events during the Iraq invasion show how things have advanced since Vietnam. No example is more emblematic than the guarding of Baghdad's Ministry of Petroleum while allowing Iraqi archaeological sites, museums, and libraries, not to mention hospitals, to be looted and destroyed. A message was sent: only the West, especially the Americans and British, on their own terms, are to preserve and define the world's heritage and health. In Baghdad, about a million books and ten million documents were destroyed in the fires of April 14, 2003, alone. The loss in antiquities and artifacts from that period has yet to be fully catalogued. The seizure of state archives and the targeted and systematic assassination of Iraq's academics, chillingly depicted in *Cultural Cleansing in Iraq: Why Museums Were Looted, Libraries Burned and Academics Murdered,* presents a new phase in which a policy decision has been made to openly destroy and dissolve a state.

When one examines the details of how this came about, it is hard not to think in terms of well-planned policy masked by collusion and collaboration. In effect, this brutal enforcement of a program of sanction, the destruction of materials establishing new (or no) versions of the past, present, and future, becomes its own kind of structural adjustment of a nation's imaginative possession of its history and culture. The destruction of the state, no matter how repressive it had been, ratchets up old models of domination.

The importance of culture to the American "security" argument is acknowledged in only superficial ways. The case of Iraq can clarify things. "On the eve of the invasion of Iraq an American delegation of scholars, museum directors, art collectors, and antiquities dealers met with officials at the Pentagon," Chalmers Johnson writes in his book *Nemesis: The Last Days of the American Republic,* and "specifically warned that Baghdad's National Museum was the single most important site in the country." As far as Mesopotamian antiquity is concerned, it was the single most important site in the world. While assurances of protection were being given, "sixty New York-based collectors and dealers organized themselves into a group called the American Council for Cultural Policy and met with Bush administration and Pentagon officials to argue that a post-Saddam Iraq should have relaxed antiquities laws. Opening up private trade in Iraqi artifacts, they suggested, would offer such items better security than they could receive in Iraq." Johnson goes on to provide concrete context: "In monetary terms, the illegal trade in antiquities is the third most lucrative form of international trade globally, exceeded only by drug smuggling and arms sales." And so "the literal heartland of human civilization" was ruined "for any further research or [even] future tourism."

As Lebanese video artist and writer Jalal Toufic has pointed out, the seemingly unending proliferation of new art museums and libraries in the West, along with the cataloguing and inventorying of books and objects (such as in Macmillan's *Dictionary of Art* in 34 volumes, with 41,000 articles, 6,802 contributing scholars, and 15,000 black and white illustrations), has been occurring at the same time "Afghans, Bosnians, Iraqis, etc. have been divested of much of their artistic tradition, not only through material destruction, but also through immaterial withdrawal."

Such efforts touch upon an essential crisis of cultural commerce and transmission—what Toufic calls "a surpassing disaster," that historical moment when a people undergoes cataclysmic collective trauma. Once a collective has undergone such a disaster, the materials of their tradition, their language, idioms, perceptions, and legends, and, finally, their experiences, become unavailable. They are, in effect, "withdrawn." The withdrawal occurs not just through destruction but through official expropriation, and so the journey back, toward repossession of—and gaining access to—materials and experiences that were once one's own, under new conditions, becomes daunting. Handing down an ossified and expropriated tradition may ultimately be worse than losing it altogether and starting from scratch, as Toufic alludes to in recounting the circumstances of "a Kashaya Pomo chief and scholar" who "expressly discontinued the transmission of a tribal dance," a familiar form of resistance. Toufic concludes: "Something must have indicated to her that the discontinuation of the transmission of the dance would be less detrimental and problematic."

The process of absorption of indigenous materials and the consolidation of national narratives and myths is very much a part of the deep mechanics of American cultural and political life. In an eerie echo, the *9/11 Commission Report* reveals how trauma can be usefully bureaucratized, its expropriation routinized. 9/11 is described not as a disaster, but as "an event of surpassing disproportion." What, precisely, are the proportions? What does this "event," already no longer described as a "disaster" or "destruction," surpass?

It may be no accident that the surge of interest in translation and information from and about the Arab world, building since 9/11, reached a peak at a moment of conquest and defeat, when Iraq—what we think of as the "cradle" of civilization—was subjected to severe humiliation and physical destruction. "Liberation" by the American-Anglo alliance, having already starved and suffocated Iraq through a decade of brutal sanctions, made sure to keep their client-tyrant in place until his removal was electorally expedient.

How are those of us involved in transference and translation to respond to such circumstances? What is our role in the politics of imagination and transmission? Have we reached a point where NOT translating, providing access to, handing down, works from the Arab world might be more legitimate? When we decide to participate, how do we insulate and protect such works and ourselves, not merely from assimilation, but from collaboration?

Implicated by our uses of language, we need to discover new ways to both renounce power and take it up. The insularity of American intellectual life presents serious problems, but a superficial internationalism that gentrifies on a global scale can only deepen this insularity. Writers and translators can, and often do, end up playing somebody else's game, and become complicit, perpetuating the same rules with new players. The act of transmission is never innocent. It must be permeated with a kind of vigilance that recognizes, as the American poet Jack Spicer once put it, that "there are bosses in poetry as well as in the industrial empire."

The way that one ushers in and makes use of newly introduced and revived texts is key. Are they there to ease one's conscience or do they present formal, intellectual, philosophic, and ethical challenges? When we remain casual in the face of Syrian poet, activist, and former political prisoner Faraj Bayrakdar "inventing an ink from tea and onion leaves," smuggling poems out from prison on cigarette papers, we sanction and participate in an indifference that can only come back to haunt us. To encounter, translate, and help disseminate, as I have, writers like Abdellatif Laabi —the Moroccan poet, novelist, playwright, journalist, translator, editor, and former political prisoner—is to try to point to these traps of complicity and collusion, precisely by bringing in voices aware of them under more extreme circumstances. Translation can be an act, a way to erect a picket line against the bosses, to reclaim some part of our suppressed and isolated humanity and participate in it in new ways. When Laabi writes: "We will need a nakedness / that even our skin cannot distort," he offers us entry, through his suffering, back into the "infinite crumbling world" we have been taught is out of our hands and no longer worth struggling for.

The only legitimate course is to meet other realities through a thorough interrogation of our own. Under the imposed monolingualism of these United States, this is difficult. It is hard to get news that matters, that isn't propaganda of one kind or another, that might be able to challenge our ethical and intellectual assumptions and priorities. While in some ways we may be closer to understanding a history we could call our own, most people in the United States remain ignorant of the effects of their government's policies abroad. This is no doubt because of the country's vast global military, corporate, and cultural reach. As concentration and consolidation in media and publishing reach unprecedented levels, the channels through which translated texts or autonomous representations of other cultures can be transmitted and emerge into the public realm have narrowed, even with the internet.

The translation of writers from parts of the world that we directly affect and are directly affected by us is hardly an esoteric branch of literary studies. Academic discourse, which often interiorizes, domesticates, ignores, or theorizes work whose intentions were originally public and political, can neutralize this power, example, and force. Instances of this can be seen in the treatment of work by Vietnam veterans, suppressed people, political prisoners, and writers of all kinds involved in popular movements at home and abroad—from rural and urban America to Central America and the Middle East, particularly Palestine, to Africa and Asia. Such works, within the framework of "multiculturalism" or serving the rhetoric of human rights, are treated as mere "texts" and forms of "hybridity" often serving to buttress the class bias, allegiances, and organization of literary and political hierarchies.

Lessons about the function and ethics of writing and literacy, the place writing has as testimony, the relationship between a writer and his or her potential or actual audience, can be learned only by those searching in earnest, unwilling to buckle under orthodoxies with their small and large rewards. As narratives fall through the cracks or have the oxygen sucked out of them, the right to narrate and intervene erodes, creating a vacuum filled by a discourse of sympathy and expertise. In particular, the lack of personal relationships between North American intellectuals and especially their counterparts in the Middle East has made it much easier for official propaganda to dominate the discursive space available. The absence of this human connection has removed our primary line of defense, allowing an ensuing vacuum to fill up with disinformation, with things that occupy the space where real exchange would arise.

The experts continually tell us that, for example, the Arab world has no Solzhenitsyns or Havels. The facts get in the way of such a claim, but they are also not that easy to get a hold of. The number of writers, intellectuals, and political activists in the Arab, Middle Eastern, and Islamic world who have been censored, imprisoned, tortured, assassinated, or disappeared, and who have put their experiences into writing fully as rich and philosophically complex as anything we are familiar with constitutes one of the great human sagas of our times. There is no single place to go find a narrative of these events. The need for an archaeology to excavate and represent this, and do so systematically, is absolute and essential, and belongs in the realm of public health.

As a start, the relative positions of the terms we often use to describe such situations must be reversed: when one uses the rhetoric of human rights, and thinks about the typical report on human rights, one's first reaction is to be angry or shocked at the extent of the repression by the regime in question. What if we were to think of it instead as a general index of the enormous extent of *resistance* that requires such repression?

How did we get to such a point? How have the issues at stake—so important for the world, for its complex and diverse history, sense of itself, its symbols and roots and myths—been rendered invisible to the public of a country with more than some say in everyone else's affairs? Accountability for this systemic failure must be laid at the doorstep of American intellectuals and their lack, not just of responsibility, but of response, on almost every human, creative, historical, and political level.

While those involved in cultural transmission and translation face the risk of appropriating, trivializing, and displacing a work from the realm of significance to that of indifference, the risks of not doing such work may be greater still. Translation and transmission can constitute an intervention at the heart of power and not only preserve the "innate quality" Adonis called an essential "constituent of consciousness," but help us work towards that "symposium of the whole" Robert Duncan called for where "all the old excluded orders must be included." The destruction of other cultures and states goes hand in hand with the discourse of sympathy and expertise. To protect against assimilation and collaboration requires more than fitting newly introduced and revived texts into existing frameworks. Defining what information is for us, where it comes from, and where to find it becomes an essential survival skill. But this retrieval and definition also starts at home, with materials we need to reclaim as our own, outside the codes and constraints of administrative control. Inaction, indifference, a lack of solidarity and lack of curiosity together mark something ominous—the inability to cross a picket line, one that we have put up in our own imaginations, one we cannot cross and that we have forgotten even exists.

Ramsey Scott/*Loggernaut*: I'm interested in your connections to the ideas, languages, and cultural ties you associate
with Israel/Palestine, New England, and the former Yugoslavia. What is your connection to each of these regions?
How have the cultural legacies you've been left with from
these places influenced your work and thought?

Ammiel Alcalay: To quote Robert Hunter and the Dead,
"what a long strange trip it's been." These things seem to
change fairly significantly in different phases of one's life. In
my case, I've been feeling more and more tied to the New
England part of myself (even though I live in Brooklyn).
Getting back to that has been quite circuitous. Growing up
"first generation," with parents and extended family speaking a bunch of different languages and acting differently
(yelling out your "strange"-sounding name in the super-
market, for instance), does mark you. On the other hand,
the more I think back to the kids I grew up with, middle-
class and working-class kids, the more I realize how many
of them were in similar situations—Italian, Greek, Chinese.
There wasn't any official definition or discourse around it
so we weren't encouraged to "share" in that patronizing but
sometimes useful way kids are now. But Boston, Gloucester,
and later Cape Cod (where I lived for several years working
in trucking and automotive stuff), left indelible marks on
my sense of place, landscape, light, speech patterns—the
textures of everything that becomes "familiar." Not to mention the Red Sox, which could be the subject of a whole
other interview.

This is not at all to say that the eight years I spent in

Jerusalem didn't also etch indelible materials into me. But I would concur with Olson's great line that "people don't change, they only stand more revealed." In terms of ex-Yugoslavia, since my parents came from there as refugee/immigrants, they preserved a kind of "frozen" sense of the place, circa late 1930s, up till 1941. Although I never lived there, it seemed completely familiar on the many long visits I made. If I hadn't had such extended experiences and encounters with generational memories of other places, I don't think my work would have developed the way it has—in other words, I don't think I would have felt the need to engage in all the different aspects or facets of things that I have engaged with. I learned a tremendous amount by being elsewhere, by involving myself in other languages and ways of being public as a writer. That makes my sense of place and language complex and unlikely to be easily contained.

The experience of being politically involved while living in Jerusalem, before and during the first intifada, the Palestinian uprising of the 1980s, is irreplaceable. It really was a popular revolution, despite the fact that it was suppressed and then politically co-opted. There was something exhilarating and expansive about being there. What I encountered in Jerusalem, having been politically active and conscious in high school during the crucial years of the late '60s and early '70s, were surprisingly familiar ways of thinking, acting, and being.

In one's life, there is a constant negotiation and renegotiation between places and times and activities. As far back as I can remember, I've gravitated towards things and people that are local, or genuine, of a place, whether it be a bookstore, a garage, or a corner with people hanging out.

When I managed a laundromat in the West Village in the mid-1970s, there was a contingent of retired longshoreman out talking on the sidewalk every morning and every afternoon. Tom Iacovone, one of the last ice-men in New York City, was someone I refer to in *from the warring factions*. When I was a kid there was a guy named Mr. Chase who came to paint our house. Besides being a house-painter, he worked on the Boston & Maine railroad, I can't remember whether as a brakeman or an engineer, but I remember that I would fake any and every possible kind of illness so I could stay home from school and hang around him, carrying his bucket of spackle, watching him work the walls and listening to his stories. When I was in Jerusalem the first time, in the late '70s, I worked as a kind of general gofer and assistant at this very old organization called the Council of the Sephardic Communities. Most of the people there were old Jerusalemites, from families that had been there for hundreds of years. Just by hanging around, I learned and intuited a tremendous amount, things that led me to understand what I found and didn't find in books. During the intifada, we had a close friend who was a Mennonite and she ran the Mennonite Center. It became a kind of clearing house for all kinds of people and activities. I remember a huge party there, celebrating the release of an enormous group of political prisoners sometime before the first intifada started—it was these people who had, as it were, done their post-doctoral work in prison, and who formed the grass roots leadership of the revolt. By spending time there and listening, engaging with people like that, I was able to understand things in ways that were completely unavailable elsewhere.

This has characterized my approach, for instance, to the

literary world. I'd much rather work with a small press and get deeply involved in the endeavor, meeting the people and working with them, than strive and hob-knob with big name types. That doesn't interest me because there is little or no exchange involved—those kind of people are just moving ahead, with little or no concern for anything common or collective. I feel more and more strongly that all of this must be part of an intellectual ethics, a way of putting into "thinking" practice how we take up or don't take up power, how we exercise power relationships, breaking some of them down rather than falling into them and simply accepting what's given. That's the point where collusion and complicity start. But everything changes as the context changes. I put a tremendous effort into translation and enabling access to various literatures and traditions. As that gets taken up in a more organized way by others, I find it less urgent and have shifted my energies elsewhere.

Things always seem to work at cross purposes and not always as we might have initially hoped: as I work to make things accessible, some of those things do end up entering the market as commodities, in some other form. This is an almost inevitable cultural process but it gets exacerbated in the present circumstances. In our post-NAFTA world, Americans feel they have a *right* to literatures from other parts of the world, much like they have a right to Chilean cherries in New York in the middle of January, Australian wine, or an endless flow of products made somewhere else. When I say I think it may be wise to NOT translate certain things, it is partly because we are only reproducing the process of getting something at "no" or "low" cost. This occludes the work involved and the price so many pay for real knowledge. If you have to learn a language and immerse yourself in another culture to the point that you can begin discerning things about it, there is a significant cost and a significant renunciation of one's own powers in American English. There is no replacement for taking such personal initiative because its transformative effects are real and profound, and that much harder to package and throw away. After this whole circuitous journey, up until now at least, I've come back to thinking about this continent and its writers in a way that may be closer to the intuitions I had when I was much younger, almost as if I had to undertake these journeys and involvements to verify those original intuitions, or figure out what they mean.

Scott: What experiences on this continent can you point out to that might've been at the root of these "intuitions"?

Alcalay: Well, the experience of playing badminton with the 6 ft. 7 in. Charles Olson in the back yard as a five year-old is kind of indelible. I was lucky enough to grow up having all those small press books and little magazines around the house. My parents were interested and involved in such things—we had *Black Mountain Review*, *Evergreen*, *Big Table*, *Yugen*, etc., around, so when I started exploring, these were the things I encountered. Kerouac, Burroughs, Olson, Creeley, Duncan, Douglas Woolf, Denise Levertov, Diane di Prima, LeRoi Jones/Amiri Baraka—these were familiar names. When I started writing poetry as a teenager, I sent it to the late Vincent Ferrini, and had a great correspondence that continued until Vincent was in his 90s! Vincent was that rare poet who spans the pre-Cold War political poets of the '30s with all the post-1945 trends, from the Beats to Black Mountain, San Francisco Renaissance, and all the other labels that get us to one section of the shelf without letting us see the whole library.

For many years I had found myself questioning this "Americanness" as against some other sense of history or collectivity I centered around the Mediterranean, what I've called the Levant. In coming back more strongly to myself as a poet rooted in this language and culture, I'm exploring a whole new range of questions. What is it that causes this explosion of creativity? Looking only, for example, at the music and writing in the United States, but also elsewhere, from 1950 to 1970, as an example, you find a period comparable to any sanctioned period of "greatness" in cultural history, whether the T'ang Dynasty or the Abbassids, the Italian Renaissance or the Elizabethans. What is the obverse of American "exceptionalism," not in the negative political policy sense, but in a positive cultural and experiential sense? Are there things in our continental histories that have created the conditions for this kind of dramatically original creative expression? Haven't all the origins and erasures on this continent created different kinds of political and social space, different boundaries, different memories and different kinds of forgetting? These are only some of the things that I've been coming circuitously around to investigating and considering. But as I do this, I'm also very aware of what kinds of uses opening these questions up might be put to, like the processes I've described regarding my work in translation. The powers of assimilation and subjugation, as well as "market forces," are relentless and always need to be kept in mind as one proceeds.

Scott: Could you expand a bit more on the political contexts of translation?

Alcalay: This at-first-glance counter-intuitive idea of NOT translating has become increasingly important to me. Capital is like water, it will take up whatever space it can occupy—if you've ever dealt with leaks, whether on a roof or in plumbing situations, you know exactly what I mean. Not to mention even stronger forms, like floods. The same way with cultural capital. As things heat up with Iran, suddenly Iranian women are a major cultural and literary topic; this is not to say they shouldn't be, just that the timing is always somewhat "fortuitous." Moreover, representations are incredibly selective and completely dictated by class assumptions— we learn about certain kinds of oppression regarding personal freedoms but learn little about basic categories like infant mortality or literacy, things that, ultimately, have a much deeper impact on Iranian women than wearing head scarves or modest clothing.

After over twenty years of activity as a translator from several languages and an advocate and activist for the visibility of many more, I'm both encouraged and discouraged. A few important public initiatives have characterized our lack of translated texts as a national crisis; older and newer small presses continue to bring texts from elsewhere into circulation. On the other hand, we remain wedded to the American con-game that you can get something for nothing—translated literary texts arrive without their context: no collections of letters, biographies, social, political or literary histories; no gossip or controversy. In the highly regulated trade zones of our post-NAFTA delirium, where labor is occluded by finished product, it is a most difficult task to insulate the text against the slings and arrows of fashion, foreign policy shifts, and the market. Some translations might do more harm than good, reinstating the illusion that we have actually added a significant element to our vocabulary, when we might not even be remotely prepared to comprehend what it is we're getting. Often this helps to buttress and reconstitute privileged ideas of art and the literary artifact in our tradition, removing texts from social, political, economic, historical, and spiritual contexts that might create friction, cause controversy, spark actual debate, or undermine what I have called the discourse of sympathy and expertise. More disturbing is the fact that in this post-NAFTA world, along with the post-9/11 idea that it might not be a bad idea to be informed about other parts of the world, all kinds of people are able and willing to step in as speculators, in some sense panning for the gold of some unknown potential Nobel Prize winner by suddenly showing interest in all kinds of previously obscure literatures. This is an imperial maneuver. I think of Thoreau's wonderful line that goes something to the effect of, "If a man comes to your door trying to help without having been asked, turn around and run."

The way all this operates allows for a kind of laundering—just like money laundering—in which people deeply discredited in their own countries can come to us, the uninformed, and seek rehabilitation through translation and adulation. Our mediocre, and insular, intellects then use these works as opportunities to display their apparent courage and social consciousness. This ranges from the farcical to the truly demonic. There will be no shortage of Baathist writers lauded by gullible westerners who don't know the simplest facts about Iraqi repression or literary history and will simply take those seeking rehabilitation at their word. The racism of many popular Ashkenazi Jewish Israeli writers towards Arabs and Arab Jews, something that is common knowledge amongst the victims of that racism in Israel, rarely gets dealt with here. Huge and very consequential reputations are built on completely faulty premises. You can find these kinds of examples in almost any culture, if you get to know it well enough. Since we have no real venues for the deeper public debate such cases demand and require, these things and more pass unnoticed.

Scott: The "intellectual ethics" that you mentioned previously bring me to another question that you've written about, and that has to do with different strategies that can help, as you've put it elsewhere, "insulate" texts from other places and make them matter. Could you comment on this?

Alcalay: After many years of thinking through this intuitively, I've come to the conclusion that the key is to make such texts available at the points closest to the production of innovative work here. In other words, I look for those venues or sources that the writers I identify with here would go to. This allows for creative tensions that can challenge writers not involved in commercial production to question some of their assumptions and possibly explore a new referential vocabulary and other possibilities. The equation seems to hold: when books appear in more commercial venues, they enter the discourse at a stage further from the initial production of innovative writers and have less of an effect. At the same time, this may not necessarily be an indication of how writers actually act—that is, "experimental" or "innovative" writers may be as bound to formal codes or constraints as "commercial" writers. Yet, a number of books that I've translated with smaller presses remain in print while other books, brought out commercially and to more fanfare, are no longer available. The first account of someone describing his experience in a Serb camp, *The Tenth Circle of Hell* by the Bosnian poet Rezak Hukanović, published by a major press with prominent reviews in all the major newspapers, is now out of print. It had an immediate effect, got its nano-second of air time, then disappeared, while the other stuff has remained (like the work of Bosnian poet Semezdin Mehmedinović or *Keys to the Garden*), and keeps reaching and influencing people in deeper ways.

Scott: One difference between some of the writers that you've tried to bring into the American context and contemporary poets in the United States is, in my view at least, the question of what constitutes the political. Are Americans misguided in distinguishing between "political poetry" and other forms? Are they misreading poets like Mahmoud Darwish when they read him as a writer whose primary interests or themes are political ones? In other countries and for writers living under duress, it seems as though such distinctions might not exist.

Alcalay: Absolutely, I think you are absolutely right in how you phrase this. The difference, I think, is that here there is the well-crafted and insidious illusion that "politics don't matter," especially to certain segments of the population. Some people have the luxury to pretend politics don't exist, the world is ordered simply as it is, generally to their advantage. This serves as an excellent class and caste barrier, making it very clear who belongs where, what lines of legitimacy will be drawn and so on and so forth. I was flabbergasted to read a story in *The New York Times Sunday Magazine* about a young novelist who got a $500,000 advance for his first novel and a $1 million advance for his second. I know the literary agent in question and I've heard great things about the writer. However, I firmly believe that when phenomena like this exist, there must be a reason behind it, and there must be—whether conscious or not—a complex set of social, political and economic mechanisms at play. Being much more used to great writers who have generally remained on the brink of poverty, something I would never romanticize, I have to see the current *overpayment* of a select group of writers as an attempt to glut the market and create a useless commodity out of writing—something apparently necessary but, like the VCR that could be pro-grammed two years in advance, useless.

The kind of writing I'm used to is, first and foremost, a necessity for the writer. Only then, in my opinion, can it become a necessity for its readers. The audience for this kind of writing tends to be smaller in number. Again, I would never promote an elitist view. I have no problem with writers working for large audiences. I think someone like Stephen King is a great writer, and a necessary one. He also happens to have a more conscious and active politics towards writing, through his support of the National Poetry Foundation, than many who might identify a Stephen King as the problem. I once had a dispute along those lines with Susan Sontag when King got a well-deserved National Book Award. In terms of writers from other places, we read them reductively by only focusing on the political conditions out of which they write. For someone like Darwish, this has been a central problem. Much of his writing over the past twenty years directly addresses this.

Scott: I'd like to get back to some individuals and experiences you mentioned in your first response as indirect influences on your writing and your sense of place: Mr. Chase, the longshoremen at the laundromat, and the head of the Mennonite Center in Jerusalem. What is the difference between locating inspiration in these people and the experiences that surround them, as opposed to, say, citing your first encounter with a William Carlos Williams poem?

Alcalay: I don't see a difference. My experience of encountering Williams's *Spring & All* is as real to me as anything, sometimes more so. The same goes for everything I remember reading that was formative for me early on, whether it was Jack London, Jack Kerouac, Kenneth Patchen, Richard Wright, Emily Dickinson, or Sappho. Just like music you hear, places you see, or people you meet and become attached to or learn something from, early reading experiences are crucial. While I have stressed the experiential, I think reading is an encounter that can be life changing, consciousness changing. It is absolutely necessary for sustenance. Robert Duncan at some point is speaking about a critic who relies on taste, and I'm going to paraphrase this from Jed Rasula's *The American Poetry Wax Museum: Reality Effects, 1940–1990,* one of the few truly essential literary histories we have of post-WWII American poetry: "'Since he has no other conceivable route to knowledge of that work, taste must suffice. But I can have no recourse to taste,' Duncan says, adding that the work of Olson, Levertov and others 'belongs not to my appreciations but to my immediate concerns in living.'" The key is not to make the separations that society wants us to make. Books are real, books are part of the world. Un-branded, unexpected, non-commodified experience is rapidly becoming a thing of the past. Books and poems may serve as some of the surest and last pathways back into experience, back into the values of experience, and so back into the world we actually live in.

REPUBLICS OF POETRY

1

Copy of notes in pencil, jargon/corinth edition of maximus

for kristen case

————————

the strophic structure is itself an archipelago

dolphins mire & blood
            [I think a bunch of my notes are
             quotes from eliot, dry salvages, I think]:

Where blood-begotten spirits come
And all complexities of fury leave
Dying into a dance,
An agony of trances,
An agony of flame that cannot singe a sleeve

feather to feather [cantos/paterson]

   [then on the blank left page I have this:]

lexis=eliot
syntax=hopkins   back   of it
figures=yeats   coleridge
                  wordsworth   Arnold curiously enough
                                the wedding of history
                                 and archetype
      Wreck of the Deutschland '31
Arnold—art as criticism
Adorno—committed—O. as a more radical critique
                  took on more at base

>   than WCW or Pound
>   thus closer to Stevens in terms of
>   anticipation—Stevens retreats /

>   O. attacks

DeMan on Keats & Ode To (Fanny Brawne)
& confrontation with self (dread of) connie
only mentioned in end of maxis (my wife my car etc.)
                    or betty?
promotion of the "impersonal" broken through
by mother/father, occasionally son

>   [then this on part 3 that begins
>   "the underpart is, though stemmed" etc.]

the dative
Mandelstam on Dante
p. 42 Eliot [where / what that is I have no
            idea but I'll check my old eliot]
also Yeats Speaking

"But that which matters, that which insists, that which will last,
that! o my people, where shall you find it" etc.

Ash Wednesday V

the whole series of "whens"
when all is become
when even our bird
when, on the hill etc.

this is the "cuando" that dante
LEARNS how to use,
finally, by canto 26

pejorocracy=pound's word

[then this, near section 5]:

Language in general is worn out & used up, an indispensa-
ble but masterless & arbitrarily employed means of communication, as indifferent as a means of public transport,
["how / that street-cars, o Oregon, twitter / in the afternoon"] as a streetcar which everyone enters & leaves at will.

Heidegger 1935 Introduction to Metaphysics

(o Gloucester-man, / weave etc.)

"Custom is the greatest of Weavers"—Carlyle
custom=costume
tailor
veil

found my copy of the waste land—section III.
The Fire Sermon, my notes:

The Librarian & I, Maximus

"I Tiresias, though blind etc.

I, Maximus, a metal hot from boiling water etc.
l. 229 perceived the scene (the Librarian)

section V Ash Wednesday, last line: O my people
I see now, it's Burnt Norton—the echoes are everywhere:

"Quick said the bird
"Round the corner
"Go, go, go, said the bird
"at the still point, there the dance is
"After the kingfisher's wing
"Only by the form, the pattern

end of Section III

also Dry Salvages—all over the place

"Lady, whose shrine stands on the promontory"

2

At the time of the appointment of poet Dana Gioia to head the National Endowment of the Arts, the nation's leading arts agency, *The New York Times* wrote of Gioia that "He is a registered Republican who voted for George W. Bush and his father before that. His poetry is not political."

To seek proof texts, one just needs to look around. How did we get to a place where such sentences can be uttered by their speakers and accepted by their editors with a straight face? What do such sentences tell us about how things are organized? What does it mean when dominant assumptions are considered "not political," while anything calling them into question is?

I want, through a long involved story, to take us through this question. Part of it has to do with what has come to be called American Exceptionalism. Historian and theorist Perry Anderson's concept is that we are on a large continent with oceans on either side, with a population of migrants that tend to lack any cultural memory rooted in the places they've come to inhabit. Such a geographical, social, and political sense of real exception might constitute a start.

As a first-generation American, I have a certain lien on some other world, having grown up within other languages. This has always been an issue, in my life and in my relationship to writing, poetry, and poetics. What is it that I recognize and seek out in a text that comes from some other part of the world, that embodies some kind of plural collective memory, some plural collective moment? And what is it in American texts that often does almost the opposite? That almost declares its solitude and isolation? That declares its aloneness?

Two examples worth thinking about have to do with the issue of contact, how superficially it has been treated, the nature of filters and lenses, and the ways our vision gets directed. The examples are from Algeria and Israel—Algeria of the decolonization period in the late 1950s and the early 1960s, up until the mid-'60s, with its relationship to African-American culture here, and the Israel of a very radical shift, post-June War, post-1967. I want to examine a little bit what the meanings of these shifts are and some odd and, from this perspective, remarkable facts from these periods.

First, a little history. In the relationship of the United States of the post-Revolutionary period, 1780s, 1790s, to Algeria and Morocco, then called the Barbary States, Morocco was the second country to recognize the United States, after France. But the United States did not reciprocate. It did not send an envoy for a number of years. The Moroccans, at a certain point, started to get bugged about this and began capturing ships and taking captives. Algeria, on several occasions, declared war on the United States. This had to do with sea rights and triangulated conflicts with France and so forth. In 1800, while there were about one million enslaved Africans in the United States, there were about seven hundred American captives in Algeria. A number of those people, upon return, wrote captivity narratives. A number of these were abolitionist and anti-slavery tracts, such as the recently reprinted *The Algerine Captive* by Royall Tyler, originally published in 1797. They were comparing the conditions they lived in under "slavery" in Algeria to conditions of enslaved peoples in the United States. There's some evidence that Frederick Douglass read some of these pieces, published in *The Columbia Orator*.

The role of North Africa in our national consciousness

from this period, and its subsequent relation to "the Middle East," is largely unknown and unexplored. For example, an earlier version of what becomes our National Anthem was written by Francis Scott Key to honor Decatur after Tripoli was vanquished in 1805. It's quite chilling, given the post-Cold War context. The two last stanzas are:

In conflict resistless each toil they endur'd,
Till their foes shrunk dismay'd from the war's desolation:
And pale beamed the Crescent, its splendor obscur'd
By the light of the star-spangled flag of our nation,
Where each flaming star gleam'd a meteor of war,
And a turban'd head bowed to the terrible glare.
Then mixt with the olive the laurel shall wave,
And form a bright wreath for the brow of the brave.

Our fathers who stand on the summit of fame,
Shall exultingly hear, of their sons, the proud story,
How their young bosoms glow'd with a patriot flame,
How they fought, how they fell, in the midst of their glory,
How triumphant they rode, o'er the wandering flood,
And stain'd the blue waters with infidel blood;
How mixt with the olive, the laurel did wave,
And form a bright wreath for the brow of the brave.

We can see, through this, how crucial it is that circumstances of cultural transmission can become obscured and then naturalized, in this case in the genealogy of a song repeated or at least known by all Americans.

A certain kind of French theory in the U.S. academy is part of the story here, but only a small part. The way this theory is presented, under the guise of a politicization of studies, has tended to depoliticize the *context* of that theory, a context that arises out of serious debates over decolonization, over identity, over otherness, over language, and over the body—the language and body literally being those that can be and are tortured. If one goes back to earlier sources, and earlier texts, and looks at how these things were discussed and debated in the 1950s, you find an intellectual history that is only slowly starting to come back. It's an important history. In many cases, the texts people are reading are inadequate, if not willfully misleading. There is another catalog of texts, however, that could more explicitly and effectively open up issues relevant to our political world and to how this political world has been apportioned since WWII.

Academic politics has to do with cultural space and cultural space can only be occupied by so much. Once it's filled, it's filled, and if something is there, other things can't get in. One of the reasons for the predominance of certain kinds of theory and its list of texts may, paradoxically or deliberately, be that such an operation fills available space, excluding or supplanting, among other things, theoretical aspects of our writing, poetics, and critical imagination. This imagination is best expressed, perhaps, in poetry and works emerging from a milieu in which poetry is central. In a lecture on Charles Olson by someone who may be even less familiar to you, Ed Dorn, who had been Olson's student at Black Mountain College, Dorn excoriates this dominance of theory over writing or poetics when he talks about what he calls "the structuralist preference":

Those Methodists detest authorship. They prefer to maintain authority in their own hands and to scoff at the worthlessness

and ignorance of writers, in order to enact their own rites of
explication, or exploitation. In other words, authorship is an
authority signal. Anyone who chooses that interpretation of
the function of words is of course quite anti-art.

Writing in turn gets relegated to the creative department,
which comes to mean the "non-thinking" department. This
has had an enormous effect on our ability to define ourselves and define some of those I'll talk about further, particularly Olson, who presents, I suspect, a more radical and
critical project than what is presented as theoretically radical and critical in the academy. One of Olson's primary
concerns was to determine what and where the knowledge
is that one should know, and how one should get to it.

I want to go back and do a little tracing of some of these
histories and see where the twain meets and where it separates. In an earlier version of what you are now reading, a
lecture given at the Cornell Forum, I asked, doing an informal poll, how many people were familiar with or had read
the work of the poet Robert Duncan. There were a few
hands. I asked about the main subject of my talk, Charles
Olson. A few more. Then I asked how many people had read
or were familiar with the work of French theoretician Michel
Foucault. There were many more hands for Foucault, most
everyone, in fact.

There's an instructive passage by poet and textual scholar Susan Howe not directly related, but certainly germane,
to this problem of American writing and the overlay of
Continental theory. It's from *The Birth-mark: unsettling the*
wilderness in American literary history:

"What is an author?" asks Michel Foucault in the essay that

directly inspired and informed my writing about Anne Hutch-
inson, Thomas Shepard, John Winthrop, Anne Bradstreet, Mary
Rowlandson, James Savage, and Emily Dickinson. Foucault's
influence is problematic. This wide-ranging philosopher and
library cormorant's eloquent, restless, passionate interrogation
of how we have come to be the way we are remains inside the
margins of an intellectual enclosure constructed from memo-
ries, meditations, delusions, and literary or philosophical spec-
ulations of European men. "What is a picture?" Jacques Lacan
tells me, at the perceptual level, in its relation to desire, reality
appears to be marginal. What are the guises of human sciences
when women do speak? In Emmanuel Levinas's terminology:
"A work conceived radically is a movement of the Same
towards the Other which never returns to the Same." After
1637, American literary expression couldn't speak English. I am
a North American author. I was born in 1937. Into World War
II and the rotten sin of man-made mass murder.

The problem of "intellectual enclosure" is hardly just a
European one, of course. In 1944, Robert Duncan wrote the
text "The Homosexual in Society," published in Dwight
McDonald's *Politics*. At the same time that he wrote that
text, he sent a long poem, I think an elegy, to the *Kenyon
Review*, then edited by John Crowe Ransom. In the interim,
during the time that Ransom was supposed to answer,
Wallace Stevens had sent in "Esthétique du Mal." In this
interlude Ransom had read "The Homosexual in Society"
and had a fit. He wrote back to Duncan and said, "I read the
poem as an advertisement for a notice of overt homosexuality
and we are not in the market for literature of this type. I cannot agree with you that we should publish it... I cannot agree
with your position that homosexuality is not abnormal." What

this did was to remove Duncan from any possibility of entering the "normative" literary canon, a condition that held for a long time, there being no *Collected Poems* of Robert Duncan, no *Collected Prose* of Robert Duncan, years after his death, for one set of reasons or another. Duncan still remains outside the general curriculum. Either way, as Rasula notes, quoting Duncan himself, in *The American Poetry Wax Museum:*

Duncan later recognized the incident as good fortune instead: "So I was out, just read out, out, at a point when I would have been in at the wrong place... I'm glad I wasn't in there; I would have been read not as an advertisement but a conformist of the first water.

In "The Homosexual in Society," there's an astonishing sentence where Duncan describes—again, looking for precedence, uses of language, where things are coming from—his own very rarified, private world of a group of homosexuals. He's discussing this in relationship to Hart Crane, the fate that Crane had at the hands of critics, and Crane's attitude toward his own sexuality. Remember, this comes out in 1944. Duncan writes:

Where the Zionists of homosexuality have laid claim to a Palestine of their own, asserting in their miseries, their nationality; Crane's suffering, his rebellion, and his love are sources of poetry for him not because they are what make him different from, superior to, mankind, but because he saw in them his link with mankind; he saw in them his sharing in universal human experience.

This is really an extraordinary paragraph, because Duncan is making a crucial set of distinctions between universals and particulars. This is part of the story I want to trace: how do we get from complex, multivalent ideas of human experience to narrowly construed, narrowly configured ethnic, gender, or national identities? Even if the ideas of identity expand, they are based on a very narrow beginning. Even when you have a plurality of ethnicities or genders or national identities, you still find a narrowly constructed notion of identity. Duncan's much broader way of describing things, the kinds of links he makes and their specificity, are almost impossible to imagine today.

The second part, it seems to me, may be of even more significance, and to get to it I want to speak about Olson, who was born in Worcester, Massachusetts in 1910. His father was born in Sweden in 1882 and was carried to the new world when he was only a few months old. The poet's mother, Mary Hines, was born in an Irish family that had just come to the United States. Working from the age of fourteen to support his mother and sisters, Olson's father moved from a milk route to iron work, becoming leader of a crew of master builders that raised the huge factory stacks of New England. From there he went on to work in the postal service as a letter carrier, becoming very active in his union and in workers' rights. Olson always felt that his father's premature death, in 1935, was partially the result of conflicts with higher-ups in the post office.

Olson was one of the few children of immigrants enrolled in graduate school at Harvard, in the newly formed "History and American Civilization" program, a program very different from what would become the Cold War model of American Studies initiated at Yale, under Norman Holmes

Pearson, a former O.S.S. officer. Olson's teachers included F. O. Matthiessen and Frederick Merk. It was through Matthiessen that Olson met another student, Pete Seeger, who was working for Matthiessen at the time. Later, in 1940, after he'd done the groundbreaking research on Melville that would result in *Call Me Ishmael*, Olson found himself in New York, working for a journal called *Common Ground*. Bumping into Seeger in Greenwich Village, Olson was invited to a gathering at which he met the musicologist Alan Lomax and the singer Woody Guthrie. After hitting it off with Guthrie, Seeger suggested Olson take a look at some of Guthrie's writing. This encounter led, fairly quickly, to Guthrie getting a contract with the publisher Dutton for what would become *Bound For Glory*. In his biography of Guthrie, Joe Klein tells the story:

It had started with Charles Olson, an old professor of Seeger's from Harvard, who'd come to Almanac House for dinner one night. Pete had told him about Woody's writing ability, and Woody had shown him some things he'd written. Olson was suitably impressed, and asked Woody if he'd like to write a story about how people out in the country learn to become musicians for Common Ground, *a small scholarly magazine with which he was associated. Woody responded, within a matter of days, with a lovely story called "Ear Players," about his mother singing ballads, and the shoeshine boy in the barbershop in Okemah who played the long, lonesome railroad blues on his harmonica, and how he learned new songs on the road to the Gulf Coast and California. The story was going to be published in the magazine's spring issue.*

Some time after this, Olson ended up working during

WWII in the Roosevelt Administration's Office of War Information. Unlike the isolationists or America Firsters—like General Smedley Butler who saw U.S. involvement as a disaster that would lead to the "racket" of imperialism—Olson came into the war effort as an idealistic New Dealer, from a milieu in which isolationist ideology was common. He'd been Chief of Foreign Language Information under the Common Council for American Unity and then, in 1942, served as Assistant Chief of the Foreign Languages Division of the Office of War Information. In 1944 he became Foreign Nationalities Director of the Democratic National Committee, a crucial position dealing with securing votes for FDR's re-election. He would probably have been appointed to a high-level position had he not, then, turned his back, around the end of the war, on the Democratic party, having already resigned as assistant chief of the Office of War Information Foreign Language Section in May 1944. According to *The New York Times* of May 19, 1944, Olson and his colleague Constantine Poulos charged that George W. Healy Jr., O.W.I.'s domestic director, had "hamstrung" the activities of their division. The article goes on: "Mr. Poulos, acting chief of the section, and Mr. Olson, assistant chief, contended that what they termed interference by Mr. Healy and Dowsley Clark, who is director of the O.W.I.'s news bureau, had prevented them from functioning to offset Axis propaganda aimed at creating dissension among America's 35,000,000 citizens of foreign ancestry." Certainly this must have signalled a major policy shift, coinciding with the emergence of former Axis figures being filtered through enemy lines to come to work for the United States. Despite his earlier position, Olson, following the death of FDR, the rise of Truman, and detonation of the bomb, left in disgust and in full awareness of what was to come, realizing the nature of the Cold War's gathering momentum.

While still living in Washington, having turned his back on party politics to declare himself, of all things, a poet, Olson began visiting Ezra Pound, who, as far as I know, was the only prominent American cultural figure charged with treason during WWII. Pound had been interrogated in Pisa, and was headed for prison in May of 1945 for Italian radio broadcasts supporting Mussolini, while the CIA was hiring Nazis and Axis collaborators by the truckload, utilizing their expertise in numerous spheres of policy. As Christopher Simpson writes in his groundbreaking *Blowback*:

The U.S. "national security state," as it has since come to be termed, established itself very quickly in the wake of the showdown at Potsdam. Before three years had passed, the emerging intelligence community had begun undertaking small and medium-scale campaigns using former Nazis and Axis collaborators as operatives in a coup plot in Romania, the subversion of elections in Greece and Italy, and attempts to manipulate favored political parties throughout the Soviet-occupied zone of Eastern Europe. One can well imagine what the USSR's interpretation of these U.S. initiatives was at the time, considering the Marxist-Leninist dictum that the United States is inherently imperialist in character.

One hardly needs to fall into Cold War dialectics, taking, for example, the Soviet side, to see the implications of these phenomena for foreign and domestic policy. Nonetheless, their relation to cultural framing, from 1945 till the present, is almost completely unexamined.

At the time his visits began, Olson's significant work on

Melville was behind him, Melville being still at that point an "undiscovered" American writer, even with the work of Raymond Weaver and a few others. As we know, Pound was turned into an example of some kind, considered unfit to stand trial and declared insane. Olson's visits are recorded in a remarkable book edited by Catherine Seelye, *Charles Olson & Ezra Pound: An Encounter at St. Elizabeths.*

Olson looks at Pound through the eyes of a young writer, with admiration but also as somebody coming from an immigrant working-class background, revolted by Pound's fascist and anti-Jewish outbursts. In his best writings from this period, Olson had begun wrestling with a fundamental political and cultural question: how does one approach authority, with authority? The real issues that should have been brought up by Pound's trial were not touched, not even broached. This allowed Olson to reassess the role of political authority and his official involvement in public life. He wrote a text called "This is Yeats Speaking," in which he puts himself in the voice of W.B. Yeats:

The soul is stunned in me, O writers, readers, fighters, fearers, for another reason, that you have allowed this to happen without a trial of your own... There is a court you leave silent—history present, the issue the larger concerns of authority than a state, Heraclitus and Marx called, perhaps some consideration of descents and metamorphoses, form and the elimination of intellect... What have you to help you hold in a single thought, reality and justice?

These are the questions Olson opens up in 1945, 1946. They have enormous implications, implications that spin out in a whole host of directions. I believe they are at the root of his proposing a set of conditions for which he will later use the short-hand term the "post-modern."

While the claim of precedence is, in itself, unimportant, Olson, in a letter to Robert Creeley, is the first to use the term in the sense that we might think of it, though the first use is, as far as I know, chronological, by Arnold Toynbee, in *A Study of History*. It seems like an arbitrary date for him, dating the post-modern at 1870. In Olson's case, it's different, possibly signifying a dividing line of some kind. Less than a specific moment, it seems to capture a process of thinking that ranges from letters to anthropologist and O.W.I. colleague Ruth Benedict in 1946 to letters to friend and poet Robert Creeley in 1951. Pound gets the Bollingen Prize in 1949 and that prize is championed by the same John Crowe Ransom who had rejected Duncan, placing Duncan beyond the pale. You also have, at this time, around the body of Ezra Pound, a crucial divorce between aesthetics and politics. You have the construction of a means through which to administer culture on a level that is deep and very hard to detect. As opposed to Olson's intervention, which Pound said "saved his life," the literary rallying of support for Pound held different implications. As Rasula put it:

The defense of Pound actually had little to do with Pound himself, and operated on another level than the textual issues that preoccupied critics of the award. What was crucial was the preservation of the administrative system that had assumed custodial control of poetry (not just Pound's poetry) as surely as the man was impounded in a mental asylum.

The debate around whether to give Pound the prize or not is about whether the poetry is great, is transcendent—whether or not it goes *beyond* politics. Politics becomes expendable. At the same time, on another front, it "doesn't matter" what Pound's politics are. I think that's partially how we get to a sentence concerning the U.S. government's top arts official, of whom it is said that, fortunately, "his poetry is not political." Following the visits to Pound, Olson writes in 1945:

If we the people shall save ourselves from our leaders' shame, if we the people shall survive our disgust, if we the people shall end our own confusion, we must see this big war for the lie it has become. Make no mistake, it is a lie. Unwrap the charters and pacts, recognize the deals, stomach the people's hope for security, tighten the soil over the men, always little men who are dead. Call the big war what it is—a defeat for the people.

Olson had joined the war as a New Dealer. He emerges after it not only closer to isolationists and America Firsters, but, as Ed Dorn characterized it, as "republican—in a real way." Olson came to characterize himself as a "ward and precinct man," local to the core. He was trying to see more deeply into the American political and cultural problem. This arises around the issue of how Pound's *mistaken* authority could have been summoned as a position of authority, so that he could then bring up other possibilities.

Olson leaves official life, even though he had access to power and could have made a career out of politics in Washington. But he chooses, instead, at the beginning of the Cold War, like many other important American poets and writers, to opt out, to go underground and work in relative isolation, not, as the Olson scholar and poet Charles Stein has pointed out, as a withdrawal, but to secure another perspective from which to enact a different political life.

None of the poets associated with this group or associated with what has come to be called the New American Poetry had any mainstream academic or professional affiliation to speak of—until the mid-'60s when, for a moment, it looked like institutions might be changing. The whole schema of professionalization that we are accustomed to today was alien, removed from reality for these people. Olson's relation towards the seats of academic and national political power had been developing and is unequivocal by his last letter to Pound in 1948:

BUT you have to deal with us Olsons... your damn ancestors let us in (AND AS ABOVE I DON'T THINK THE BATH-TUB WAS SO CLEAN WHEN THEY DID). We're here. And to tell you your own truth, you damn well know anglosaxonism is academicism and shrieking empire. LIFE out of Yale, CULTURE out of Princeton, and the BOMB out of Harvard.

It is striking to see how finely honed Olson's sense of things was. This converges in his use of the term post-modern in his 1951 letter to Creeley:

> *my assumption is any POST-MODERN is born with the ancient confidence that, he does belong.*
> *So, there is nothing to be found. There is only (as Schoenberg had it, his Harmony) search) tho, I should wish to kill that word, too—there is only examination.*

Olson's conception of the post-modern, curiously, very curiously, has resonance with the great historian Marshall Hodgson's definition of the technical age, both in his posthumously collected essays and in *The Venture of Islam*, where he speaks about the technical age and the idea of different velocities of technology, how that affects people and society. In the letter to Ruth Benedict, from 1946, Olson writes:

The EXPANSION of peoples, materials and sensations that the AGE OF QUANTITY involves itself in, DEMAND a heightening of that servant of clarity, the CRITICAL FUNC-TION, wherever: that is, the above increases in the quantity of experience is also an increase in the sources of confusion, and so, to cut them down requires more labor than previously... that the job now, is to be at once archaic and culture-wise— that they are indivisible.

In another August 1951 letter to Creeley, Olson writes:

I am led to this notion: the post-modern world was projected by two earlier facts—a) the voyages of the 15th and 16th Century making all the earth a known quantity (thus, geographical quantity absolute); and (b) 19th Century, the machine, leading to (1) the tripling of population and (2) the same maximal as the geographic in communications systems and the reproductive ones.

In other words, that, the QUANTITATIVE, which, as I guess you know, has been the rock I have been trying to crack, is so embedded that one should not be surprised that it has forced all old functions to behave anew.

This echoes a passage in the 1946 letter to Benedict:

It is my feeling that <u>the record of fact</u> is become of first impor-tance for us lost in a sea of question... In New History, the act of the observer, if his personality is of count, is before, in the

*collection of the material. This is where we will cut the knot...
I think if you burn the facts long and hard enough in yourself
as crucible, you'll come to the few facts that matter, and then
fact can be fable again.*

This is remarkable in its applicability to a number of
aspects of the paradoxical situation we find ourselves in:
information overload on the one hand, and containment
—excluded areas—on the other. How do you categorize
information, how do you deal with knowledge, how do you
find it, how do you transmit it, how do you make, as he
says, "fact fable"? How do you turn fact into a narrative so
it can move somewhere? Where do you do this from? What
does it mean to be "at once archaic and culture-wise"?

In this same year of 1951, Olson applies for a Fulbright
to study Sumerian civilization in Iraq. His application is
rejected. I'm convinced that if Olson had lived in a world
where he *could* have gotten a Fulbright to Iraq, the cultural
history of the post-WWII period might have looked very
different. In his proposal to the Committee, from his
Selected Letters, Olson writes:

*My desire is to go to IRAQ to steep myself, on the ground, in
all aspects of SUMERIAN civilization (its apparent origins in
the surrounding plateaus of the central valley, the valley city-
sites themselves and the works of them, especially the architecture and the people's cuneiform texts).*

*The point of a year of such work at the sites and in collec-
tions is a double one: (1) to lock up translations from the clay
tablets, conspicuously, the poems & myths (these translations
& transpositions have been in progress for four years); and
(2), to fasten—by the live sense that only the factual ground*

gives—the text of a book, one half of which is SUMER. (The other half is the MAYA, and the intent, in putting these two civilizations and especially their arts together, is to try and make clear, by such juxtaposition, the nature of the force of ORIGINS, in the one case at the root of Western Civilization and in the other at the root of American Indian Civilization.

The further intent is that such a study throw a usable light on the present, the premise of such a study of origins being, that the present is such a time, that just now any light which can lead to a redefinition of man is a crucial necessity, that it is necessary if we are to arrive at a fresh ground for a concept of "humanism."

Such a proposition, coming from a highly trained scholar refusing the straightjacket of administered knowledge, constituted a radical break with almost all acceptable uses to which knowledge and research could be put. The scope of Olson's interests, his combination of curiosity and erudition, poetic creativity, political experience and sense of rooted history, coupled with his willingness to pursue apparently esoteric knowledge without a specialized degree, must have alarmed the Committee readers of his proposal, given the function the Fulbright Program was created to serve. Indeed, while serving as rector and teaching at Black Mountain College, in the mountains of North Carolina, Olson had a visitation from the FBI. Meeting the world on his terms, Olson was woken up by the agents and met them at the door naked, reaching for a towel when he realized who they were, welcoming them in. He later wrote to Creeley, whom he'd brought to Black Mountain to teach:

I imagine I did say to you that I doubted State wld take a risk

on me at such outposts of the empire as Istanbul or Teheran,
simply, that in such places, they can't afford more than pink-
cheeked servants.

Olson is clear about what apple carts he might be upsetting and what this seemingly abstruse research might mean in terms of possibilities for the formation of the intellectual, of fields of knowledge, the formation of a new curriculum, and what all this would mean to the established structures of power.

To get at this "examination" Olson called for, it is helpful to get into the milieu around decolonization, how different people behaved, and what some of the paths taken and not taken have been. There are many parallels: in the early 1960s, Olson writes a text called "Proprioception," using a term he had been familiar with that came up through phenomenology from the French philosopher Merleau-Ponty. It's a term that has significance in the debate around Algeria because of its connection to "otherness," emerging in the work of Frantz Fanon, for example, through different routes.

Around the time I was digging into this Olson material, I was reading a lot about Algeria of the 1950s and '60s and thinking about it in relation to political and intellectual responses by the parties seemingly with more power, i.e. the French—though the Algerians and the Vietnamese who opposed the French ultimately had real power, they won! In terms of how these things are perceived across time, I wanted to compare the responses in the seats of "power," in the metropoles, to what was going on, more in Algeria, less in Vietnam, along with the American response. A couple of things struck me. Number one, I was interested in the move, particularly in the United States, in black, African-American communities, from a possibility of a certain kind of internationalism to the constraints of an increasingly identity-based nationalist agenda, a move mirrored in different ways in many other communities in the United States. I was looking for indices, sign posts of this. The Red Scare, particularly on the West Coast, and the industrialization of cities and the increasing economic constraints on black communities, had a lot to do with the ability to participate, let's say, in worker organizations, in a trade unionism that was international in scope. What you have as one of the last gasps of a *certain kind* of internationalism, by the 1960s, is the Black Panther Party identification with foreign liberation movements, Third World movements, African liberation and so forth, with segments of the leadership going into exile in Algeria. Some part of this was of course self-preservation. This is not to place a value on any of these things, but to indicate that, at that time, they were in the realm of the possible.

I began to look at a journal published by Abdellatif Laabi, published originally in Morocco, in French, called *Souffles*, which came out from 1966 until 1972. In 1972 it was shut down by the authorities, and about two hundred people involved in it were imprisoned for long periods of time. Laabi was imprisoned for eight and a half years. The group included a very famous political prisoner and part of the political opposition, Abraham Serfaty. As an anti-Zionist, Serfaty's case was suppressed by the Israeli and American Jewish establishment, despite the cruel and unusual punishment he was subjected to for seventeen long years. It was in looking through old issues of *Souffles*, that I saw, in 1969, that Serfaty had hosted the delegation of the Black

Panther Party to Morocco and Algeria. He delivers his "salute to the African-Americans" at the cultural festival in Algeria. This is at the same time that COINTELPRO was running campaigns and planting infiltrators at home to paint the Black Panther Party with the brush of anti-Semitism, to subvert any cooperation and coalition between blacks and Jews, a linkage crucial to previous Civil Rights organizing. This takes place *after* the foundations upon which Cold War policies had been erected were beginning to crumble.

The irony of this future Jewish political prisoner in Morocco hosting the Black Panther Party at the same time as COINTELPRO's smear campaigns and fabrications are running in the United States pinpoints how a single historical incident can illuminate and set in relief wider geo-political and cultural relationships of a period. The obscuring or erasure of such events and facts provides a parallel to Olson's formulation of the "post-modern" and the almost complete obliteration of the origins of that term by its current use. These are crucial splits, breaks and connections we know little about; a recuperated memory of them is essential.

As I was doing more and more work on Algeria, I began to see that there was a clear cut-off point for these astonishing developments. If you look, from about 1956, '57, '58, '59, '60, '61, '62 up until about 1965, there's quite a bit of material that's appearing in the United States. It's being translated, primarily from French, specifically regarding the Algerian question. That's the context, for example, for a writer like Albert Camus. Only later, when removed from the context of debates on Algeria, does Camus come to represent a more amorphous position under rubrics like "humanism" or "existentialism," serving as a figure of choice in American Cold War discourse, as a model of "authenticity" for the young, as opposed to, say, the "disengaged" beatniks. The similarities of these operations to the labeling of people as "post-structuralist" and "Jewish" (with "exilic" or "diasporic" being the favorite adjectives), is startling: Jacques Derrida and Hélène Cixous specifically come to mind. In their adoption into a new, deracinated thought system, the fact Algerian Jews were granted French citizenship as early as 1897 by the Crèmieux Decree, while ninety-seven percent of the Algerian population, Muslims and Berbers, remained non-citizen colonial subjects, is seldom remarked upon. As the work of Camus became available, an important book by Henri Alleg, called *The Question*, is translated. Alleg was a European Jew, and the editor of an Algerian daily, captured and tortured in 1957 in al-Biar, one of the infamous torture chambers in Algiers. That book—the first to be banned in France since the late 18th century—was published immediately in the U.S., in 1958. This translation of Alleg's book, significantly, was reprinted in 2006, precisely when similar questions about complicity and torture were being raised in the United States.

Alleg's 1958 text was followed in the United States by a number of works by the late Germaine Tillion. She was an anthropologist and student of French anthropologist Marcel Mauss, whose *Essay on the Gift* exerted enormous influence in many different fields. Born in France, Tillion had done her field work in Kabylia in the Aurès mountains of Algeria in the 1930s. She joined the French resistance and, as the leader of a resistance group, was put up for the death sentence by the Vichy government on something like five different occasions. She ended up in Ravensbruck, in the category of prisoners destined to die in captivity. Her mother, also arrested for resistance activities, was killed in the gas chamber there, a month before the camp was liberated. Tillion survived and went on to do her doctorate under the great Orientalist Louis Massignon, known for his work on the 10th century Muslim mystic and martyr al-Hallaj. Because of her experiences in Algeria, she served as a liaison between Saadi Yacef, one of the original Algerian resistance leaders and a founder of the FLN, and the French. Many might inadvertently be familiar with Yacef, since he plays himself in Italian director Gillo Pontecorvo's masterpiece *The Battle of Algiers*, used after the Iraq invasion and occupation for counter-"insurgency" training by U.S. military and government officials. Tillion's role was crucial in negotiating several ceasefires during the war in Algeria while her books were coming out in English. At this time, as well, the work of Pierre Bourdieu on Algeria came out in English. The classicist Pierre Vidal Naquet's book *Torture: Cancer of Democracy,* on Algeria came out. Fanon's *Wretched of the Earth* sold 3,300 copies when it came out in 1961 in France but was reprinted twice before reaching the bookstores in its first American edition in 1965, eventually going through five paperback reprints in the Grove Press edition within a single year.

This list of things that were available then is part of what I mean by our having, by comparison, a woefully inadequate or misleading inventory of referential texts today around which theoretical constructs revolve. It is hard to believe and harder to remember that these books were part of the landscape in the United States, a part of intellectual discourse. There was a book about an Algerian prisoner, Djamila Boupacha, co-written by Simone de Beauvoir and Gisele Halimi. Gisele Halimi is now a prominent, still-practicing French human rights lawyer, a feminist, and Tunisian Jew. She signed on to become the prominent Palestinian political prisoner Marwan Barghouti's lawyer, in an important case in Israel.

I find it helpful to watch the fates of different people, people who have continued to maintain certain principles or certain stands on things and those who have changed their positions over time. On my way to lecture at Cornell, I read in *Le Monde Diplomatique* a long front-page piece by Maurice Maschino, on neo-conservative tendencies among French intellectuals. Maschino was a draft resister during the Franco-Algerian war and ended up going into exile in Tunisia. He was one of the first people writing reports about Algeria, from Tunisia, in 1956 or 1957. According to the article I was reading, Maschino seems to have maintained a certain sense, being able to connect Israel/Palestine, issues of racism, Iraq, and U.S. policy on the Middle East. My point in bringing these examples up is that they stand out against the trend.

Another dramatic instance of the quality of transmission in the distances traveled from the mid-'50s through the early 1960s up to the present can be seen in the case of Claude Lanzmann, the French director of *Shoah*. In the early 1960s, as a member of the editorial board of Jean-Paul Sartre's influential journal *Les Temps Modernes*, Lanzmann had gone to meet Frantz Fanon in Tunis and serve as an initial intermediary between Fanon and Sartre. Thirty years later, in 1994, Lanzmann made *Tsahal*, an epic apologia for the Israeli Army. In 2004, he played an influential part in a campaign to prevent the screening and distribution of *Route 181*, a film co-directed by Palestinian Michel Khleifi and Israeli Eyal Sivan; a scandal ensued in France when the film was pulled from a major festival by the Ministry of

Culture for "public safety concerns."

The swing from anti-colonialism to pro-Zionism consumed French and European intellectuals fully as much as Americans. Sartre was instrumental in this shift: having once endorsed Fanon's *Wretched of the Earth* with a preface not nearly as subtle as Fanon's text, promoting the idea of violence as a cleansing action, Sartre then publicly defended Israel's actions in the June War of 1967. Fanon's widow Josie insisted that Sartre's preface be removed from all subsequent editions of *Wretched of the Earth* "because of the pro-Zionist and pro-imperialist position taken by its author with respect to Zionist aggression against Arab peoples." None of this is common knowledge, nor has it been included in how we might think about, for example, the roots of "French theory" in America, the constructs of existentialism, postmodernism, postcolonialism and so much else. Scratching below the surface of debates following 9/11, one can find similar fault lines and shifts. The exchange of letters in the *London Review of Books* that went on for several months following a "roundtable" issue on 9/11—featuring prominent intellectuals, critics, and writers from both sides of the Atlantic presents a textbook case in such uses of authority.

I think that for us, it's crucial to practice this activity of investigating shifting allegiances and the consequences they bring with them, looking at breaks and splits, to begin to enact possibilities Olson, for one, was exploring, and that others have picked up on here and there since. While it is important to call out those working to disappear or obscure the legacy of the 1950s and 1960s, it is equally important to recuperate and retrieve those figures and histories that have fallen by the wayside and are no longer part of the general intellectual framework—figures and histories that open up models for experience of the present and an imagination for the future. This is not simply recuperation, but activation of the past in new contexts. While Archie Shepp was playing at the 1969 Pan-African Festival in Algeria, with thirty Tuareg musicians, segments of the U.S. Army were in open revolt. In Congress, there was open discussion, using official figures, of how ten to fifteen percent of American soldiers were on heroin. You're looking at whole units, during Moratorium Day in 1970, going on strike, demonstrating against the war while in the middle of it, with other units refusing to fight and having to be replaced. You're talking about strategy documents from the Naval War College analyzing the relationship of the Civil Rights movement to what's going on in the Army and to what's going on in U.S. cities. A hundred and twenty five cities have anti-police riots or revolts. 1968, '69, and '70 are very, very, very tumultuous years.

After having spent so much time with friends who lived through the early to mid-'90s siege of Bosnia, I'm coming to think more and more that, sometimes, even if you live through something, you don't really understand what it is about until long afterwards. We need everything we can possibly gather: conversations, memoirs, names, dates, anything that will begin the work of connecting past to present.

Go back, for example, to those last years in which the war in Vietnam effectively ends but soldiers are still there, '67, '68, and '69. Look at how people organized, what kinds of things were effective, how people operated. The erosion in opposition and dissent since then is remarkable—you're talking about, in 1969, 1970, five hundred and fifty underground newspapers in this country with a circulation of about five million. A magazine like *Ramparts* had a circulation of 300,000 in 1967 and 1968. The kind of headlines that were coming out in underground papers are extraordinary compared to today. One hundred and forty-four underground papers on U.S. military bases, with headlines like "Don't desert, go to Vietnam and kill your commanding officer." Some of the stories of individual and collective courage and resistance from this period appear in Zeiger's *Sir! No Sir!,* a film that suggests a thread from the resistance of GIs in the Vietnam War to the Gulf War and occupations of Iraq and Afghanistan. There are many more such stories, if one digs to find and recover them.

It's unimaginable but extremely valuable for our understanding to grasp dissent and opposition, what assertiveness can mean and how these can be, and have been, tied to thinking, research, action, and placing the body, as well as our public activities, literally, on the line. These are crucial to imagination, the imaginative faculties, to narrative, to poetics. To think about such things enables us to see how constrained we are, how constrained things have become, and to experience an opening that is not limited to the present.

Amiri Baraka, the great African-American writer, in an interview that director Henry Ferrini, poet Anne Waldman, and I conducted for Ferrini's film *Polis Is This: Charles Olson and the Persistence of Place,* elaborated on how Olson, attuned to the concrete relation of politics and imagination, brought something crucial to the endeavor of knowledge and poetry different from the direction things took:

Charles was coming out of a political and educational background, the work he did with Roosevelt in the 1940s, being the chancellor at Black Mountain, meant he had an enormous amount of information. Information is actually ammunition, because a lot of people don't have the information. They might have what they think of as an emotional charge. But to be able to have that, contain that with their wide sweep of information is a huge factor. You are talking about somebody who can link up the Roosevelt campaign with Mayan practices in one swoop. I think the problem now is they have reduced poetry again to abstract metaphor and they are not trying to teach you anything. They are trying to be ironic or to make you feel sad or happy, but it is not a teaching instrument anymore. The idea of you teaching, and then to be emotionally raised up, that to me is what a poet is supposed to do. The educational process, the political process along with the emotional charge, that is supposed to be one thing. And with the whole motion of the 1960s, what the poetry began, they are covering it up again. It is like the door opened and the door closed. It is a near tragedy, but one that has to be fought back against. You have to fight that because what they do, they bring in another wave of academic people who are just talking about nothing at all. They refuse to talk about the world. What is going on now is like the fifties. You have another set of loyalty oaths. With that, you get a cover, a muting and a mutation of the arts themselves. So what passes as art suddenly has changed and is mutated. The unfortunate thing for us, I think, is that a lot of people of our own generation are dying at this point when we are in a real key kind of transitional period. You see people drop all around you. Great people, people who could help explain the world. These people preserve the life of the future. Without that history the future will be born dead, born as a corpse.

Given the enormous stakes, these matters raise a number of further questions. How might one open things up in the context of different levels of autonomy, whether it's an academic setting or some other setting one finds oneself in?

Where is this kind of creative, historical, and intellectual work done, what is it about, who is it for? How can one begin to slough off the decorum and change the terms of activities, through different relationships and different contexts, reconsidering what such things might mean, either in the world of a small community we create or out in the larger world?

DISCUSSION FROM THE CORNELL FORUM:

Deborah Starr, Moderator: What you're doing, to a great extent, is shifting the narrative of how we got to this point of conflict. That shifts its meaning. You've given us a sense of the need to recover lost narratives and alternative sites of resistance as you situated them, initially in contrast to privileged sites of radicalism, particularly within the academy. I would be curious to hear you articulate a little bit more why you think that Israel has become the screen through which everything Middle Eastern is filtered at this point. Although it is usually articulated through political science or international relations discourse, it seems to me there may be some connection between the kinds of attacks taking place on alternative views of the Middle East in the U.S. academy, as represented by something like Campus Watch, and the kinds of things reflected in Olson when he spoke of "LIFE out of Yale, CULTURE out of Princeton, and the BOMB out of Harvard."

Ammiel Alcalay: I spent about eight years, off and on, living in Jerusalem. I learned a lot about America there, witnessing the rapidity with which nativity was eroded by the process of transformation, people forced or squeezed off the land to become laborers or refugees. I grew up in New England, so I grew up in and with all these place names of peoples who are pretty much no longer there, or at least not there to the extent they had been. It made me think and internalize, in a new way and at a more conscious age, certain things that had always been a part of me. The experience of Jerusalem drove it all home.

Beyond the kind of geo-political, military, economic and other more obvious aspects of the relationship of the U.S. to Israel, what else is there and how does it get manifested? Besides the pop imagery, the settler and westward expansion, and the presence of references to Native Americans in Palestinian literary discourse, there is, I think, more to it. I find some of the contemporary parallels to Algeria mortifying in the sense that, if one thinks about movements now to legalize torture in the United States, from a legal perspective, Israel is the state that we have the closest public, open relationship with and that we claim follows our tradition as a democratic country. This is not something the United States would claim in terms of its client states in Latin America. It would not make these claims for other places in the world, but this claim is made towards Israel where torture is a publicly acknowledged and institutionalized policy upheld by the courts. This creates very real political precedence and a set of very real political problems.

I was reading Pierre Vidal Naquet's *Torture: Cancer of Democracy*, and it struck me that in all of the publicity, in all of the different and superb work done, both by Israeli human rights groups like Betselem, and other, older pioneering Palestinian groups like Palestinian Human Rights Database, and others, I am as yet unaware of anything that looks at this issue both conceptually and institutionally, that is, in a larger sense, outside the specifics of the individual cases. A lot of the work merely reinforces the roles everyone is already in—victim, perpetrator, state institution, and so on—and legitimizes the state as the body allowed to condone, condemn, and decide. This relates to a point I brought up before: when we look at a situation using the discourse of human rights, we emphasize the repression without necessarily thinking of the resistance. When people look at instances of human rights abuse and torture in Israel, they are not considering its function and structure—psychologically, socially, politically, culturally, economically—within the state itself. And I don't mean just the corrupting nature of the practices, which is how it is generally considered if it is considered at all, but more in terms of criminalization, imprisonment, racism, and militarization in this country, with all its economic and political implications. To not think about these things critically is stultifying and prevents us from acknowledging the potential of our power. There is certainly a parallel to the different forms of repression and coercion operative in the United States—as liberals and progressives bemoan measures taken by the Bush administration, few point out that the need for such pervasive and repressive measures indicates that the populace is NOT down with the program, and could thus be disruptive. Things have to be taken beyond the accusatory level, to try and conceptualize what is going on and figure out where the pressure points might be to exert actual change.

Audience: After September 11, I saw a headline, that said "Why?" It was rhetorical—Americans don't want to know why, and it was amazing how quickly the discussion about "why" disappeared. I tend to be pretty vocal in my condemnation of U.S. policy, particularly in the Middle East, but Israelis don't ask why—I mean, a suicide bomber goes into a shopping mall or something and blows himself up, they don't ask why, they know why. So, as much as there are parallels between Israel and the United States, there are some differences. How is it that this discussion never gets started?

Alcalay: I'll read you a quote by Melani McAlister, from her book *Epic Encounters: Culture, Media, and U.S. Interests in the Middle East, 1945–2000*. In a chapter on the 1979 Iran hostage crisis, she offers one of the best descriptions I've seen of this difference you bring up:

Terrorism's presence on the world stage enabled a narrative that constructed the United States as an imperiled private sphere and the Islamic Middle East as the preeminent politicized space from which terrorism affected its invasions. For more than a decade that narrative had worked to produce a type of American identity, defined by the production of individuals who were "free of politics." Within this world of vulnerable families and lovers, terrorism threatened precisely what had to be threatened in order to establish the disinterested morality of the state's militarized response in the international arena.

In the Israeli case, I think there's a different dynamic at work, and I don't think it's just a question of them not asking why. To begin with, there's a different level of consciousness there and here—things that one can speak about normally in Israeli discourse are almost impossible to speak about in American discourse. There is a presence there, people understand what is at stake, whichever side of the political spectrum you may fall on. But I think that there is also a combination of cynicism, racism, and, ultimately, dehumanization occurring which expects "those people" to commit "those" kinds of acts. So that a different kind of "why" can be asked, or not asked, than the one that is not asked here.

Audience: So much of our discussion, at least at the Cornell Forum, has had to do with a sense of a certain political impasse that we're at right now and the difficulty of getting a discourse of political dissent going. I thought that what you really addressed in your remarks is the lack of a mode of cultural criticism, a cultural kind of frame, and you got to the very heart of it, to address how that lack might be part of the impasse. I wondered if you might talk a little bit more about why you were interested in Charles Olson's notion of the post-modern, because I think you're suggesting an alternative conception of postmodernism which might be more politically viable than what we have now.

Alcalay: What we've gotten is what I would call industrialized postmodernism, it's off the assembly line. I feel that a lot of the theoretical language and the way it's taught and how it's used is really colonizing, it's a subjugation of the material that it's supposed to be examining, and a kind of training in subjugation. Olson's interest in archeology was not happenstance, it was an attempt to begin to allow the objects to determine the theory. It was, as he said, to "be on the ground," to examine the stuff in its proper place and see what emerges from it. I find much of what we're doing now is very much the opposite. However radical it may seem internally, what it does is to entrench power, at various levels, disciplinary power and categories of thinking—it encloses people and encloses thought. In other words, only a certain kind of border crossing is sanctioned and legalized. This domesticates the principle and precludes a truer border crossing that might more fundamentally disrupt, and open up, ways of thinking and approach. What you say points to a real problem. There's some terrific political work and analysis going on, but the cultural connection is buried much deeper and is more marginalized. It's almost as if the people who are doing politics think, "Well, that's later, we can't really deal with that now, this is more important, we'll get to culture and other things after the political work." I think that's very counter-productive. Politics needs to be done holistically. All the parts need to mesh. If they don't, the political work is hollow, it doesn't get any traction and can't last. Without investigating the borders of our imagination, the "changing same" of politics cannot take root.

3

I've been thinking a lot about a quote of Olson's I first encountered many years ago, in a short review of a book about Billy the Kid, originally published in 1954 and reprinted in the 1967 edition of *Human Universe and Other Essays*:

It's this way. Here's this country with what accumulation it has—so many people having lived here a millennia. Which ought to mean (people being active, more or less) an amount, you'd figure, of things done, and said, more or less, as in other lands. And with some proportion of misery—for which read "reality," if you will wait a minute and not take "misery" as anything more than a characterization of unrelieved action or words. That is: what strikes one about the history of sd states, both as it has been converted into story and as there are those who are always looking for it to reappear as art— what has hit me, is, that it does stay, unrelieved. And thus loses what it was before it damn well was history, what urgency or laziness or misery it was to those who said and did what they did. Any transposition which doesn't have in it an expenditure at least the equal of what was spent, diminishes what was spent. And this is loss, loss in the present, which is the only place where history has context.

What needs to be done to ease this pressure of loss, to relieve the past? One can't help but try to contextualize things through the present, through the immediate present. As I was thinking about that, I was considering a letter by Robert Duncan to Olson in 1963, May 9th I believe. It was one of the things in the *H.D. Book* in which Duncan outlined the idea of generations, writers belonging to certain worlds, worlds they were born into and those worlds having certain qualities or characteristics. He mentions a remark by Gertrude Stein in *The Making of Americans,* something to the effect that an American doesn't know what he or she is doing until they are about twenty-eight years old. Duncan agreed, saying he was twenty-eight when he wrote *Medieval Scenes.* Then it took him another two years to figure out whether he knew if he knew what he was doing. Which made him thirty. And so, I took twenty-eight to thirty as being this generational marker and began thinking from the present backwards about how one might contextualize Olson in the present. Getting at this context, looking at all the origins and erasures, has a lot to do with detecting shifts and transmissions between and across generations.

In a scene from one of my favorite movies, *The Big Lebowski,* by the Coen brothers—this film now has a whole subculture around it—two guys, played by John Goodman and Jeff Bridges, have a close friend who has just died of a heart attack. After having his body cremated, the friends are confronted with a problem. They have been given their friend's ashes by the funeral home, but, unable to afford an urn, they buy a large coffee can instead. They decide to hold their own private service for him and are about to spread the ashes out over the Pacific Ocean. The character Goodman plays, Walter Sobchak, is a Vietnam vet who isn't, let's say, fully balanced:

WALTER SOBCHAK *(Goodman): …and as a surfer he explored the beaches of Southern California, from La Jolla to Leo Carillo, and up to Pismo. He died, he died as so many young men of his generation before his time. And you took him, Lord, you took him, as you took so many bright flower-*

ing young men, at Khe Sanh, at Lon Doc, and Hill 364.
These young men gave their lives, so Donny, Donny who
loved bowling… And so, Theodore Donald Karabatsos, in
accordance with what we think your dying wishes might well
have been, we commit your final mortal remains to the bosom
of the Pacific Ocean which you loved so well. Goodnight,
Sweet Prince—

[Goodman opens the coffee can with Donny's ashes in it; a
wind blows towards them and the ashes fly away from the
ocean and all over Goodman's friend, the Dude, played by
Jeff Bridges]

WALTER: *Oh, shit, dude I'm sorry.*

THE DUDE: *Goddamnit Walter, fucking asshole.*

WALTER: *I'm sorry.*

THE DUDE: *It's a fucking travesty with you, man. What was*
that shit about Vietnam? What the fuck does anything have to
do with Vietnam? What the fuck are you talking about?

That's what I wanted you to hear, that question: *What does*
anything have to do with Vietnam? This is how I began to
think generationally backwards. It takes us back to that
extraordinary quote from George Bush Sr.'s inaugural
before the first Gulf War: "The final lesson of Vietnam is
first that no great nation can long afford to be sundered by
a memory." Going back further, there is a quote from the
period right after Olson's death, the early 1970s:

We were sent to Vietnam to kill communism but we found

instead that we were killing women and children. We knew the saying "War is hell," and we knew also that wars take their toll in civilian casualties. In Vietnam, though, the greatest soldiers in the world, better armed and better equipped than the opposition, unleashed the power of the greatest technology of the world against thatched huts and mud paths. In the process, we created a nation of refugees, bomb craters, amputees, orphans, widows and prostitutes and we gave new meaning to the words of the Roman historian Tacitus: "Where they made a desert they called it peace." We wish that a merciful God could wipe away our own memories of that service as easily as this administration has wiped away their memories of us. But all that they have done and all they can do by this denial is to make more clear than ever our own determination to undertake one last mission. To search out and destroy the last vestige of this barbaric war, to pacify our own hearts, to conquer the hate and the fear that have driven this country these last ten years and more. So when thirty years from now...

—that "thirty years from now" would be around 2001—

...our brothers go down the street without a leg, without an arm or a face and small boys ask why, we will be able to say "Vietnam" and not mean a desert, not a filthy obscene memory, but mean instead the place where America finally turned, and where soldiers like us helped in the turning.

These are the words of John Kerry, speaking before the Senate Foreign Relations Committee, April 22nd 1971. One could look at this text and be amazed at the distance Kerry traveled in his rise to political power. But one could also see evidence of something else, if one looks at things in light of

American politics and the precedent here of assassination and political blackmail. Holding the validity of the 2004 election results in abeyance, we might reconsider our perceptions of the importance of that election no matter how distant it has now been made to seem. Maybe the Democratic party didn't want to inherit the wars in Afghanistan and Iraq and the economic mess just yet. Maybe the Democratic party didn't want to win the election and didn't want John Kerry to become president, given his political history. Maybe his previous experiences, as a Vietnam vet and through investigations he initiated as a Senator, particularly the precursor to the Iran-Contra hearings, the Kerry Commission, with his subsequent investigations into the financing of terrorism, gave him access to structural knowledge. Kerry's staff was the one to first expose the illegal activities of Oliver North, uncovering the financial network behind the illegal transfer of arms to the Contras. After being denied a place on the official Congressional Iran-Contra Investigative Committee, Kerry exposed what the U.S. Senate ended up calling "one of the largest criminal enterprises in history." This enterprise, the Pakistan-based Bank of Credit and Commerce International, known as BCCI, was a model for international terrorist financing with deep roots in both parties and ties to senior and junior Bush administrations. But it was Kerry's decision to go after a major Democrat, Clark Clifford, implicated and indicted in the BCCI scandal, that would have marked Kerry as an enemy to his party. The deep politics of this are truly deep, as pointed out to me by Fred Dewey, since Kerry's attack on Clifford was also on one of the original architects of the national security state and the two-party fix. Given Kerry's history, maybe he understood that winning put his life and family in danger.

Given our history, these are plausible conjectures.

As a result, Kerry's formulation from 1971 has made me think about the enormous stakes in memory, where we place it, how we catalog it, where it goes and what happens to principles over time. We are living in a supposedly "postmodern" world. The characteristics of that supposed world are very unlike the characteristics of what I think Olson meant by that term when he used it in his letter to Creeley in 1951. So I want to telescope us back to see where Olson and others might fit as a path not taken by this culture, as those who may have had their finger on the pulse of debates, of arguments and issues that have largely become non-debates, non-issues, false debates, false issues. To put it another way, Olson and Duncan and others put their finger on matters that have become more and more important, however forgotten, buried, or unrelieved they may be.

According to Robert Duncan, Olson's 1910 birth meant that he was born in a "pre-World-War-world." He writes that Olson was "initiated into childhood—learned to walk and talk 'before the war' the last possible member of a creative family that we now sketch as having its *time* from 1882–1914." Duncan then goes on to characterize 1945-on, in this generational mapping, as "the state of War economy with the idea of world destruction." This echoes something Muriel Rukeyser said in the 1940s:

We are a people tending toward democracy at the level of hope; on another level, the economy of the nation, the empire of business within the republic, both include in their basic premise, the concept of perpetual warfare.

This observation by Rukeyser was made a half century before

the U.S. state openly and publicly described this as official doctrine. Rukeyser also provides the link between Duncan and poet and activist Denise Levertov, through a review of Duncan's first book, *Heavenly City, Earthly City*, that caught Levertov's attention in 1948. It was Rukeyser who would accompany Levertov to Hanoi in 1972, when Levertov's relationship with Duncan was strained to the breaking point.

The relationship of Duncan and Levertov, with their differences and debates revealed in nearly five hundred letters exchanged between the poets from 1953 to 1988, can tell us a lot. The letters explore, as their co-editor Albert Gelpi writes, "how the imagination can and should address violence, how poetry can and should engage politics." For Duncan, life and the practice of art were already politics: "I write as I do and live as I do not because these are 'right' but because I want this kind of living and writing to come into existence."

What had been a life for Duncan, open homosexuality and a long domestic relationship with the artist Jess Collins, was being turned, by society, into a "lifestyle." For Levertov, "words" had "to be filled with, backed up by, imaginative experience," something Duncan felt implied a reliance on "truth anterior or exterior to the realization of poetic form." By contrast, for Levertov, commitment to "the movement" had nothing overtly to do with poetic form, while "taking on the burden of action," as she says in *New & Selected Essays*, could be a source of "unforeseen blessings."

Surely Olson's early piece "Against Wisdom as Such," directed at Duncan, continued to resonate and had something to do with Duncan's convictions. As he wrote to Levertov, Duncan preferred to believe in what he called a "Robin Hood or guerrilla existence. Not for the future. But from the beginning of life." That letter, from March 30, 1968, has Duncan taking Levertov to task for thinking that, in writer and social thinker Paul Goodman's words, "We assume that the Americans do not *really* will the Vietnam War but are morally asleep and brainwashed."

[This is] an assumption that I do not make in the face of half a century of living in America, of having American parents—I see the Vietnamese War (as I saw the Second World War) as a revelation of the truth of the potential evil of 'America'—Blake, Hawthorne, Melville, Lawrence—Whitman in his 'Eighteenth Presidency'... the Vietnamese War as a revelation of the truth of American Karma, what Commager calld [sic] the consequences of the unacknowledged, unrepresented crimes. There are those, even among those who feel Vietnam is a revelation of the evil, who think the carnage of Berlin, Dresden, Hamburg, Tokyo, Hiroshima 'was in a good cause.'

Like Olson, Duncan's companion Jess Collins was somebody who could have made a mark officially, participating at the highest levels of the country's establishment. Jess was a chemist who, while in the military, worked on the Manhattan Project and later at Hanford. He had a dream, I believe it was in 1946, that the world would be destroyed. He left his chemical engineering career behind and enrolled in art school.

Olson's case is even more revealing. He'd gone far as a child of immigrants, but he retained the consciousness of his class background. He went to Wesleyan University and at the age of twenty-two was already doing the kind of primary research that would establish his scholarly credentials in a field he would then begin to question and, eventually, leave behind. After pursuing research in the newly defined field of American civilization, Olson wrote in the 1930s about Melville. Olson's subsequent move into politics and his work under the Roosevelt administration was a very clear turn away from the academy, just as his turn away from party politics would signal an even more radical stance towards knowledge, history, experience, community, narrative, and form. In a letter to Van Wyck Brooks from Washington, dated August 6, 1945, Olson announces that the "Melville Book is finished." This would be *Call Me Ishmael.* As Ralph Maud, the Olson scholar, points out, it was chronologically after the atomic bombs dropped on Japan that "Olson direct-ed his attention to the cannibalism of the Essex story... Olson told Ann Charters that he wrote the introductory 'First Fact' on the ferry back from Nantucket on what was presumably Monday 20 August 1945." The sentiments Olson began to express after the war, about political corruption and "the big lie" war had become, referring to the "big war" as a "defeat for the people," were more apparent and visibly popular, that is, widely shared and in the open for the public, *before* the war than after it. With the Cold War looming, Olson, like Jess, chooses to move, to find a different vantage point from which to work.

It would be good to recall some of poet Bob Kaufman's activities in this context. In a documentary radio show writ-ten and produced by David Henderson—poet, Jimi Hendrix biographer, and one of the founders of the Umbra Arts Work-shop—brother George Kaufman recounts Bob's experiences:

Bob and I lived together in New York when he was a seaman. I was a merchant seaman then too. He represented the National Maritime Union at conferences in London and

France after the war. Then he got into politics. He was an area
director for Henry Wallace's [presidential] campaign in 1948.
The Progressive Party. [Bob] ran into some real problems. He
was an area director in the wrong area and he ran into some
real serious problems with the police forces definitely trying to
see his point of view wouldn't be heard in that area of the
country. He was arrested many times, brutally beaten, thrown
into jail cells with no heat and freezing conditions and kept
there for a long time. But that never stopped him. He still had
his own way of thinking.

Bob Kaufman's case, maintaining his "own way of thinking,"
eventually entailed complete withdrawal in the form of a
vow of silence taken after the assassination of JFK. He kept
that vow until almost the end of the war in Vietnam. When
I talk about Olson responding, turning away from this very
real possibility of either becoming a very significant academic or person in Democratic party politics—he might have
been offered the head of the Democratic National Committee or Postmaster General, the latter a classic patronage re-
ward for good party service—it is to show that, for Olson, it
was clear the world, and America's role in it were going a
certain way and he was going in another direction, an alternative direction.

When, in "This Is Yeats Speaking," Olson asks "what
have you to help you hold in a single thought, reality and
justice?", he addresses this in its broadest possible terms—as
a call for a new kind of ethics, a new kind of work based on
new materials. He's quite clear about the Cold War, what
institutional affiliations in such a climate are about, what is
happening, and where he has to go. He attempts to go across
time, through place, by going to the Yucatan. He begins to

research, and conceive of, culture in a holistic way, something that's begun to return more recently, connecting archaeology and astronomy, anthropology, ecology, neurology, biology, and linguistics, relating these and looking at production and culture as being of a piece, as humanly connected. Olson's conceptualization of these things anticipates the most advanced contemporary thought, theories linking genes to language and migration.

Olson went to the Yucatan to study the Maya at the same time he applied to get his Fulbright to go to Iraq. He was simultaneously fascinated with the Ancient Near East and the antiquity of the Ancient Near East. Olson was onto the fact antiquity itself has an antiquity. He was relating the case of North America and the "Old World." Like Meso-America, Mesopotamia had an antiquity that you would have to go back to, to the Neolithic and Paleolithic, and you would have to look at it in a full sense, in relation to the pre-history of the Americas, to begin understanding anything. You had to go back, as broadly and concretely as possible. Clearly moving along Olson's trajectory, poet, writer, and translator Clayton Eshleman has dedicated significant creative and intellectual energies to just this sort of inquiry in his *Juniper Fuse: Upper Paleolithic Imagination & the Construction of the Underworld.*

The concern with Pound, the interest in the antiquity of antiquity, awareness of the politics of knowledge, all these form a kind of pre-history to Olson's taking up poetry. Olson had two personal relationships, two friendships that were very important to his awareness and consciousness about what took place in Europe during WWII. My dates and some of the details on all this may not be fully accurate, but I believe the first of these friendships involved Corrado

Cagli. Cagli was an Italian sculptor and painter and his sister
Serena married an old Alcalay family friend, Mirko Basaldella,
an Italian sculptor and painter. I remember Mirko from my
childhood, impeccably dressed, a chain-smoker, able to sculpt
out of any and all possible materials, making little figures of
bulls out of tongue depressors when my brother or I were sick,
masks made from the hoods of automobiles or monumental
totems from bronze or driftwood. Cagli had apparently come
to this country from Italy because his daughter, I believe,
was studying here. In checking his biographical information,
I found the following: in 1938, as racial laws were instituted
in Italy, because of his Jewish origins, Cagli fled to Paris, then
to New York, where he got a studio. In 1941 he became an
American citizen and enlisted in the army. He was one of the
people to enter, now as an American soldier, the Buchenwald
concentration camp. He made a series of remarkable drawings of what he saw. One of Olson's most important poems,
a poem that really marks the terms of where the human race
is at the time, a poem I have cited often in my work, from
1946, is "La Préface." He would publish a chapbook with it
and Cagli's drawings together. The poem refers both to what
Cagli saw and to what another friend, Jacques Ribaud, a
mathematician and French Resistance fighter experienced.
Ribaud became close to Olson in that period. He had been
interned in a camp and was the person who ended up
weighing, as the poem notes, "80 lbs." This is "La Préface":

The dead in via
> *in vita nuova*
>> *in the way*
You shall lament who know they are as tender as the horse is.
You, do not speak who know not.

"I will die about April 1st..." going off
"I weigh, I think, 80 lbs..." scratch
"My name is NO RACE"   address
Buchenwald   new Altamira cave
With a nail they drew the object of the hunt.

Put war away with time, come into space.
It was May, precise date, 1940. I had air my lungs could breathe.
He talked, via stones   a stick   sea rock   a hand of earth.
It is now, precise, repeat. I talk of Bigmans organs
he, look, the lines! are polytopes.
And among the DPs—deathhead

at the apex

of the pyramid.

Birth in the house is the One of Sticks, cunnus in the crotch.
Draw it thus: (   ) 1910 (
It is not obscure. We are the new born, and there are no flowers.
Document means there are no flowers

and no parenthesis.

It is the radical, the root, he and I, two bodies
We put our hands to these dead.

The closed parenthesis reads: the dead bury the dead,
and it is not very interesting.
Open, the figure stands at the door, horror his
and gone, possessed, o new Osiris, Odysseus ship.
He put the body there as well as they did whom he killed.

Mark that arm. It is no longer gun.
We are born not of the buried but these unburied dead
crossed stick, wire-led, Blake Underground

The Babe
        the Howling Babe

I grew up with stories of both the lucky ones who landed in Italian DP camps and others who disappeared without a trace. The starkness and drama of this poem stuck with me from when I first encountered it as a teenager, even though at the time I couldn't articulate why.

In a remarkable article called "Warlords of Atlantis: Chasing the Demon of Analogy in the America(s) of Lawrence, Artaud and Olson," André Spears writes:

"La Préface" not only announces the start of Olson's career as a poet, but also, in line with Artaud's continued work on the Tarahumara, the poem views humanity's radical, archaic commitment to the creative impulse as the most immediate means for contending with the midden of history.

In *Juniper Fuse*, Eshleman also points to "La Préface" as a marker, and specifically investigates the phrase "'My name is NO RACE'   address / Buchenwald new Altamira cave":

Olson's presentation of Buchenwald and Altamira (shadowed by Odysseus' response to the Cyclops' question), with space rather than a verb between the two nouns, presents the reader with an overwhelming question: What do these two nouns have in common? The answer that I find suggests that the astonishing ancientness of the human creative impulse, which was discovered in this most inhuman century, may somehow offset total despair.

This is further articulated by Rasula in *The American Poetry Wax Museum*:

Olson abandoned a budding political career for poetry in the aftermath of the atomic bomb and the disclosure of the Holocaust. But the appearance of the Collected Poems, *edited by George Butterick (1987), made it clear that Olson turned to poetry as the most imaginatively expedient means of reckoning the cost, to the species, of such historical traumatization.*

Spears describes Olson's chapbook *Y & X*, from 1948, with Cagli's drawings:

This collection, like Olson's first major volume In Cold Hell, In Thicket *(1953), opens with "La Préface" ("Buchenwald new altamira cave"), the poem that stands as the clearest instance of his writings' ideological rootedness in the moral collapse of Western civilization after World War II... In addition, "La Préface" is the most succinct exposition of the archaeological scale by which Olson proposes to elaborate an enduring poetic response to the trauma of global warfare.*

As Spears notes, Olson's temporal scope never abandons specifics in the insistence that all human time connects:

As an "archaeologist of morning," Olson is positioned to bring to his poetry the globalism and "post-modernism" of a Pleistocene perspective on history, from which he looks as far back as the discovery of fire and the invention of language to relocate humanity in the present.

Despite a severe language barrier, Olson's encounter with Cagli proceeded through gesture and symbol. In this short poem, Olson was able to convey a profoundly human encounter and transfer of vital knowledge across what he once defined as the limitations any one of us is inside of. He did this through "a nail" drawing "the object of the hunt," "via stones a stick... a hand of earth."

My parents came from Belgrade and were refugees in WWII. They ended up in Italy where they were in hiding. My late father was a painter and he had his first exhibits in Rome right after that war, 1945–46. Then he ended up working as an art guide in the Vatican. And one of the people my father met in Rome was sculptor and artist Mirko Basaldella, Cagli's brother-in-law. After my parents came to the United States in 1951, this thread led the family to Gloucester where a drawing by my father appeared in the first issue of Vincent Ferrini's magazine *Four Winds,* in 1952. That led to more involvement with all these people. First, there was Mary Shore, an artist in Gloucester who later married Ferrini, the poet to whom *The Maximus Poems* were addressed. Through Ferrini, we came to know Olson.

Olson had returned to Gloucester in the '40s, and Ferrini is somebody he goes to find and talk to because he realizes, through a poem by Ferrini he encountered in a small magazine, that here's maybe somebody he can talk to. This is occurring as Olson is rethinking the nature of political life. Ferrini is mentioned at a number of points in *The Maximus Poems,* and has been consistently misrepresented as a secondary and transient interlocutor, as if his labor, his publishing poetry since his debut *No Smoke* in 1941, his political toughness and connection to the local fishing industry did not embody part of a presence that Olson relied on. Olson's thoughts are precise when he declares Vincent Ferrini and Shore "the one brother and sister that

I have." This brings us back to one of the reasons Olson settled in Gloucester. He felt he found, in Vincent, a living connection to a possibility in American poetry and expression that had been almost completely obliterated or forced underground. As Olson saw it, Ferrini provided the key link between the activist, public poets of the 1930s and the "post-modern." Of Italian immigrant background, Ferrini had been a union organizer at General Electric during the Depression years, on some very tough terrain, in Lynn, Massachusetts, then moved to Gloucester, spending the rest of his life as a frame maker, poet, and activist in, and on behalf of, Gloucester. In light of this, it is important to note, for instance, that at Black Mountain College, Olson urged one of his great students, Michael Rumaker, to read Anzia Yezierska's masterpiece *Bread Givers*, a forgotten book that was later revived. He then convinced Rumaker he ought to write to her and Rumaker, indeed, began to correspond with Yezierska. While much has been made of Olson's relationship to women, his allegiance to immigrant and working-class roots is seldom explored, particularly given that his three prize students at Black Mountain, Rumaker, John Wieners, and Edward Dorn, all came from working-class backgrounds.

Withdrawing into small societies, very small societies of peer groups, like that in Gloucester, then the societies that get built up around small magazines and presses and around Black Mountain—these are acts that, as Olson put it, propose "the initiation / of another kind of nation." In the early *Maximus Poems* there is this kind of frontal attack on Ferrini and *Four Winds*. It's a crucial matter that has been taken out of context to obscure deeper ties. One of the things that Olson is trying to say here is—if you're going to have an independent society, which is this magazine—an independent community—then it has to be as good as any other endeavor. I think at some point he compares it to a fishing vessel where everybody on your crew would have to be tested, you wouldn't want to have somebody on that boat, on your crew, just because you heard they were good. That could be very dangerous. So Olson engages Ferrini. This is a key point about Olson's endeavor. It is the context that *The Maximus Poems* have been put in that makes this hard to understand—the false assumption is that one needs all kinds of erudition in order to approach something, one needs to know this, that, and the other thing. It's as if there were two strains of American poetry: those deriving from Pound—one needs all kinds of esoteric knowledge in order to even open their books—and those deriving from Williams—their work is vernacular and emotional. These origins and splits are posited so that everyone else becomes derivative or an imitator and can then be erased. Poets are not looked at in the complexity of their own historical or poetic experience, and experience that is the result of generational differences and allegiances. Poets become codified, in Robert Lowell's terms, as part of either "the raw" or "the cooked" schools.

Rasula points out that "after 1960, when it was clear that Charles Olson could not be conveniently ignored, it became fashionable to dismiss or belittle him as a derivative poet, overly indebted to Pound and Williams." Edward Bruner in his book *Cold War Poetry*, comments further on this:

What remained invisible to [Robert] Lowell was Olson's innovative return to bounded geography, for that in turn forced a recovery of the issue of civic welfare (the problem of the "polis")

as it was powerfully dramatized in the first three books: an inter-
est in working-class values and history from down under, a no-
nonsense revisionist approach to the founding of Massachusetts
as a business venture and a deromanticized portrait of the sea
as the ultimate dangerous working condition.

There's that famous poem by Olson where he talks about walking by that "bad sculpture" of a fisherman at the shore in Gloucester and he writes: "no difference / when men come back." All that is remembered is when they are lost at sea. It is helpful to read *The Maximus Poems* in light of the fact that work worth doing always entails risk. The price one might pay for making a mistake in dangerous working conditions becomes an example for Olson, just as the example of his father's union activities and the price his father paid for them shape Olson's intellectual ethics. Holding to an ethical standard, especially in building and maintaining a community is part of Olson's engagement with Ferrini at *Four Winds* or with poet and editor Cid Corman at *Origin.* It directly inspires the astonishing situation of a magazine like *Yugen*, edited by LeRoi Jones/Amiri Baraka and poet and writer Hettie Cohen/Jones, affirming the possibility of linking up the most vibrant but isolated and far-flung elements of thought and poetry throughout the country, with only a circulation of a few hundred copies.

To date these things generationally, and put oneself into such histories—my own ties to this world, through experiences and memories of going to Gloucester as a child, growing up around these journals and people—is essential to figure out how to take things off the shelf and put them back into the "polis," into the living context of a place and its location in a more collective, plural, geographical history.

Olson was very clear about how all these things were being compressed and ruined at just the moment they were most necessary—the things people needed to hold on to their experience and retain crucial independence. In the initial poem of *The Maximus Poems*, "I, Maximus of Gloucester, To You," he writes:

But that which matters, that which insists, that which will last,
*   that! o my people, where shall you find it, how, where, where*
*   shall you listen*
when all is become billboards, when all, even silence, is spray-
*   gunned?*

The question of the commercial, of ownership, Olson's insight of looking at Massachusetts as an enterprise of business and work, and the founding of the country as such an enterprise, not having any romanticism about that, pays dividends as things go on. The idea of engaging in a small society, of engaging in the exactitude of that—this is an aspect of Olson that has not been fully examined or acknowledged. Olson set the tone for what would become these independent societies of small magazines. In *Letters for Origin*, his correspondence with Cid Corman, his initial letter is clear:

But take a look at any little magazine, take a look at the PNY issue starring Apollinaire. What happens? The oldest thing here in these States: backtrailing, colonialism, culture scratching!

Any such endeavor has to have its own integrity, its own reason for being, its own purpose, its own standards, and its own work, otherwise it's not worth doing and can't be tested.

One can trace something like *Origin*, Ferrini's *Four Winds*, *Yugen*, *Floating Bear*, and so many other small magazines, to the growth of core principles in the underground press, to the growth of the idea of independence, of autonomy of thought, of means, of distribution. It is there that one can locate different kinds, different scales and activities of remembering and forgetting amidst the indices and life of public memory. It's in these kinds of things that one can begin to make a case for Olson as a major force in American thought and culture after WWII. A lot of things that happened afterwards would be unimaginable without that presence, without that work that was taking place from the mid-'40s through the '50s and begins to explode in the '60s, in the mid-'60s and later '60s—Olson's research, his many friendships, his involvement in creating and sustaining crucial clusters of activity and attention.

The role of authority in all of these matters and how it is both formed and deformed is something Olson is very concerned with, especially how individuals, through the practice of an ethic, can temper the deformities, or not. I'll leave the reviewer nameless for the moment, but in 1975, in the *New York Times Book Review*, there's a piece on Volume III of *The Maximus Poems*, in the Grossman Viking/Compass edition, Seelye's *Charles Olson & Ezra Pound: An Encounter at St. Elizabeths*, and *The Post Office*, Olson's memoir of his father, published in Bolinas by Donald Allen's Grey Fox. The review fills a whole page. It gives an indication of how Olson was already being framed five years after his death, by someone ostensibly sympathetic to his work. This comes at a point when I think even someone like myself (around twenty at that time) figured, well, maybe a whole cadre of scholars will come along and embalm the poet and entomb him in some kind of academic dust. This didn't happen—the few scholars who devoted themselves to Olson were unique and dedicated individuals. I'm thinking primarily of people like George Butterick and Ralph Maud, but also Ann Charters and Donald Allen very early on, Don Byrd, Charles Stein, Al Glover, Sherman Paul, Charles Boer, younger people like Benjamin Friedlander and others that I'm sure I'm leaving out, not to mention people like Ed Dorn, John Clarke, Duncan McNaughton, or Fred Wah, all of whom enacted Olson's poetics and ethics in diverse ways, through independent scholarship. They didn't do it out of any sense of careerism —quite the contrary, as *The New York Times* opinion of Olson makes clear. It is here that we can see that the paths not taken in the academy parallel those not taken in the culture and society generally. A major national paper codifies the general mechanics of how to handle Olson: he is defined as someone with great ambitions and a grand scheme but who is, on the whole, in the words of *The New York Times*, "a failure." How this is done is clever. The operation undertaken is all about the arbitrary nature of authority, that is, authority with no, or arbitrary, standards—an issue Olson had faced frontally with the Pound case, in "This is Yeats Speaking." With no overt and disclosed criteria for what might constitute a "success" or a "failure," innuendo and the public and private spheres come into play, as if in a secret trial based on evidence and criteria that never make it into the record and are never stated.

The review opens with what, superficially, would seem to be praise:

For twenty years or more Charles Olson has been a cult figure in American literature and a prophet of the Black Mountain poets...

To start with, these poets did not exist: there were no Black Mountain poets, just poets who went to Black Mountain.

...even to their second, third and successive indistinguishable generations.

It is not enough to pull in one generation, we must tar them all as "indistinguishable."

It is a fact to my mind, it is also a misfortune both for the man, i.e.: this posthumous reputation and for literature itself. We know what happens to cult figures. When the bubble bursts it bursts completely and they go down into academic oblivion. I hope this won't happen with Olson. But I fear it may.

The definition of Olson, the enclosure of Olson as a cult figure, encodes him at the outset as not being worthy of serious attention, much the way we are asked to treat "conspiracy theorists." We are made to feel sympathetic with the reviewer. He has a heart. He feels sorry for Olson, and so should we. We are forced into joining him in the unpleasant task of literary execution. The paper draws this conclusion:

The Maximus Poems...*is a huge and truly angelic effort. It needs prolonged reading and extended commentary. Here, all I can do is record my feeling that Olson succeeded only in parts. The whole is a failure.*

This business of killing through compliments is, indeed, a fine art. Through it, *The New York Times*, in a sense, sealed the official view of what this work, and this poet, should and should not be considered as. This takes on a bit more significance when one considers that the reviewer, Hayden Carruth, served his apprenticeship as an editorial assistant at *Perspectives USA*, a Ford Foundation-funded Cold War vehicle for promoting certain American views globally.

The New York Times April 1, 2005 obituary of Robert Creeley—whose friendship with Olson proved so important and fruitful—bears this out, in the choice of quotations and the inclusion of a critic of little literary standing as an obligatory detractor—"There are two things to be said about Creeley's poems," John Simon wrote. "They are short; they are not short enough."

Such stratagems serve to buffer and neutralize the effect and importance of our key poets as writers and thinkers, not so subtly disappearing vibrant and critical history to maintain administrative control: "Robert Creeley... helped transform postwar American poetry by making it more conversational and emotionally direct." The obituary then goes on to emphasize Creeley's relationship to William Carlos Williams's "vernacular style, casual diction and free-verse rhythms." While couched in genteel terms, the analogue of this would be to extol a "natural sense of rhythm" in the work of Langston Hughes. How different if the reporter started: "Robert Creeley, following in the line of classic American poets and thinkers like Dickinson, Emerson, and Thoreau was one of the formulators of the concept of 'post-modernity,' a category that has come to mean something different from what he and fellow poet and thinker Charles Olson originally delineated in 1951." Had such an obituary been written, I contend, we would be living in another country.

Audience: The review, as a whole, took Olson's oeuvre as a failure. All his work was a complete failure?

Ammiel Alcalay: Yes, it was a grand effort and it was a great endeavor but a failure. In this kind of thing, there is no indication of what, as I said, success might entail. Or what the terms are to begin with. What would success mean? To whom? What is the meaning of that whole terminology?

Anne Waldman: You have talked about why Olson left the Office of War Information and those kinds of decisions. I was interested in your statement that, had he stayed, he could have been a player. Can we get more context there? And about his not getting the Fulbright to go to Iraq?

Basil King: There was also the painter, Ben Shahn, who worked with Olson under Roosevelt and the two of them left pretty much at the same time…

Alcalay: The reasons were myriad. Roosevelt dies. The "big lie," Olson's interpretation of the result of the war, was a bitter response to hopes he might have once held. I think he could not see himself partaking in what was coming, he saw very clearly what kind of machine was being put into place, a machine both beholden to and creating special interests, that was going to effect all aspects of life, especially the endeavor of research, of intellectual thought and activity, the transmission and location of knowledge.

Waldman: It's unfortunate in a way because you want people like that "inside." I feel like this myself—sort of clamoring at the gates and wanting to be more effective. How do you become more effective, when you have to sort of swallow, and you're inside this thing... How do you get opportunities to make that radical shift?

Alcalay: I don't know what the answer to that is. I mean I think one can take it either way. I recommend people read the Robert Duncan/Denise Levertov correspondence. Duncan pulls out of the whole situation and probably has, ultimately, more effect on life as it gets lived by actual people than many others. His exclusion from official culture, once he wrote "The Homosexual in Society" in 1944, is rarely looked at, for example, in the context of gay culture though his actual life, as he chose to live it with Jess Collins, embodied a radical individual political decision with far-reaching consequences. Obviously, in Olson's case, to continue on in party politics was, from a temperamental position, a non-starter. He was outside. His poetics were a constant calling forth of a polity, a constituency, he clearly wanted a forum and wanted to create something that wasn't there yet.

Waldman: I see him as "the archaeologist of morning," through those images of him at the end, those little pieces of paper, gathering information, the shards, the mind that's so myriad, and yet trying to hold it all in consciousness.

André Spears: To follow-up on what you've said about Olson as the poet of the American path not taken... It's wrenching—Olson would be turning in his grave now over what's happened in America. But maybe not. I'm just wondering—talking about Truman and Roosevelt, thinking about Reagan and Bush—are you saying that rather than being the poet of an American path not taken we should look at another path that perhaps is being taken but perhaps not revealed, or one that is concealed and not acknowledged? Is that what you mean with this business of the small community, the small poetry magazines? How does one not despair, how do you not despair at this, how do you read a poet or a path not taken, an American path not taken without despairing, without positing at some level that there already is a path, but it's hidden? Is that what you're implying?

Alcalay: I'm trying to be specific about the time of these endeavors. Times change, obviously, but what I meant by a path not taken was that Olson was onto a lot of things about the—I don't want to use the word "nature"—but the elements out of which this country has mythologized itself and established itself and how that all actually works. He was on to this through his research and thinking about Melville, about Massachusetts, about the West and the gold rush, then Iraq and Mesopotamia, the Mayans, and the nature of the "West" as a whole. A lot of what has manifested itself are things that were nascent throughout this period. He has these lines: "having descried the nation / to write a Republic in gloom on Watch-House Point." And that's kind of where it ends up—"in gloom on Watch-House Point." From Gloucester, from my own roots and the ways I have gone about absorbing the possibilities of these roles, looking at this nation, the Olson lesson, it seems to me, is that one cannot be intellectually reclusive. One can be involved as a poet with poetry as fundamental fact, as a fundamental basis for facts and how one absorbs knowledge about the world, how one responds to the world. That can take different forms. One can engage in different ways with real life institutions and real life issues and problems using fundamental knowledge that is gained through encounters like these, through that kind of encounter that Olson has with Cid Corman, in establishing the critical parameters that would go into *Origin*, for instance. That might seem like a small act, but it doesn't have to be. Ultimately, in the scheme of things, it isn't small at all. When I go into thinking about how I'm going to do an editorial for a newspaper—what it is going to lead to or mean—I always keep in mind the effects Olson had on people, personally, in the human realm, through letters, through the force of his suggestions or ideas. When I came back from spending a number of years in Jerusalem, I was privy to precise and useful information because of the people I knew and met and all the activities I had been involved in. Had I chosen to, I could have attempted to market that experience to a place like the Sunday Magazine at *The New York Times*. I had the contacts, and certainly there was interest. But I realized that by doing that, I would be doing something to that experience and information that I didn't want to do. It would become part of that system and so become disposable. Instead, I set about to write a long letter to Robert Creeley. He had been invited to read in Jerusalem and I thought he ought to know what he was getting into, since the public relations propaganda machine there relied on using cultural figures. In other words, it was clear to me that passing this information and point of view on to Bob, a single individual, was more important in the larger scheme of things than publishing it in a mass circulation magazine. My letter was eventually published, with Bob's blessing. Olson was very clear about this sort of transmission from person to person. It's a very particular American genius, if you will, that Olson locates in Charles Peirce, and prior to William James, in pragmatism as practice, *how* one practices. This comes to fruition in Olson's study of [Alfred North] Whitehead—and here is yet another path not taken, for how many people today read or think about Whitehead? My point is, I think it's a question of not exactly the results but the process, how work moves between people and what kind of solidarity remains in the integrity of memory, as activities and meanings become codified for general consumption.

Audience: The Italian artist that you mentioned, are you saying by that that there was a European influence?

Alcalay: Olson's meeting with this particular artist, Corrado Cagli, was very personal and immediate—Cagli was bringing him news about what had happened, what was happening in Europe, and very first-hand news, as Olson also got from Jacques Ribaud. If one looks historically, as far as I can tell, the poem that I read is the first to respond particularly to what was happening. Cagli was the conveyer of that experience and knowledge and Olson, unlike many in the U.S., was receptive, and receptive in a unique and defining way.

Audience: Are you saying that Olson approached this years before it was generally acknowledged?

Alcalay: Olson transmitted this very immediate personal news into indelible markers. This is where we are: "no race," "new Altamira cave," "address Buchenwald." This is where the race is, the human race. That's our new address. Any other way of looking at it is not realistic. My whole connection to this—my parents had been part of this emigré artists' scene in Rome and then when they came to this country, that was our connection to Gloucester, through these people Olson had known. Again, one looks at this huge oeuvre of Olson's—the essays, *Call Me Ishmael, The Maximus Poems, The Collected Poems*, etc.—all produced by somebody who lived in poverty in a tenement in Gloucester. One of my father's favorite stories about Olson was of calling the Olsons on a hot summer night to see if they wanted to go to a movie and Charles's wife Betty saying "Well, Albert, I don't think we can do it, we don't have any money." And Charles saying in the background, "Wait a second, I just got a check for three bucks from the *Partisan Review*, so let's to go the movies." That's where things were at. And I think that's something to keep in mind—the costs, both personally, to him, and family-wise, to his own relationships, to his children, and what it meant at that stage to opt out, what it meant to stick by that, for better or worse.

Audience: It strikes me that during the time of the '50s and '60s, if you were a college student, an English major, you were under the New Criticism, which was only the text, no background whatsoever.

Alcalay: Olson was very prescient about this in the letter to Ruth Benedict I cite, the letter where he asks when are we supposed to cut the knot with all the information and the facts and how do you turn fact into fable. In teaching a literary text, even a single poem, I think one needs about eighty or a hundred books around it, just to think about it, to think historically—where does this thing fit? We're still coming out of an era where the poem is an artifact and there's nothing outside it. Olson was very clear about this when he looked at Melville. There was a world there that had to be plumbed, a world that had to be known about, that had to be extrapolated from. One can see this in Amiri Baraka's *Blues People*, a very Olsonian project. One can see it in a writer like Susan Howe, in her book *My Emily Dickinson*, where she reconstitutes a world of the real in which Emily Dickinson's poems can then be situated. I think that's why Duncan's generational thing is so valuable. He said, alright, so this is a person who lived, breathed, and was nursed in this particular time. What does that mean, what are the constituents of that world that go unconsciously into the making of that text or that poem? How did that person live? What choices did they make?

Audience: Because of the isolation here there is very little cultural space in which to opt out—I'm thinking of Germany now, for instance, where you still seem to have this cultural space, at least that's been my experience…

Alcalay: It's hard to put oneself in any time and space outside one's own. It'd be easier to ask a person who lived in Olson's time. A quote that keeps coming back to me: Gary Snyder said that in the 1950s, you would hitchhike a thousand miles to stay with a friend. That says something about relations of friends and space and what you would do in order to be with somebody then. Olson felt at home in Gloucester. In clips from the outtakes of the show done on Olson in the 1960s, for what was then National Educational Television, you see him walking around the neighborhood. He's a figure, he was a letter carrier summers, he knew everybody. He'd been going there since he was five, and his mother moved there after his father died. He went out sword fishing a number of times and on other expeditions. He was a known figure, everybody knew him. There's a terrific book, *Maximus To Gloucester,* that the writer Peter Anastas edited, with a forward by the poet Gerrit Lansing, another key Olson friend and interlocutor who still lives in Gloucester. Peter Anastas is a Gloucester writer whose parents had a soda fountain that I used to go to. Peter edited Olson's letters to the Gloucester newspaper, they had to do with a variety of urban development issues, local civic things that were going on. He was very much part of that, while also having this voluminous correspondence with people who were all over the place. The letters are an incredible resource. Another person who plays a crucial part in all of this is Frances Boldereff. Many of Olson's key ideas were developed in correspondence with her. Boldereff was a Joyce and Blake scholar. Just a remarkable correspondence. Key ideas get fleshed out in this intense two-to-three year period where they're corresponding sometimes two, three, four times a day. All these paths and paths not taken: the connection to Ferrini in Gloucester and the movement through him across worlds of poetry, from the '30s, through the Beats and the post-modern; the voluminous correspondences with people like Boldereff, not part of any official literary or cultural history but who was deeply influential; the students from Black Mountain like John Wieners, Ed Dorn, or Michael Rumaker who form individual paths or constellations all their own—even in this brief catalog, we can see Olson as focal point from which not only paths must be taken, but from which a fundamental remapping of what we think we know of our history and experience can begin.

4

*Since 1955, poetry or verse as some would prefer it be called
has, despite all forebodings that it was dying, taken through a
handful of writers in the United States, a stranglehold on
established modes of thought, analysis & attention.*

—John Wieners, 1972

*One night in a restaurant on Elmwood street, Charles [Olson]
and John Wieners and Harvey [Brown] and whoever else was
at our table began smoking joints. Nobody did anything about
it. The revolution was underway, and poets were the political
leaders. Charles was to be the president of that Republic. Later,
during the summer when he tried to make the Berkeley Poetry
Conference into a political convention, some, including a few
of his best friends and supporters, did not return after inter-
mission. That, really, was the end of that. When he returned
to Buffalo, he raged about it at Onetto's; I'd never seen him in
such agony. He had been wrong, he thought. But then his conviction would return and he'd curse his false friends for desert-
ing him. There remains a marvelous "conspiracy theory" to be
created about this conference and the "politics" surrounding
it. As a result of Intelligence Agency action or not, by the end
of 1969 all living revolutionary leadership was dead or in hiding. Rock music had met its limit at Altamont and Ed Sanders
would soon investigate the "Manson Family" murders...*

*Recently I had a brief exchange of e-mail with a young
academic who is interested in how [Olson] and Robert
Creeley shaped their careers... Her interest strikes me as genuine. But I have been unable to communicate to her the
dimension of spirit in which Charles lived and worked. There
seems to be no explaining it to the next generation.*

—Albert Glover, 1997

If we are the seminal fluidity, then we contain already,
as Whitman knew, everything, "diddling" (Poe) as well as
the Good, however forced sometimes the dilation as seen
from old heroic organization before the shit rolled like
termite droppings into the load-bearing bridges for everyone
to cross into Dealy Plaza, Dallas "takes us" November
22, 1963, and not only Oswald and Ruby, but Guy Bannister,
Shaw, Ferrie, Bloomfield and Permindex, now Roscoe White
and more aliens up from the South, Watergate's Sturgis,
Union survivors up North, all those insane in Honolulu
since the birth of the Nation/Hail to the Chief shot
American Transcendentalism out of the feudal individual
and delivered into the hands of Walt's "unprecedented
average," thank you Abe, thanks Jack, now it's up to us.

—*John Clarke*

Charles Olson's life and work have appeared throughout
the cultural landscape in varying degrees of visibility. Though
much is still unedited, much is available—*The Maximus
Poems*, unfinished at his death in 1970; *The Collected Poems,
The Collected Prose*; collections of correspondence between
Olson and Edward Dahlberg, Robert Creeley, Cid Corman,
and then Frances Boldereff, in *Charles Olson and Frances
Boldereff: A Modern Correspondence*. While Olson is the subject of many books and several biographies, the vast scope of
Olson's stance, its breadth and achievement has not been
coherently mapped. The deeper one delves, the clearer it
becomes that we can't make sense of North American culture in the 20th century, and situate ourselves in the 21st,
without him. Looking back, there is even the 19th century,
given *Call Me Ishmael*, his groundbreaking work on Melville
and the American whaling industry—what Olson calls the

first, most emblematic industry in America.

Olson was rector of Black Mountain College in one of its most creative periods, the final one from 1954 to 1956, and has become titular head of what has come to be known, in poetry, as the Black Mountain School, a school that means far more as a critic's category than it ever did in reality. Olson's voracious intellectual appetite broke all restraints. Little escaped his high-energy scrutiny: historical geography, paleontology, archaeology, the Tarot, anthropology, psychology, Native America, the Mayans, Ismaili Islam, westward expansion, economic history, physics, architecture, even rock painting. His study, work experience, and writing extended from local zoning battles to urban demographics, from machine politics to the mechanics of the literary and academic worlds and even the military-industrial complex, always taking the cosmos and the place of humans within it into acccount. This immersion in different systems of knowledge and ways of knowing was unquestionably crucial to Olson's notion of the "post-modern" and infuses his multi-, inter-, and intra-disciplinary approach. As the unparalleled Olson scholar Ralph Maud points out, Olson hoped to provide a "sense of belonging" among fellow writers, thinkers, and artists, but always in a "human universe," rather than as a humanism. Such a generous and inclusive notion, echoing Robert Duncan's "symposium of the whole," used words like "community," "the post-modern," and "humanism" in a way very different from how such terms are now generally used.

Olson grew up in Worcester, Massachusetts where his father worked as a letter carrier. He attended Worcester's Classical High School, went on to a brilliant academic apprenticeship at Wesleyan and Harvard, then embarked upon his career in the Roosevelt administration. Olson's background and experiences made him acutely aware of the concrete aspects of work and labor's divisions across a full spectrum of activity, whether physical, political, or intellectual. This is evidenced in a 1952 letter to Merton Sealts, a Melville scholar, blasting the official world of Melville scholarship that refused his labors:

> *... god damn these insolent fucking imposers—users—vulgarizers of a man they hold their jobs by: my god,*
> *Merton, how can they be so dishonest as to peddle him whom they owe their feeding of their children to?*

Certainly this is as accurate and biting a description of the academic food chain as we have. This leads, later in the same letter, to an astonishing and comprehensive challenge: "how to carry out what I am sure is the moral imperative of any worker in any field: to be responsible to the public for the conduct of the other workers in that field?" The idea that we hold each other accountable in this way, that knowledge is a group endeavor sustained through communities no matter how small or seemingly inconsequential, and that scholarship meant responsibility and was antithetical to any kind of profit carried through to his deathbed. He writes his last letter in answer to a query from a graduate student, Nimai Chatterji, curious as to whether Olson knew of connections between Ezra Pound and Rabindranath Tagore.

In our current hyper-specialized, polemical intellectual atmosphere, it is hard to imagine the existence of a figure like this. Never a "public intellectual" in the neutered sense we might now conceive, Olson was more akin to a public intelligence. His stature does not conform to the tyranny of reduced expectations. His relationship to Pound is a case in point. Olson never shrank from addressing the implications of the older poet's politics. In notes from 1945, before he began meeting the incarcerated Pound, Olson wrote:

What constitutes "our" side is not easy to see or state: to go no further than the term "democracy," left or center, it is too lazy, too dead of the past to include the gains of the present and advances to come. But the enemy, because he attacks, stands clear. A "fascist" is still a definition.

We shall not try this Pound, this Streicher. We have not moved out, as some men who died in Spain, far enough. These men are not enemies of the state, traitors, instruments of nations, German, Italy, alone. They will come closer to trying us, for they have gained, in their conspiracy, a critical vantage. They are already international, as we are unprepared to be. We have not yet shaped, because we have denied this civil war, a justice with sanctions, strong and deep enough to measure the crime. Our own case remains unexamined. How then shall we try men who have examined us more than we have ourselves? They know what they fight against. We do not yet know what we fight for.

It does not surprise me that Ezra Pound will not be tried.

Increasingly removed from access to public printed space, and not yet having fully established the communicative world of the little magazine, Olson chose to spend most of his creative years living in abject poverty in a small tenement apartment at Gloucester's edge, amongst Italian immigrant fisherfolk, dilapidated warehouses, and trucking depots. Letters served as a lifeline to the outside world. In 1968, he wrote to New York poet Joel Oppenheimer: "I have become like a true nearctic one, & almost now live on a floe far far into those currents which I suppose cld just as well be the Early Nile." Charles Stein, as noted before, puts it clearly: "Olson does not withdraw from politics: his understanding of what constitutes political action deepens and expands." This seems to me absolutely key. When Olson wrote, in a 1953 letter to Robert Duncan, that "truths are as mortal as the life in any of us," he was insisting on a fundamental redefinition of primary terms, one that extends far beyond the established confines of the literary. When asked by David Ignatow to contribute to a journal of "political poetry" in 1960, Olson—having been a politician—challenged Ignatow's notion of the political: "the restoration of 'vision' (that man lives among public fact as among private fact, and that either is solely a face of the double of the real) is conspicuous and crucially demanded." Ignatow did not respond.

It has been more than forty years since the death of Olson in 1970. It has been more than sixty years since Olson, in 1951, applied for, and failed to get, a Fulbright fellowship to study in Iraq. While the signs were there, the country Olson lived in would probably be unrecognizable to him now. It might, however, fulfill his vision of where things were already heading. What Olson, following Pound, called "pejorocracy" has come to stay. More even than "sound, itself" is "neoned" in, as Olson wrote in the first *Maximus* poem, in the early 1950s. The year after he died, in 1971, following urban uprisings, the Black Power movement and many other insurgencies, including the Winter Soldiers born of Vietnam Veterans Against the War, attempted to lead the country into "a turning" that Olson had anticipated and called for years before. This turning was answered by repression and economic and psychological warfare, imploding into covert wars, imprisonment expanded on a massive scale (from 200,000 in the early 1970s to over 2 million presently), and a flexing of imperial muscle installing us in Afghanistan, Iraq, and virtually every country on earth. The suppression and denial of the "turning" Olson sought, while he could see the response to its necessity already in his lifetime, has now turned us inside out, making our lives and experiences unrecognizable to us.

If you wore an army jacket in 1969, 1970, or 1971, it either meant you were a veteran or that you identified with the soldiers and veterans fighting the war against the war in Vietnam. That was still the case when I took classes at City College in New York in the mid-1970s. The draft had passed me by, but a number of the students studying Ancient Greek with me were older and survivors of the war in Vietnam. They were eager to find and lose themselves in texts as archaic and startling as their experiences must have been. Olson would have understood this.

By the late 1970s, I had set off on part of a journey through languages and places whose logical cohesion lasted close to twenty years. On the surface, this journey seemed to lead away from the poetry and ways of thinking I was most intimately connected to, away from a rooted sense of place and language that, even as a first-generation American, held deep claims on me. Yet, as I came to see, in leading back to that part of me I can call home, this journey helped me grapple with these claims, giving me tools I could not have imagined before. Olson's work in turn helped me rediscover old things while finding new things to confirm my innermost sense. In a 1950 letter to Melville scholar Roland Mason, Olson wrote:

I am struck with the feeling that the rest of the world is just now getting what the Americans have been putting up with a long time; that we are "experienced" in the dread business of this reality—that Melville had the under-parts of what Rimbaud didn't even know; that the Am Civil War itself was the predecessor of what this century is the international civil war of; and that the same victor now will be the gross thing which won, here, then: MATERIALISM.

For me this sort of understanding has led to the poetry and personal relationships I began to forge as a teenager, and to a slow but ongoing immersion in Ancient America, an essential element missing in our generalized and circumscribed histories. In the interview for the Ferrini film *Polis Is This*, Baraka talks about the significance Olson's trajectory had for him:

To me, Olson's concept of the polis was just simply the idea that you had to be grounded in the concerns of the people, that the people are finally the makers of history, and that you have to be grounded in what is historical in that sense. What are the concerns of the people? Why are they these concerns? The whole question of putting the hinge back on the door. That is, trying to find out what had been hidden from us by the emergence of this new one-sided society. That was important, particularly for me being black because I knew part of that was the connection to Africa. Where are the foundations of the world from? Charles was saying, "you have to go back, you have to go back." One of the most important parts was language, you know, the expression of life is language, and you have to grasp languages. At the time, people were concerned about the same thing. What is language and life? What do they reveal in themselves?

The relegation of Olson to some nether world of "influential" but unread poets has occurred through any number of restraining orders and forms of administrative detention, much of it dedicated to blocking this business of "going back." Larger bureaucratic nets trap us and enable the terms of debates to remain unchallenged and limited, cutting off areas of exploration that are as vital to our sustenance as the air we breathe. Much like the intensive psychological conditioning that produced acceptable trajectories, horizons, boundaries, and limitations of discourse during the Cold War, we find ourselves now in the midst of a "one-sided" society that has erased its origins, development, and all consciousness of the consequencees of this development. This form of society wreaks havoc on our lived experience of the past. This brings us to concerns Olson, almost alone, expressed when he said, already in 1945, confronting the treatment of Pound, that "our own case remains unexamined." For Olson, Pound's trial was made to appear like a leftover from WWII but may have been, instead, a harbinger of a new order to come.

In 1945, my parents, having survived WWII as refugees from Yugoslavia, were living in Rome. In May of that year Pound was captured by Italian partisans and handed over to the Americans for interrogation. During the same month, as detailed by Christopher Simpson in his book *Blowback*, Gustav Hilger, a war criminal instrumental in SS efforts to capture and exterminate Italian Jews, surrendered to U.S. forces and was "quietly shipped to Washington D.C. for debriefing at Fort Hunt." Far from being publicly tried as Pound would be, for the next few years Hilger "shuttled back and forth between the United States and Germany under the sponsorship of the U.S. State Department," working under grants from the Carnegie Corporation and given posts at Harvard's Center for Russian Research, Johns Hopkins University, and other academic places serving as CIA covers, under the guise of "academic freedom." While Pound was in the cage at Pisa as the "demonstrable" traitor, another key Nazi figure, Reinhard Gehlen, "Hitler's most senior military intelligence officer on the eastern front, surrendered to the Americans, along with his top aides." Former Nazi officers, intelligence personnel, and scientists were recruited to build up essential parts of American and NATO overt and covert operations, serving as key elements for the United States government in Europe and the Middle East during the Cold War. "Bloodstone" was the first such operation and others, including Overcast, Paperclip, Pajamas, Dwindle, Apple Pie, Panhandle, Credulity, and Sunrise followed. As macabre and absurd as some of these names are, as Simpson writes, "in a very real sense, the men and women who engineered Bloodstone were the same ones who designed U.S. Cold War strategy for every administration from 1945 to 1963." The consequences deepened and became part of general foreign policy, as "former Nazis and collaborators on the U.S. payroll who were also fugitives from war crimes charges began to demand U.S. help in escaping abroad in return for their cooperation with—and continuous silence about—American clandestine operations." All this should sound familiar, especially in light of the subsequent American record with the *mujahadin* in Pakistan and Afghanistan or Saddam Hussein in Iraq, not to mention earlier model campaigns like the Phoenix Program in Vietnam—so cogently described by journalist Douglas Valentine—and other "counter-revolutionary" operations in any number of places around the globe.

Such "deep politics," in the sense poet and historian Peter Dale Scott has defined them in *Deep Politics and the Death of JFK*, get left by the wayside again and again, especially in trying to think through the relation of politics to history and culture. While all these Nazis were being brought into the government, Pound, a poet, was indicted in 1945, taken from Italy, and imprisoned in the District of Columbia Jail in Washington. After his formal arraignment, he was transferred to a hospital in order to undergo psychiatric examination. There he was declared "insane and mentally unfit for trial." After being placed in solitary confinement in the penal ward at St. Elizabeths Federal Hospital for the insane (now designated headquarters for Homeland Security), Pound underwent a sanity hearing on February 13, 1946. As scholar and translator Richard Sieburth writes in his superb presentation of Pound's *Pisan Cantos*, "The jury returned a verdict that the respondent was of 'unsound mind'... In this juridical limbo—neither innocent nor guilty and because adjudged *non compos mentis*, no longer a legal subject with power of signature—Pound would reside at St. Elizabeths for the next twelve years." Never a real trial, the Pound case played an important cultural, historical, and political role. It established the shadowy image of the poet through whom art's relationship to politics can be administered and cordoned off, and used as a surrogate form of debate, like a condom placed over organs of policy and their effects. As mechanisms get jump-started by events, a series of stand-ins takes up the space of the actual, making it difficult, if not impossible, to talk about things outside their categorical function.

The case of Olson, and his concern with "putting the hinge back on the door" to the past, follows a similar course.

The poet comes to represent the inherited weight of patriarchy or is made out to be the priest-shaman-leader of a
cult, reducing the poet, the research, and the work as a whole
to unintelligibility. This sort of process occurs throughout
society now: 9/11 becomes Pearl Harbor, or vice versa, while
talking to the "terrorists" becomes Chamberlain appeasing
Germany. Deployment of these formulas has its own history and makes knowledge gained through experience and
changes in consciousness, the only place non-technical
knowledge might arise and matter for the public, difficult
to achieve.

As in various past moments of political crisis, it is worth
consulting codified and contemporary official doctrine to
identify the politics at work. Turning to the *9/11 Commission
Report*, one finds parts of it as if written and vetted by staff
members versed in literary and historiographical theory:

*In composing this narrative, we have tried to remember that
we write with the benefit of hindsight. Hindsight can sometimes see the past clearly—with 20/20 vision. But the path of
what happened is so brightly lit that it places everything else
more deeply into shadow. Commenting on Pearl Harbor,
Roberta Wohlstetter found it "much" easier after the event to
sort the relevant from the irrelevant signals. After the event, of
course, a signal is always clear; we can see what disaster it was
signaling since the disaster has occurred. But before the event
it is obscure and pregnant with conflicting meanings.*

*As time passes, more documents become available, and the
bare facts of what happened become still clearer. Yet the picture of how those things happened becomes harder to reimag-
ine, as that past world, with its preoccupations and uncertainty, recedes and the remaining memories of it become colored*

by what happened and what was written about it later. With
that caution in mind, we asked ourselves, before we judged
others, whether the insights that seem apparent now would
have been meaningful at the time, given the limits of what
people then could reasonably have known or done.

What is really at stake are war mechanisms, primitive triggers to reorder the past to make it conform to the "logical necessity" of the present. Colonization takes place across the board: there can be no liberty or liberation, no "outside" (in Jack Spicer's sense), nothing beyond an all-encompassing present that does not merely *contain* the past but *dictates* its meaning and limit. The *Report*'s conclusion states: "We believe the 9/11 attacks revealed four kinds of failures: in imagination, policy, capabilities, and management." In section 11.1, titled "IMAGINATION," a new encoding is proposed: "Considering what was not done suggests possible ways to institutionalize imagination... It is therefore crucial to find a way of routinizing, even bureaucratizing, the exercise of imagination."

Against continual Orwellian scenarios presented by liberals and progressives, perhaps it would make more sense *not* to divorce something like the *9/11 Commission Report* from the general culture, to see it as *following* and not leading, as *confirming* what has already taken place these past years since the end of the war in Vietnam. How has the exercise of the imagination been routinized and bureaucratized? We experience, for example, the "shock" of Abu Ghraib divorced from the concrete, bureaucratic realities and effects of vastly increased incarceration at home, with all its racism and organized brutality. In *Prisons: Inside the New America*, poet and novelist David Matlin, having taught in the New York State prison system for years, writes:

This is a triumph generating barrenness and dread at the secret core of our daily lives so tangled we don't any longer know how exactly its touch rots everyone of us. The pictures from Abu Ghraib, swelled with perversion and self-satisfied hate, are only hints of our domestic abyss we have already perfected and begun to export. This is not a threshold looming before us as a People, it is a threshold we passed through long ago and we have been for at least two generations perfecting its ransoms.

As part of exporting "our domestic abyss," we need to consider the "ransoming" effect of Abu Ghraib on human rights and civil society movements in the Arab world as well. As the exposure of prisons in North Africa, Syria, Palestine, and other places galvanized widespread resistance to state repression, military dictatorship and occupation, and when names like Tazmamart, Tadmor, and Ansar turned into rallying cries for liberation, Abu Ghraib arrived to take over as a focal point onto which all eyes then turned. The magnetism of such a well-publicized and locateable site of crime, through the unabashed American use of imagery, diverted the energies of indigenous movements away from endemic, regional problems. This caused movements and activists to shift and displace their indignation and activism towards violations by the United States. While focusing on American violations surely has value, for American policy-makers, this displacement signalled a tremendous gain: no matter how horrible the story or imagery of Abu Ghraib, it was "our" story, to be exposed, judged, or suppressed solely on our terms.

Poetry and writing become a kind of test case for these processes, with their own set of "acceptable violations," "demonstrable traitors," and so on. A fairly fixed set of roles, theories, and vocabularies become routinized and bureaucratized. Adopting, using, and mouthing them will let you become a "player" in one of the many current gaming schemes. Described by Jack Spicer in a 1947 review of Henry Miller's *Remember to Remember*, this was already a world in which "a reviewer, not sitting very high off the floor of the exchange finds himself casting down worried glances at the tape and hoping fervently that he is ahead of the trends of the trading." The stakes that a poet like Spicer openly engaged in, however, refusing to take a loyalty oath during the 1950s and losing his academic position as linguist, were of an order we can barely recognize now. As poet, scholar, and editor Peter Gizzi writes of Spicer: "He's less interested in a dialogue with the dead than in inhabiting the same space with them, as in a poem, a room in a pub, or on a baseball diamond. That is to say, he's more interested in sharing this space with others, putting it into play—making it public. If one opens the circuitry between the living and the dead, one has to be willing to shed the notion of social acceptability, of clearly delineated public and private realms, of property."

This comes closer to the kinds of purposes poetry is put to by someone like Matlin. Taking the work of writers like Robert Duncan, H.D., William Carlos Williams, and Olson into workshops with hardened criminals, Matlin quotes Frank O'Hara, stressing how the words of poets allow us to "experience the 'traumatic consciousness of emergency and crisis as personal event,' and assume responsibility for being alive 'here and now,' no matter how accidentally."

As poets, writers, artists, and intellectuals found themselves—some rapidly and others gradually—shocked into or out of recognition of public life following 9/11, a variety of issues started getting talked about in ways that hadn't arisen for years, old denials and suppressions returning in new guises. In one of the most acute pieces posted on the Buffalo poetics list at the time, the poet Taylor Brady wrote the following in response to a post by prominent literary critic Marjorie Perloff:

I'm disappointed that your warning against too-broad strokes and too-hasty judgment only seems to apply from the inside out, as if history were a one-way mirror in which certain groups bear the burden of a constant agonized self-reflection, while others survey the scene of this inspection and pronounce on its correctness. And I regret that the internalization of this model kept many of us on the left from articulating a reasoned response, kept us talking about respectful silences and periods of mourning, not wishing to appear unseemly, in the crucial first hours during which the Bush administration prepared for war.

Amiri Baraka's poem "Somebody Blew Up America" came along to work as a perfect test balloon, forcing buried issues out of hiding, putting poetry in the news and pushing hard at this "delineation of public and private realms," at the ownership and decorum of emotions and ideas, exposing the "reasoned response" and "respectful silences." People who hadn't objected to or been outraged at the endless information gaps regarding 9/11 or the call to war suddenly found ample strength to voice their outrage over a mere poem, and whether one or two of its hundreds of assertions were or were not "factual." Baraka was judged "unfit" and was fired as New Jersey Poet Laureate.

This division over poetry and the larger question of "self-reflection" takes us back to the Berkeley Poetry Conference of July 1965, an event that Baraka, then LeRoi Jones, had been invited to but could not make due to unfolding events in New York. Malcolm X had been assassinated in Harlem in February, a night described by Baraka in his autobiography:

February 21, 1965, a Sunday. Nellie and I and the two girls were at the Eighth Street Bookstore, at a book party. I had a cap, hunting jacket, and round dark glasses, the dress of our little core. I was being personable and knowledgeable... Suddenly, Leroy McLucas came in. He was weeping. "Malcolm is dead! Malcolm is dead! Malcolm's been killed!" He wept, repeating it over and over. I was stunned. I felt stupid, ugly, useless.

In what became a symbolically charged and reductively interpreted event, Baraka acted by moving out of the downtown bohemia of Manhattan to Harlem. As he describes it:

The arrival uptown, Harlem, can only be summed up by the feelings jumping out of Césaire's Return to My Native Land *or Fanon's* The Wretched of the Earth *or Cabral's* Return to the Source. *The middle-class intellectual, having outintegrated the most integrated, now plunges headlong back into what he perceives as blackest, native-est... When we came up out of the subway, March 1965, cold and clear, Harlem all around us staring us down, we felt like pioneers of the new order.*

In a poignant moment caught on film in the out-takes of a National Educational Television show, there is a shot of

Charles Olson shuffling through papers to get at a letter from Baraka. As he picks it up, Olson says something like "how could anyone refuse such a call," alluding to the allegiance Baraka felt towards Malcolm X and his need to move out of the world he, Baraka, had inhabited—and into the world Malcolm had been seized and disappeared from. Olson was clearly haunted by the situation and the power of Baraka's move. While searching for materials in the Olson Archives, I came across a fragmentary message from this period, written by Olson in a notebook and addressed to Baraka:

My dear Leroy,

I haven't ignored a damn thing. Please keep coming directly to me.

And of course, there is the astonishing *Maximus* poem "I have been an ability—a machine—" that traces the parallels between his father and Baraka's father, also employed in the Postal Service, and refers to waves "of / migration... like Leroy and Malcolm / X the final wave / of wash upon this / desperate / ugly / cruel / Land this Nation / which never / lets anyone / come to / shore..."

Poet Nathaniel Mackey, heir to the legacies of both Olson and Baraka, has described in *Paracritical Hinge* the impact of Olson's now legendary performance at the 1965 Berkeley conference:

Poets of my generation tend to look askance at the large claims for the poet that poets like Olson and Duncan make, especially where they warm over romantic senses of the poet's mission or smack of moralizing self-aggrandizement. It is as though the analogy they draw between the poet and the politician boomer-

angs, what they say sounding like campaign rhetoric at times, as hollow as a political candidate's claim to integrity. What strengthens Olson's position and protects it against the charge of naiveté, however, is his willingness to acknowledge himself to be an heir to the corrupt power he condemns. He can own up to certain spoils the poet gathers from the workings of that power, can admit, as we have seen, that imperialism gives "a language the international power / poets take advantage of." In this we see the workings of not a clean but a troubled conscience.

Olson sometimes speaks of political power as something from which he is excluded, promoting a sense of a priori exclusion as a way of confirming his poetic vocation. But there is another side of his thought that admits that for a white male poet like himself, born in a white-supremacist, male-supremacist society, political power, relatively speaking, is a birthright from which he isn't excluded but about which he has to make a choice. A man who was once on the threshold of a political career, as he was in the 1940s, more believably speaks of renunciation than of exclusion. That is exactly what we find him doing, exhorting others to choose "to be these things instead of Kings." For him poetry is analogous to a vow of poverty, a moral act of renunciation, as he writes very early in The Maximus Poems:

> *In the land of plenty, have*
> *nothing to do with it*
>
> > *take the way of*
>
> *the lowest,*
> *including*
> *your legs, go*
> *contrary, go*
> *sing*

Mackey then describes the consequences:

The sense of poetry as something like a form of penance makes it a matter of conscience, his way of sublimating or attempting to sabotage his birthright, the complex of privileges and guilts we can, with Amiri Baraka, call white karma. At the Berkeley conference Olson makes an interesting remark: "I'm the white man. I'm that famous thing, the white man. The ultimate paleface. The noncorruptible, the good. The thing that runs this country, or that is this country. And thank God —And in fact the only advantage I have is that I didn't." His righteousness, what here he calls his "advantage," consists only of abstention, of writing poetry in place of running the country.

Olson declared himself as "the ultimate paleface" at Berkeley and some of the people most affected by the risk Olson enacted on stage were those in the Detroit contingent, including the legendary writer and activist John Sinclair, one of the founders of the Detroit Artists' Workshop. Sinclair would become manager, manifesto-writer, and much more for the MC5, a crucial influence on the punk movement. At the Berkeley conference, Sinclair read with Ed Sanders, a poet who had already embarked upon a remarkable trajectory through publication of his *Fuck You: a magazine of the arts*, formation of the legendary Fugs, and opening his Peace Eye Bookstore in New York's East Village. Sinclair, by 1968, would become a national figure at the forefront of new alliances, shared influence, and exchanges between movements like the Black Panthers and white radicals, becoming a founder of the White Panthers. Another member of the Detroit contingent, poet and filmmaker Robin Eichele was also a founder of the Detroit Artists' Workshop, along with Sinclair and Sinclair's partner (and later wife), artist and photographer Leni Arndt, trumpeter Charles Moore, and another dozen artists working in different forms. Eichele described Olson's performance:

So, it was a political convention, a rite of veneration, confession, immolation, or whatever you want to drop on it for a name. It doesn't really matter much. It was Olson, in public, putting his edge to the world and heaving, cutting deep and wide at the dictate of his concerns. He ran a lot of people out (invited them to leave if they didn't like the program) and did do violence to the poems as poems. But, for me, once I got on to what he was up to, he had me on his vector, holding on where I could, but riding that wave of energy and joy as it broke wildly in all directions. It broke a lot loose in me, merely by its form, how the man does slice into something (everything) and does work to be that inclusive of the universe. He stood as he says, taking on the risk of a public place, Discrimination on his left shoulder, Exaggeration ("the only question in poetry is how to exaggerate") on his right shoulder, and as he was reminded when he strayed from the podium, a microphone (the hold of the Virgin Mary as he called it) at his neck.

This "taking on the risk of a public place" occurred on July 23, 1965, and it would be hard not to see a parallel in Bob Dylan's performance at Newport two days later, on July 25th, when Dylan went electric, much to the chagrin of a very vocal segment of the audience. Just as Eichele describes Olson doing "violence to the poems as poems" and running "a lot of people out," the response to Dylan's performance suggests a similar quality of momentous divide. Dylan's comments seem pertinent: "Whatever it was about wasn't about anything they were hearing. I had a perspective on the booing, because you've got to realize you can kill somebody with kindness too." For some listening at Berkeley, like Eichele or Anne Waldman, Olson's refusal to read his poems "properly" redefined the concept of the poet's public role. Olson became a reference point for what might be possible in spheres of activity seemingly far removed from poetry.

Sinclair's introduction to Olson had come with a reading of "Projective Verse" in 1964, followed by Olson's inclusion in Donald Allen's defining anthology *The New American Poetry*. In his introduction to the *Collected Artists Worksheets*, Sinclair wrote:

The beautiful thing about the whole "movement" here in Detroit is that we all started equally—we were literally "nowhere," and we have somehow been able to make a very precise place for ourselves in this city, solely through our efforts, making all the "mistakes" we had to make, taking all the chances we didn't even know were chances.

Wayne Kramer, another founder of the MC5 recounts:

We had been championing Detroit music for years. "High Energy" is how we described it at the time—no holds barred, pedal to the metal. Combining the R&B we heard on WJLB and WCHB, the blues of Howlin' Wolf and John Lee, the new sounds coming in from the Rolling Stones and The Who and the Yardbirds, and the powerful force of the avant-garde "free-jazz movement," we toiled away in small clubs all over the Mid-west. Night after night, we worked at perfecting our sound and our stage show. The music was in our blood, and it dripped everywhere. It was very messy. We rehearsed in a storefront studio in the Cass corridor (we called it the Warren/Forest then). It's on the corner where East Warren Avenue meets the John C. Lodge Expressway in the "inner city" of Detroit. The district was close to Wayne State University and was a little rundown. There were cheap rents and a general feeling of "live and let live." North of this, on the corner, was a series of two-story commercial structures with storefronts below and what used to be a dentist's office above. The reefer smoke billowed out of these buildings. The storefronts housed the Detroit office of the Committee To End the War in Vietnam, the Fifth Estate (the underground newspaper), the Artists' Workshop and, later, the MC5's rehearsal space. The upstairs became the band's communal home. From there I watched the city of Detroit go to war in the riots of the long hot summer of 1967. I watched tanks and armored personnel carriers from my bedroom window. Tanks rolling across Warren Avenue. I was arrested by the Army just up the street for being a suspected sniper—I had a telescope in my window... That corner in Detroit was, for me at least, the center of the known universe. Late nights were spent tripping on acid, smoking the best Mexican herb to be found, listening to Sun Ra, John Coltrane, and Albert Ayler, and plotting the future. Our political idols were the Black Panther Party and crazed poets like Allen Ginsberg, Charles Olson, and Ed Sanders.

The question of decorum gets to the heart of acceptable speech, acceptable public behavior, the institutional life of writing, and the reach a poet's take on the universe can have. Such descriptions, and the one to follow, come closer to a deep sense of how Olson's energies and work incited people, from "nowhere," sometimes with, sometimes without expressed debt, to challenge models that had been handed down to them, to take up the burdens of their own inquiries and visions. Describing Olson's arrival in Buffalo for a teaching position—two years before Berkeley, in 1963—Michael Boughn writes:

All this work was implicated in a move away from what we think of as the "literary," finally claiming for poetry an altogether other range of importance. What Olson founded in Buffalo, what followed from his arrival there, begins with that. "Literary" in this context, that is both Olson's work and the work he engendered in Buffalo, has to do with two different but related issues. It refers both to the conventions, modes and procedures of writing that mark, however broadly and ambiguously, what is proposed at any given moment as "literature," and also with the "life worlds" such practices are implicated with, something loosely called, say, the "literary life," complete with all its competitions, prizes, career paths, disciplinary bodies, canonical aspirations, and so on. The literary, then, as an institution, as institutionalized practices. Crucial to Olson's sense of a move beyond or around the literary is his notion that it's possible to reconnect with or recover energies that pre-exist their historical institutionalization into a specific, fixed grammar of social practices. And even more importantly, that to do that, to push one's self toward that connection, is to disrupt or alter that grammar, a profoundly political act.

This "profoundly political act" was the quality that first attracted Baraka:

What fascinated me about Olson was his sense of having dropped out of the U.S., the "pejorocracy." He said in his poems we should "go against" it. That we should oppose "those who advertise you out."

One can trace out the kinds of things that this "politics" led to, gave birth to, in a number of directions and locations: in Detroit, through the activities of a group of young poets, musicians, filmmakers, and visual artists; in Buffalo, through the Institute for Further Studies; in Cleveland, through the Frontier Press, with its essential list of reprinted classics and new poetry including *The New Empire* by Brooks Adams, *Peace Eye* by Ed Sanders, the Situationist text *Decline & Fall of the "Spectacular" Commodity-Economy*, *Paths of the Mound -Building Indians and Great Game Animals* by Archer Butler Hulbert, *Years of Madness: A Reappraisal of the Civil War* by W.E. Woodward, *Interlinear to Cabeza de Vaca* by Haniel Long, *The Book of Daniel Drew, Prison Memoirs of An Anarchist* by Alexander Berkman, *Spring & All* by William Carlos Williams, *Hermetic Definitions* by H.D., and books by Ed Dorn, Stan Brakhage, Michael McClure, and others; through the activities of Sanders as poet, musician, journalist, and more; through the work of Dennis Tedlock, scholar and translator of the *Popol Vuh* who, in his preface to *Finding the Center: Narrative Poetry of the Zuni Indians*, wrote: "I see the book in part as a contribution to the ongoing reopening of the ear and voice that Charles Olson called for all the way back in 1950, when he said that poetry must 'catch up and put into it certain laws and possibilities of the breath.'"

There are many, many further instances, both collectively and individually. In order not to romanticize the immediate past of our poetics or its history of struggles, in the interest of not using that past to bludgeon the present or the present to bludgeon the past, a continuation of Olson's "ongoing re-opening of ear and voice" becomes only more necessary. Sanders, who took up Olson's opening directly, called it "investigative poetics." The principles and dangers of this spirit were succinctly described as early as 1949 by Rukeyser, who had also written of poetry's ability to "extend the document":

There has been a great deal of political talk about security in this century. Growth is the security of organic life. The security of the imagination lies in calling, all our lives, for more liberty, more rebellion, more belief.

When a call to bureaucratize imagination emerges openly and overtly out of the national "security" state, how, as Olson put it, are we to "write a Republic" and initiate "another kind of nation"? While his republic was meant to come after having "descried the nation," to be written "in gloom on Watch-House Point," such a precise location, as isolated as it was, now seems almost a luxury. Have we reached a frontier *beyond* the past? As far back as 1940, the geographer Carl Sauer, a major influence on Olson, wrote:

Year by year the sweeping hands of modern industry and commerce brush away more and more of what is old. Traditions die with the old people; documents are destroyed; weather, storm, and flood erase the physical remnants; science and market standardization destroy old crops.

Sauer's response was to write of "old truth":

The terrific impact of the modern western world, however, does not repeal the old truth that the history of man has been markedly pluralistic, and that there are no general laws of society, but only cultural assents. We deal not with Culture but with cultures, except so far as we delude ourselves into thinking the world made over in our own image… From all the earth in all the time of human existence, we build a retrospective science, which out of this experience acquires an ability to look ahead.

Sauer believed in "the relevance of all human time," that it "may require a lifetime given to learning one major context of nature and culture." Poet Duncan McNaughton writes in "When time was young we were too":

> *it wasn't death at all*
> *it was what happened to time*
> *after that there wasn't any   it wasn't*
> *that there was less time   there was no time*
> *time went south.*

Has not the velocity of change and consumption, through some law of diminishing returns linked to depletion of the planet's life sustaining resources, overtaken our ability to stay in one place and allow ourselves the idleness local knowledge demands?

In *Call Me Ishmael*, Olson wrote that Melville understood "America completes her West only on the coast of Asia." Perhaps westward expansion for the United States reaches some apotheosis after the Vietnam War, with sneaker factories named after Nike, the Greek goddess of victory, and Babylon remade in our image, eradicating the likely site of Eden to displace it to the northwest, to the Middle East's "only democracy," that land of uprooted olive trees and legalized torture. A "retrospective science" that looks at "all the earth" cannot help but delve into, record, and anticipate this sort of destruction, enacting and respecting the local in

the context of great forces occurring over long stretches of
time. André Spears writes:

*What emerges in the manifest exorbitance of the Maximus
poems is the central drama of humanity's intimate relation to
a living, "migrating" earth... Human migration, for Olson,
finds its archetype in the tectonic life of earth itself... Against
a zodiacal grid of the universe, the narrative drive of the
Maximus poems—"the end of Pisces / could be the end of
species" (M 452)—culminates in a vision of planet Earth in
which the North-Western migration of Western civilization
parallels the movement of continental drift, and functions as
the representation of a gravitational or magnetic pull toward
the arctic fulcrum about which the continents continue to
rotate. This teleological locus, in turn, is the site of the periodic
glaciations—literally, the "ice" in the Ice Ages—that shape the
course of human evolution.*

To acknowledge the cosmic, cataclysmic nature of such
possibilities is not at all to give up on politics. On the contrary, it is to return politics to the concerns and experiences
of the cosmos through concerns and experiences of daily
life, wherever and however it is lived. It is at this intersection
that the thinking some poetry can enact retains, in Baraka's
words, its relation to "language and life."

Readings that see Olson merely following in the footsteps of the long poems of Pound and Williams, seeking to
create a modern or post-modern epic, miss Olson's grasp of
this relationship between forms of writing, living, and larger
social, spatial, and cosmic structures such forms parallel
and enact. A telling and conclusive quote, cited earlier, from
a piece Olson originally published in Hettie Cohen/Jones and

LeRoi Jones/Amiri Baraka's magazine *Yugen*, was raised at the first OlsonNow event, at St. Marks Church, concurrently by poet Anne Waldman and scholar/poet Don Byrd:

> *Feminine*
> *Writing so that all the world*
> *is redeemed, and history*
> *and all that politics,*
> *and "State" and Subjection*
> *are for once, done way with,*
>   *as the reason*
>   *of writing.*

What would a writing be that "does away with" "'State' and Subjection"? In Henry Ferrini's *Polis is This*, the poet Susan Thackrey describes Olson's struggle to find such a place:

He wanted always to try to get back to the beginning because he really felt that it was only there that any change was possible, and if you are talking about political change, that's the only possibility of changing form, of changing consciousness, of changing the uses of power, and specifically, I think, human masculine power, since that's the way it's been manifested since Homer and, as he would see it, since Zeus buried the Titans underground, and Charles considered himself a Titan.

While administrative attempts to limit the spread of Olson's example and struggle continue, there is no question a whole generation of women poets have taken up his challenge of form as a political matter. In poet Alice Notley's *The Descent of Alette*, it is form which must be wrested from the tyrant:

"He owns form," "doesn't he?" "The tyrant" "owns form"

Notley tells "a public story" that might "recover some sense of what mind was like before Homer, before the world went haywire & women were denied participation in the design & making of it." To seize form back might mean to change the order of things, to inhabit roles in order to refuse them: who and what we commit ourselves to makes all the difference. This leads to the complicated question of where, how, and into what we are "born":

"'When I was born," "I was born now" "fully grown," "on heroin" "When I / was born" "fully grown" "in the universe" "of no change" "nothing" "grows / up from'" ("Who sings this, whose voice?" "This person" "is in a shadow" / "down at the end of" "the platform" "I can't see him" "at all" "He continues / his song:") "'When I was born," "I was now" "When I was born," "I'm not / allowed" "to remember when I was" "the little baby" "in a darkness, joy of / darkness" "Was I the cub" "for an instant?" "if so" "only an instant," / "before I" "was a soldier" "before I" "was a soldier…'"

5

notes for bruce andrews
(stuff that I've been "up to" to be kept "in mind")

<u>it can take years to listen:</u>

heavy involvement in the people's
poetry gathering of 2003
bringing in people from Iraq, Pakistan,
Morocco, Lebanon,
Bosnia, etc.

the day the National Museum in Baghdad was looted
we did a group reading of Iraqi poetry—the American
poets that day, and throughout the events, took half
a step back, and listened

in April 2001, I performed with Najib Shaheen on 'oud,
also at the people's poetry gathering

not that many "poets" there, mostly "people"

November 2005, with simon shaheen, najib's brother,
we organized a reading of Adonis—he was presented by
myself, anne waldman, pierre joris & mark mcmorris, in the
middle of a poetry conference organized by CUNY graduate
students (anna moschovakis, noam scheindlin, matvei
yankelevitch)—an actress read the english, Adonis read only
in Arabic—

	all the poets, without knowing
[Poetry Is News]	a word of Arabic
[OlsonNow]	knew the actress wasn't
	reading the same poems:
	what happened? could
	this listening have been
why so little olson	possible in 2003,
these past 20 or so years?	if Saadi Yusef
what was the threat?	had gotten a visa?
	could this listening have
	happened if the U.S. wasn't
	occupying Iraq?

thinking how easily someone can say "unlike the old model of poetry _____," and say it so many different ways (that lack of clarity, obfuscation, are qualities to be emulated) has made me read even more diligently through a lot of the Amiri Baraka work many would rather ignore, essays from the 1970s and 1980s, as well as a book like Diane di Prima's *Revolutionary Letters* that some would now publicly declare an "embarrassment."

> "We often make our first real reading of an author
> not when we would simply desire to do so, but
> when conditions demand it."—Abdullah Laroui

Feminine / Writing so that all the World / is redeemed, and history / and all that politics, / and "State" and Subjection / are for once, done away with, / as the reason / of writing

—Charles Olson (1965)

6

It is impossible to disconnect the narratives of intellectual life from the operational procedures of documentation and official history within the "national security state," its culture, and ways of acting. What follows is a demonstration—through a kind of "immediate" investigation—of how knowledge is administered and how, in turn, such administration of knowledge can curtail our imaginative and intellectual horizons.

While looking into Jerome Rothenberg and Pierre Joris's choice of Charles Olson's "La Préface" for the opening text in Volume Two of their *Poems for the Millennium*, I came upon an interview that Jack Foley conducted with them. Foley dwells on the details of the poem before saying: "I mention Olson in particular because Olson has come under considerable attack by the language poets, who are a very important group of people." While I've been aware of various points of friction between some of those who have come to be classified as "language poets" and aspects of Olson's poetics, a lot of that history has become submerged in further false debates. Such false debates come at the cost of deeper exploration, refinement of positions, and possibilities for re-imagining and re-defining. Such structures mirror the constraints and privatizing forces within official political, academic, and media frameworks.

As my investigation progressed, I encountered by chance the extended quote that follows immediately below, as part of an exchange with Ralph Maud in his *Minutes of the Charles Olson Society*. This was a few days after having read *Breaking the Rule of Cool: Interviewing and Reading Women Beat Writers*, by Nancy M. Grace and Ronna C. Johnson. I was struck by the contradiction between what some of the practicing poets were saying, as quoted in *Breaking the Rule of Cool*, and the words of the critic who wrote the Olson Society. I was struck by this because a number of the poets were people whose work the critic had written about and, as far as I am aware of, admires. Olson is an easy target for a certain kind of feminist critique. But something else seemed at work here, given the glaring absence of contemporary reference to Olson and his concerns among certain poets, critics, and movements with related orientations. Deeper questions of gender and patriarchy seldom get explored or expressed in their biographical, political, economic, historical, or mythological context and complexity. Meanwhile, things left by the wayside or that are swept under the proverbial carpet don't disappear. They just become, in Olson's term, "unrelieved."

If one, for instance, seriously considers Muriel Rukeyser's description of "the fear of poetry," pointed out at the height of the Cold War, and then sees Olson's move into poetry (as a physically large and potentially politically powerful man, also at the height of the Cold War), as clear defiance of ruling concepts of masculinity, what the women writers below have to say about Olson opening things up takes on an entirely different meaning. Moreover, a narrow liberal feminist critique too often ignores class issues and obfuscates the character of Olson's influence. For example, how his own working-class background allied him to working-class students like Dorn, Rumaker, and Wieners, the latter two in particular later becoming active in the gay liberation movement.

The chance encounter between seemingly contradictory assertions brought up by the quotes I found seemed to open a dialogue, or at least a place where questions could be raised. Once I matched the critic's quote with quotes from women recounting their experiences, I proceeded to go through other things I had on hand, looking for relevant material. What follows is initial, but it captures how thoughts and ideas unfold in the moment of their appearance and pursuit. The investigation poses a series of questions: how do we access our history and verify our experience of it? Does a theoretical/ critical imperative (or some other superstructure) take precedence over expressions of indebtedness, ambivalence, or contradictory experiences expressed by subjects of inquiry themselves? Why are lineage or indebtedness kept secret in some cases and stated or loudly pronounced in others? Why is one person called a biographer but another a critic? How do structures of judgment and issues of "originality" reduce poetic movement and transmission, making some poets "innovators," others "disseminators," and still others "followers"? Are criteria for "success" ever spelled out on the exchange floor where people labor to stay, in Spicer's words, "ahead of the trends of the trading"? Why does partisanship buttressing official versions of events and history go unremarked, while partisanship against the grain gets framed as crude, unsophisticated, a sign of amateurism or failure, and placed beyond the pale?

I have chosen to proceed not so much as an exercise in partisanship as an enactment of it. My purpose is to bring attention to how cases are made and how histories can unfold in a public way, revealing parallels between the ways power and control over our experience get administered and distributed, and what happens to the representation of our encounters with the world.

Marjorie Perloff: In c. 1970, Philip Yanella, a professor at Temple University in Philadelphia, where I was then living, asked me if I'd like to contribute something to a special Olson issue of *boundary 2* he was editing. I had never read much Olson, being at that time very much in the camp of Robert Lowell et al., but thought this would be a chance to explore the work. Reading Olson "from the outside," as it were, I was overwhelmed by the hype—that is, by the pure adulation the Olsonites gave their hero. Everything he wrote, everything he did was regarded as special. And that included, of course, "Projective Verse 1950," an essay that was treated like some sort of milestone in critical discourse.

Now to me, "Projective Verse 1950" was very interesting but I hardly thought then, and I don't think now, that it was as momentous a statement as it has been made out to me [sic]... As for individual cases, I don't think it matters whether Olson owned this or that book by Williams or whether he had read this or that essay. My point was that *these ideas and phrasings were in the air*—Olson didn't exactly think them up. Certainly he might have known Williams's "The Poem as a Field of Action," but even if he didn't know the piece as such, Williams's priority here suggests that Olson was more of a disseminator than an originator, when it came to poetics. That was and continues to be my basic point. I did not call him a plagiarist because plagiarism is hardly the issue. Originality of conceptualization is.

...Over the past two decades I've come to see "Projective Verse" as an important statement historically speaking, never mind that it wasn't "original." Pound's own statements have been shown to be equally unoriginal in many cases. And I have come to find Olson much more interesting and exciting than I took him to be in 1971 or so when I wrote the piece. At the same time, I now understand my original animosity (and its current residue) as everything having to do with Olson's patriarchal stance, something I didn't understand in 1970 when the feminist movement had not yet been launched. Olson's sexism, evident in so much of the poetry and criticism, and foregrounded in studies like Charles Boer's *Olson in Connecticut*, where we read about Olson's expulsion of women from his classroom and subsequent glee when they "couldn't take it," is pretty hard for women to take. And I shall ask you a question I asked Chris Beach when he similarly criticized my piece in his *ABC of Influence*: how many women critics (or younger poets) have responded favorably to Olson? There's Ann Charters, but she is writing primarily as a biographer. Who else? And if women have on the whole steered clear, doesn't that tell us something?

Ann Charters: I don't think that anyone took me personally as somebody whom they had to bother with. The only one who did was Charles Olson.

Hettie Jones: And then when I met him he was just UP and I was DOWN. But he made me feel so comfortable that that disparity in size just melted away, and we just became instant friends. I hadn't met an older person who was so comforting and encouraging to me.

Alice Notley: I think I was influenced a lot by my misunderstandings of people like Olson and Williams.

D. H. Melhem: We may courteously or condescendingly admit that certain speeches and sermons are "poetic."

Perhaps Martin Luther King's "I Have A Dream" speech is very like a poem. The epigraph to this introduction, Du Bois's "Postscript" to the *The Gift of Black* (1924), may indeed be a prose poem. And some musical incursions (blues and jazz) may be admissible, in certain instances, to a kind of racy exotic privilege, but the degree and purpose must be questioned. The most incisive comment, however, remains Charles Olson's "Who knows what a poem ought to sound like? Until it's thar?"

Joanne Kyger: In 1957, when I was first coming of "age" in poetry, I was given a copy of Charles Olson's "Projective Verse," published in *Poetry New York*. I had questions about how to structure my words on the page. "Projective Verse" became my constant meditative text from then on, finding comfort in its dense, muscular, conversational rhetoric. It was my introduction to the actual breathing of a human voice. I then found a way to notate my own voice in the clarity of the field of the page, "right there where the line is born." Writing became an actuality, a physical body, a real ear, heart, hand, pen, real syllables made into real words, directly, instantly, with no hesitation energy is put onto the force field of the paper page. From Charles Olson I also found a poetics which contained history as memory of time and history as memory of place. Growing up in the U.S. with western history being taught as the history of the Greek/Roman empire, I welcomed Olson's expanded sense of the world, especially that of the American continent which he understood did not stop at the U.S. border. It included the Mayan empire which, as informal archaeologist, he personally experienced, and the civilizations of the rest of Mexico which are often, unaccountably, not included in our western cultural inheritance.

Diane di Prima: In terms of direct influence, though, I'd say that Robert Duncan and Charles Olson were it, and are still.

[In Olson]
1) the body is proposed as the ground

> As heart-beat and breath are the counterpoint in us
>   we lay listening to in the dark, as children
>   "What if it stops?"

> this body stuff—it is the first time it is so patently
> there—

[And]
2) that the work proceeds by its own laws:

"he can go by no other track than the one the poem
 under hand declares for itself" opens the door to
 various speculations and notions of the "dictated"
 poem. And Duncan's concept of "obedience" to the
 poem, if it does not grow out of Charles's sentence,
 proceeds from a like base.
      staying in the poem (the experience)
      not "memory of"
      not "emotion recollected in tranquility" etc.
              This is no easy indulgence, *for the poem is
      not all-inclusive*
      it "includes" only what is itself
      &
      is thus <u>particular</u>
Pound, and others, all the way back to Wyatt
may well have experienced this "obedience"

this following where the poem leads
but Olson was the first to propose it as a

LAW OF POETIC COMPOSITION

Charles Olson talks of the "conventions logic had forced
on syntax" and there are also the ones syntax has forced
on thought

As is obvious by now, we are the inheritors of a syntax
formed by logics other than our own:

In composition by field, nothing is excluded *a priori*
 our materials are determined by the particularity of the event

(the poem itself)

& herein lies the challenge, or one of them—
                                        to adhere to
this singularity (uniqueness)
                                        w/out allowing the attention
to wander, to be pulled off, distracted
by the Guardians of the Threshold

those keepers of the New (our self-initiation
which every poem is)
                          the darkness of our self-initiation

as there are postures of attention (readiness)
        unique to each of us

Susan Howe: It would be hard to think of poetry apart from
history. This is one reason Olson has been so important to me.

Rosmarie Waldrop: though I would not place the act, the cen-

ter of the energy totally "within," but on the intersection—
and interaction—of within and without, of I and world
(Olson's "skin"), of libido and language.

Some are more concerned with *the mot just*, with *the*
perfect metaphor, others, with what "happens between" the
words (Charles Olson)

...finally, that the vertical tendency of metaphor (Olson:
"the suck of symbol") is our hotline to transcendence, to
divine meaning, hence the poet as priest and prophet.

...What matters is not so much the "thing," not "the
right word," but what "happens...between" (Olson).

Eileen Myles: I was walking around this year thinking, I'm
like Charles Olson, because I feel as if I've just used the inside of my apartment, the street, the neighborhood again
and again and again.

Kathy Acker: WROTE DOWN "PRAY FOR US THE
DEAD," THE FIRST LINE IN THE FIRST POEM BY
CHARLES OLSON SHE HAD EVER READ WHEN SHE
WAS A TEEN-AGER. ALL THE DOLLS WERE DEAD.
DEAD HAIR. WHEN SHE LOOKED UP THIS POEM, ITS
FIRST LINE WAS, "WHAT DOES NOT CHANGE / IS THE
WILL TO CHANGE."

WENT TO A NEARBY CEMETERY AND WITH
STICK DOWN IN SAND WROTE THE WORDS "PRAY
FOR US THE DEAD." THOUGHT, WHO IS DEAD? THE
DEAD TREES? WHO IS DEAD? WE LIVE IN SERVICE OF
THE SPIRIT. MADE MASS WITH TREES DEAD AND
DIRT AND UNDERNEATH HUMANS AS DEAD OR LIV-
ING AS ANY STONE OR WOOD.

...When I first started writing, I was influenced by poetry, mainly the Black Mountain school of poetry.

Peter Wollen: Acker's debt to Black Mountain—to Charles Olson, in particular, whose work she had known since she was still a schoolgirl—is quite clear and it is strange that this should have gone unrecognized, at least as she saw it, because she was not considered to be a poet. She adapted his concern with writing as language-driven, with a certain kind of incantatory text, based on the physical cadence of the breath, while introducing these preoccupations into the writing of prose rather than poetry.

Diane Wakoski: I don't feel I'm doing anything different from what Charles Olson is doing, which is trying to discover the geography of America, which is the geography of the world, which is what human civilization is all about, and which is what my life as a poet is all about.

Olson's concerns were with archaeology, history, and language as it changes through history, so when he uses his city of Gloucester, Massachusetts, as a focus for these interests, open-ended lines which seem digressive become essential; and discovering that each subject led rapidly to another and left a field of discourse, a field of information to roam around in, his lines found themselves unhappy with simple objects and predicates. Olson found that history doesn't have beginnings, middles, and ends, as the neat composer's mind would like to think. So each poem becomes a field, a landscape of ideas, and completely baffles the critic or reader whose reading techniques were formed by the New Criticism.

I try to get away from the whole biological argument

that men are that way and women are that way, but simply that's what our civilization has been. And it's an enormous fight. I was fascinated and delighted last week when a critic, a man named Sherman Paul—who is quite a traditional New England critic, an expert on Emerson and Hart Crane who is currently very, very, very interested in open-field poetry and is in fact working on a book about Charles Olson—came to deliver a lecture on Olson, and gave both a brilliant lecture on Olson's mythology and a very interesting seminar on Olson's coming out of the New England tradition. And it was impressive to listen to him talk about the need for an open-field criticism that can in some way deal with open-field poetry. And we were all interested in a kind of minor little baby intellectual problem, which is why so much of the very masculine open field poetry like Olson's or Creeley's or Duncan's is spurned by the new critics because certainly it seems to be in the tradition of the masculine and the abstract. The real answer is (Paul spent about half an hour talking about the subject) how personal the ideology and aesthetic of the open-field poets are. That they absolutely insist their poems are personal documents. They are *not* abstract documents. That ultimately it is not Maximus speaking; it is *Olson* speaking. And by the end of the Maximus poems he is *declaring* himself to be Olson; no longer—I mean, Maximus never really started as a persona. He started as another name for Olson, but even by the end of the Maximus poems he is not… the name Maximus isn't important; it is Olson and the insistence that it is Olson and Olson's history, which if he has a big enough mind is big enough to encompass the whole of civilization. That is, if you will, moving the feminine notion of the personal in on the masculine notion of the abstract. And of course we want to think of the androgynous—not in any biological sense meaning having both physical organs, which must be really freakish rather than real, but as a spiritual combining of things—certainly that is moving towards what enlightenment must really be so that you can have the soundness of the abstract principles of the world informed by the urgent sense of the personal. And so far, there isn't a criticism. Even structuralist criticism has moved in the direction of the antipersonal. And yet the whole purpose of structuralist criticism was to deal with the eccentricities and the personalities of twentieth-century freedom and writing that comes after Freud and Marx, in a period of time where people feel absolutely authentic enough to declare themselves personal and at the same time voices, and where we don't have to think of ourselves as spokesmen for groups of people, but in fact proclaim that the personal voice is big enough to be an important voice. And in a sense this is what contemporary poetry is all about, a strange combination of the lyric and the narrative—which is the narrative for heroic epic verse, and the lyric for personal love poem; putting them together and saying that the personal voice of the love poem can be an epic voice. In other words, it can have a narrative content. It can be meaningful in terms of philosophy, history, and civilization. We don't... and I'm not claiming this for myself; I'm claiming this for all serious contemporary poetry, and I'm still angry at the critics who can't see that this is going on and who try very hard to separate out, as they say, the sheets from the ghosts, the strong intellectual (therefore reputable) poets and the weak, namby-pamby personal poets. And I do think that the whole women's movement has done a lot to emphasize the very *worst* elements of this with women claiming, "*We* feel. You don't feel."

Well, I mean, it's no better to feel if you don't think than to think if you don't feel.

Anne Waldman: I date my confirmation of a life in poetry to the Berkeley Poetry Conference in 1965 and the point where Charles Olson says:

No, I wanna talk, I mean, you want to listen to a poet? You know, a poet, when he's alive, whether he talks or reads you his poems is the same thing. Dig that! And when he is made of three parts—his life, his mouth, and his poem—then, by god, the earth belongs to us! And what I think has happened is that that's—wow, gee, one doesn't like to claim things, but god, isn't it exciting? I mean, I feel like a kid, I'm in the presence of an event, which I don't believe myself.

In the presence of an event was the illuminating phrase for me. His reading was fragmented, disturbed, and chaotic on one level, but completely lucid on another. He kept the audience there for more than four hours.

Olson continues to be a kind of "imago," as do Robert Duncan, Frank O'Hara, Allen Ginsberg, Burroughs, all for very different reasons. But that oral moment in Berkeley where Olson played the fool, the anti-hero poet at his shamanic worst, or most vulnerable on some level—that presence was like a strange attractor as I, as a young person, witnessed it. And the event still ripples in my poetic consciousness. And there's the event of *Maximus*, rich with history and mythology and language and location as a salvation for the poet, his only anchor or link to reality, as we know from the biography and various accounts. He was really possessed with this poem, people would visit him and he would be surrounded with little scraps of paper and speaking the poem, living the poem. I can identify with that kind of possession and salvation. Poets of my generation and much younger have the conversation about whether it's possible to ever have these kinds of heroic poetic figures again. It's a dying patriarchal breed, perhaps. Whether it's Spicer or Olson or Duncan or Ginsberg or Ed Dorn. Robert Creeley, Gary Snyder, Ashbery, Baraka, of course, are still active, alive, and are major poetic pioneers. But the imposing, egomaniacal, fierce, ethical poetry hero whose presence is as startling as the work—where has he gone? And can't there be women heroes? Maybe all the contemporary careerism gets in the way. And maybe the power has shifted to women who have a different, though often as uncompromising, kind of command. We'll see.

Daphne Marlatt: That etymology paper really led me into all the writing I would subsequently do… it opened up language for me.

Fred Wah: The problem has to do, in Marlatt's case, with where her language comes from. She strives for a writing which will accurately reflect the condition of the writer at the moment of the writing. This is called "proprioceptive" writing and Marlatt is one of its most disciplined proponents.

Proprioception is a physiological term and has to do with the sensory reception in our bodies responding to stimuli arising from within. The term is also the title of a short "chart" written by Charles Olson, circa 1959, in which Olson seeks to place "consciousness," a very important condition for Marlatt. Olson says the gain for proprioception is:

> that <u>movement</u> or <u>action</u>
> is 'home.' Neither of the Unconscious nor
>   Projection
> (here used to remove the false opposition of
> 'Conscious'; 'consciousness' is self) have a home
> unless the DEPTH implicit is physical being—
> built in space-time specifics, and moving (by
> movement of 'its own'—is asserted, or found-
> out as such. Thus the advantage of the value
> 'proprioception.' As such.

The "soul" is in the "body." George Bowering's outstanding interview with Daphne Marlatt... is called "Given This Body." Repeatedly in the interview and elsewhere, Marlatt has insisted on the place of the body in the origins and processes of her writing. When I talked with her recently she said, "I realize things about my living when I'm writing that I think it's necessary for me to realize and I don't seem to be able to realize them any other way."

Kathleen Fraser: ...the *visualized* topos of interior speech and thought—that full or fully empty arena of the page imagined into being by a significant number of non-traditional women poets now publishing—cannot really be adequately thought about without acknowledging the immense, permission-giving moment of Charles Olson's "PROJECTIVE VERSE" manifesto (widely circulated from 1960 onwards, through its paperback arrival in Donald Allen's *The New American Poetry*). There is no doubt that—even if arrived at through a subtle mix of osmosis and affinity rather than a direct reading of Olson's manifesto—poets entering literature after 1960 gained access to a more expansive page through Olson's own visual enactment of "field poetics," as mapped out in his major exploratory work, *The Maximus Poems.*

An urgency towards naming, bringing voice to off-the-record thought and experience—as marked by increasing eccentricities of syntax, cadence, diction and tone—would have lacked such a clear concept of PAGE as canvas or screen on which to project flux, without the major invitation Olson provided… this, in spite of his territorial inclusive/exclusive boy-talk. The excitement Olson generated, the event of the *making*—the hands-on construction of a poem being searched out, breathed into and lifted through the page, fragment by fragment, from the archeological layers of each individual's peculiar life—revealed the complex grid of the maker's physical and mental acitivity. Its "*it.*" "Olson's *acute visual sensitivity* separates *The Maximus Poems* from *The Cantos* and *Paterson*.…" (Susan Howe)—two other models for poets writing in the 1960s, who desired to break from a more standardized poem model. Olson's idea of high energy "projection" engaged an alchemy of colliding sounds and visual constructions, valuing *ir*regularity, counterpoint, adjacency, ambiguity… the movement of poetic language as investigative tool. An open field, not a closed case.

It was Olson's declared move away from the narcissistically probing, psychological defining of self—so seductively explored by Sylvia Plath, Anne Sexton, and Robert Lowell in the early and mid-1960s, and by their avid followers for at least a generation after—that provided a major alternative ethic of writing for women poets. While seriously committed to gender consciousness, a number of us carried an increasing scepticism towards any fixed rhetoric of the poem, implied or intoned. We resisted the prescription of authorship as an exclusively unitary proposition—the essential "I" positioned as central to the depiction of reflectivity. As antidote to a mainstream poetics that enthusiastically embraced those first dramatic "confessional" poems, Olson (in "PROJECTIVE VERSE") had already proposed:

The getting rid of the lyrical interference of the individual as ego, of the "subject" and his soul, that peculiar presumption by which western man has interposed himself between what he is as a creature of nature (with certain instructions to carry out) and those other creations of nature...

The excitement and insistence of Olson's spatial, historical, and ethical margins, while clearly speaking from male imperatives, nevertheless helped to stake out an area whose initial usefulness to the poem began to be inventively explored by American women—in some cases drastically *re*concieved, beginning with work in the 1960s and 1970s by such poets as Barbara Guest, Susan Howe, and Hannah Weiner and continuing forward to very recent poetry by women just beginning to publish.

Kristin Prevallet: Instead of buying gas masks and digging underground shelters (or moving to Canada), I turn my rage and confusion towards poetry, the unacknowledged legislation of worlds unacknowledged, to reveal both systems of knowing (content) and structures of ideology (form). Poetry, the work of radical linguistic, contextual, and metrical articulation, is a way to structure my sometimes perpendicular thought processes, transforming confusion and anger into form and meaning. Luckily, there are numerous trajectories in the history of poetry that active minds in search of some "tradition" can follow and, after careful apprenticeship, claim as their own. My choice for consideration here is the polyvalent tradition of Investigative Poetics and its links with Projective Verse, Relational Poetics, and even Language Poetry, which provide theoretical structures for working with language to reveal both the formal, syntactic structures that make it work, and the cultural, connotative sources that make it mean something. These enabling traditions are, obviously, specific, each with their own histories and cast of poets. And, although there are numerous points of entry into these traditions, the one most relevant to an introduction to Investigative Poetics is Charles Olson.

Sources are listed in order of citation. See the blibliography for full titles and information.

Marjorie Perloff. *Minutes of the Charles Olson Society* #8, June 1995, pp. 34–36; a reply to Ralph Maud's "A Challenge to Marjorie G. Perloff" which appeared in *Minutes of the Charles Olson Society* # 7

Ann Charters. *Breaking the Rule of Cool: Interviewing and Reading Women Beat Writers*, eds. Grace and Johnson, p. 217

Hettie Jones. *Minutes of the Charles Olson Society* #10, Nov. 1995, p. 7

Alice Notley. *Talisman* 1, Fall 1988; p. 24

D. H. Melhem. *Heroism in the New Black Poetry*, p. 4

Joanne Kyger. Personal communication sent by the poet to be read at the first OlsonNow, Poetry Project at St. Marks, Dec. 3, 2005

Diane di Prima. *Breaking the Rule of Cool*, p. 97; "Some Notes

Towards a Poetics," Lecture #3 in the 1985 Olson Memorial
Lecture series, State University of New York at Buffalo

Susan Howe. *The Birth-mark*, p. 158

Rosmarie Waldrop. *Talisman* 6, Spring 1991, p. 35; *Moving Borders: Three Decades of Innovative Writing by Women*, ed. Mary Margaret Sloan, pp. 609–10

Eileen Myles. *Talisman* 17, summer 1997, p. 44

Kathy Acker. DEAD DOLL HUMILITY; *Postmodern Culture*; vol. 1, no. 1 (Sep. 1990); in conversation with Ellen G. Friedman, Center for Book Culture (Dalkey Archive Press) http://www.centerforbookculture.org/ interviews/interview_acker.html

Peter Wollen. In "Don't be afraid to copy it out," *London Review of Books*; Vol. 20, No. 3; 5 February 1998

Diane Wakoski. *Toward a New Poetry*, pp. 315, 106–7, 303–5

Anne Waldman. *Vow to Poetry: Essays, Interviews & Manifestos*, pp. 204, 290

Daphne Marlatt. from a taped conversation between Marlatt and Fred Wah, speaking about a paper she wrote for Olson's class in Vancouver in 1963; in Daphne Marlatt, *Selected Writing*, pp. 8–9; Fred Wah on Daphne Marlatt, from the introduction to *Selected Writing*, p. 15

Kathleen Fraser. *Moving Borders, e*d. Mary Margaret Sloan, pp. 643–44

Kristin Prevallet. "Writing is Never By Itself Alone: Six Mini Essays on Relational Investigative Poetics," *Fence* Vol. 6, No. 1 Spring/Summer 2003

"YEARS TO LISTEN"

NOVEMBER 11TH: UNION SQUARE

long black braids bead and silver
earrings dashes of red under his
eyes Valerie on the ground
lighting candles I know not
of what Nation he is beating
his drum chanting for the dead

1

Muriel Rukeyser first published *The Life of Poetry* in 1949, based on talks, lectures, and broadcasts from the 1940s. It is worth repeating a specific quote from it:

We are a people tending toward democracy at the level of hope; on another level, the economy of the nation, the empire of business within the republic, both include in their basic premise, the concept of perpetual warfare.

Given this "basic premise," domestic policy is foreign policy, and foreign policy domestic; we cannot grasp what is happening around us without looking at the motivations and effects of one upon the other. We can begin with a look at the 1950s and what gets labeled as McCarthyism, but which might more usefully be called Hooverism, to use Peter Dale Scott's term. Much of that history gets revised to exonerate people we might think of as liberal who were not only complicit but instrumental in narrowing parameters of debate, expression, and articulation. We can look at cases that made the news—attacks on Middle East Studies, on Native American activist and scholar Ward Churchill, on Amiri Baraka and his firing as New Jersey Poet Laureate after 9/11, and so on. But there is a case that stands out— that of Steve Kurtz, whose life was turned upside down by the post-9/11 manufacture of fear and the mechanisms put into place to alleviate that manufactured fear. This manu- factured fear has directly and personally affected many thousands, if not millions of people, and will continue to have direct or ripple effects on many more, through searches and seizures, detention, deportation, surveillance, harassment, legal and financial blackmail, and a host of other methods invented to muzzle and terrify. Given the war on drugs, the criminalization of black males, and the construction of the ghetto/prison/industrial/complex, should any of this surprise us?

Moving across this chronology, one issue comes up: the use of attacks on the academy to privatize, incorporate, and defund education, attacks which, though in proxy focusing on faculty, are actually designed to infantilize students, mobilize them into group identities, reduce their abilities to exercise independent judgement, and force compliance. In such a climate, the biggest lies work best, perverting the scope of the terms through which we process experience. The creation of a climate of fear serves as a vehicle to drain resources and divert attention away from perpetual war, for instance, forcing us to mobilize, organize, and fundraise in "defense" of those attacked rather than in opposition and resistance to policies making security and real freedom impossible.

In a lot of the statements publicly defending free speech, I've been struck by the repeated insistence of those defending it to begin by disassociating themselves or condemning the statements of those they purport to defend. Statements begin: While I abhor the sentiments of X and completely repudiate and disassociate myself from them, I will defend X's right to blah blah blah—a very strange way to enact freedom. We might, in this context, consider Herman Melville's statement: "Freedom is the name for the thing that is not freedom."

Missing in the dominant formulation is the difference

between word and deed, thought and policy, between speech act and written word, what is outside or what is inside a chain of command, what is rendered powerless and illegitimate. What does it mean when an Amiri Baraka or Ward Churchill writes or says something? Why does it mean something different when a Secretary of Defense, a general, or the CEO of a large corporation says or writes something? These are issues Steve Kurtz and the Critical Art Ensemble have explored in some depth.

While Jack Spicer could refuse the loyalty oath in the 1950s, and pay the price of being excluded from academic work, today we no longer have loyalty oaths to refuse, being so invested in the system that the system's investment in us has ceased to be visible or contested. The roots of this sanction and ransom run deep. The first bestseller on the continent, *A True History of the Captivity and Restoration of Mrs. Mary Rowlandson*, tells the story of one of the first colonial political prisoners, the settler Mary Rowlandson, captured for ransom in 1675 from her garrison compound in an anticolonial rebellion of Nipmuck, Wampanoag, and Narragansett Indians. Intrinsic to the set of constraints imposed upon the writing of this text by her minister husband, by Increase Mather, and in turn by many other ministers, political leaders, family and community members—all with vested interests in fortifying and expanding settlement—was the embedding and entombment of experiences she had undergone and witnessed. We find here, at the very beginning of colonization, a kind of encoding and administration of experience that operates within a narrative structure serving those interests and denying the consciousness of what she had seen. This both cordons off and administers her contact with the natives and our experience of her encounters. One can draw a line from there through the Iran hostage crisis, to the case of an American soldier, Private Jessica Lynch in Iraq. All draw on a complex set of experiential, mythic, and propagandistic structures. In Private Lynch's case, her captivity and release were staged and then, finally, exposed. Like Mary Rowlandson or the hostages in Iran in 1979, Lynch no doubt went through a traumatic experience. However, the idea that in all of these cases the native populations in whose midst these acts took place—the American Indians, the Iranians, and the Iraqis—were hostages to larger political circumstances and maneuvers is either omitted from the narrative or deeply hidden between the lines. The function of this machinery is to hold us, as citizens, in check. This makes me think of one of the Critical Art Ensemble's statements: "First, organic being in the world must be reestablished as the locus of reality, placing the virtual back in its proper place as simulacra." And in another seemingly simple statement: "What we are witnessing at this point in time is the triumph of representation over being."

In the task before us of reestablishing a locus for reality, and examining these representations, we must, paradoxically, call upon and trust the projective powers of imagination. Here are lines from a poem written in 1968 by Philip Whalen that today would probably be labeled treasonous. They're from "The War Poem for Diane di Prima," 3rd section, called "The War. The Empire":

When the Goths came into Rome
They feared the Senators were gods
Old men, each resolutely throned at his own house door.

When they finally come to Akron, Des Moines, White Plains,
The nomads will laugh as they dismember us.
Other nations watching will applaud.
There'll be no indifferent eye, nary a disinterested ear.
We'll screech and cry.

In an article called "Multiculturalism and the Ruling Elite," Daniel Brandt writes: "We must be aware of our own historical legacy: psychological warfare and the secret state, the mass media and the culture of spectacle, the role of foundations and above all, the interests and techniques of the elite globalists who won the cold war."

It is a willingness to examine these operative modes and elements that I find missing in the debate promoting so-called "academic freedom." This "freedom" is a dubious concept upon which to base any sense of real freedoms, having been used extensively as propaganda around covert and overt state use of the academy, becoming ideal cover for CIA run centers and institutions particularly in what came to be called Area Studies. In focusing its formidable capabilities—particularly in their investigation of technology—the Critical Art Ensemble has embraced the idea of the amateur, the idea that the experts cannot be trusted and that we, like the Herodotus Charles Olson quoted so often in his conception of history, must *find out for ourselves.*
"Individuals," the Ensemble write, "are left with the implied obligation that they should just have faith in scientific, government, and corporate authorities that allegedly always act with only the public interest in mind." We know, of course, what the price of this expertise has been, in cases well known and not so well known—from Union Carbide's silica min-

ing at Gauley Bridge chronicled by Rukeyser up to the company's catastrophe at Bhopal decades later, from the children of ringworm in Israel to those sickened all over by depleted uranium, from Gulf War Syndrome to Gulf Spill syndrome —the catalogue is endless and ongoing.

Freedoms are not given but secured. Sometimes they have to be taken—in our relationships, our memories, and the ways we behave within structures, with our co-workers, our students, our teachers, and our bosses. And we are aware, no matter how powerless we might feel, that individual and collective actions matter. A great part of the Critical Art Ensemble's usefulness in these times has had to do with their ability to demystify processes, methods, and techniques that centralized forces go to great lengths to obscure.

In a journal entry from 1959, the poet John Wieners, experimented upon by experts through electroshock—wrote:

the different techne a man uses to make his salvation.
That   is why poetry
even tho it does deal with language is no more holy act
than, say shitting.

                    Dis-
                charge. Manifesting the
                    process of
            is it life? Or the action between this and
                        non-action? Lethargy vs.
                                Violence.
For to take up arms against the void is attack, and the price
    was
                is high

2

The most severe years of repression under the regime of King Hassan in Morocco, in the 1970s, were referred to as "the years of lead." A heroic resistance arose to this repression, mounted through songs, poetry, memoirs, and testimony. Curiously, the great 18th century English poet, Alexander Pope, in his immortal *Dunciad*, a mock epic excoriating an age of mediocrity and dullness, referred to his time as an "age of lead." Often in societies where dullness reigns supreme, repression has been so deeply internalized that citizens become their own best mutual censors and interrogators. In the United States of the past several decades, probably dating to the end of the American wars in Indochina, culture has tended to become more of a domesticating system, with willed confusion as to its public or political relationship to consciousness and human capacity. As Jed Rasula writes: "Literature can occupy a marginal social position that nevertheless embodies the centralizing labor of national destiny." I would amend this to say that literature *seems* to occupy a marginal social position while remaining absolutely crucial in the production of a certain subjectivity, the very same subjectivity resulting in a domestic and domesticated American identity that Melani McAlister has described as "free of politics." The American poet and thinker Laura (Riding) Jackson pinpointed an essential part of this mechanism in her 1928 text *Anarchism Is Not Enough*:

Art so conceived thus becomes a skilful thwarting of originality. The immediate shock to the consciousness which a work brings, which might be expected to encourage an independence

in the consciousness, a dissociation from reality (influences)
and a development of its differences from reality, is utilized to
organize itself according to its resemblances (responses) to the
particular object-work by which it is attacked.

(Riding) Jackson goes on to write:

A poem, then, in the critical scheme, is only a work in the
sense that it achieves a value equal to an exceptionally "good"
experience; it is an especially high-class object, one that makes
use of all man's powers for reconstructing reality: a model
object, as the poet is supposed to be a model man. But man's
powers for reconstructing reality are really a misuse of his
powers for constructing himself out of the wreckage which is
reality. The only true entity possible to man is an analytic
entity: the synthetic entities are all parodies of self. An origi-
nal poem is only seemingly synthetic; the words of which it is
made are both the instrument of the analysis and the sub-
stance of the pure self of the poem which emerges from the
analysis. Every poem of this kind is an instance of fulfilled
originality, a model, to the reader, of constructive dissociation:
an incentive not to response but to initiative. Poetry is proper-
ly an art of individualization as opposed to the other arts,
which are arts of communication.

In the midst of dullness composed of stringently codified
"moments" of apparent poetic movement and relentlessly
promoted social net-workers, an entity composed of 11 letters of the alphabet, forming a signifier in American English,
makes an entrance onto the scene. This signifier, "Kent
Johnson," a "name" associated with poems, translations, and,

among other things, the works of a complicated set of texts attributed to an alleged survivor of Hiroshima, Araki Yasusada, is connected to a layered series of editors, collaborators, and correspondents, all of whom may or may not be verifiably "real." While there may be others in "Johnson's" repertoire that have been suggested or that we don't yet know about, the "Kent Johnson" that is attached to *Lyric Poetry After Auschwitz, Epigramititis: 118 Living American Poets*, several collaborative translation projects of Latin American poetry, as well as the larger Yasusada project, has had a particularly incendiary and salutary effect on the American poetry scene.

There is, of course, a paper trail: in his "life," Johnson seems to provide genuine service as a teacher in a community college, and was even recognized for this, named 2004 teacher of the year in the State of Illinois. In the 1980s, during the Sandinista revolution, "Johnson" worked in the Nicaraguan countryside teaching basic literacy and adult education. From this experience he translated *A Nation of Poets*—the most representative translation in English of the famous working class *Talleres de Poesía* of Nicaragua. These were the years high continental theory dug deep into American poetry and thought while the fundamental assumption in Central America, in the words of the Salvadoran poet and revolutionary Roque Dalton, was that "poetry, like bread, is for everyone."

In *Epigramititis: 118 Living American Poets*, Johnson makes us understand that the 118 mostly not very well-known poets and their readers whom he satirizes and praises may not be so marginal. At the receiving end of Johnson's acumen and wit, these figures are, nonetheless, representative. In one of the rare studies to examine the ideological assumptions behind contemporary American literary texts, *Warring Fictions: Cultural Politics and the Vietnam War Narrative*, Jim Neilson writes:

Every literary text—and the reception of literary texts—takes place within a society in which a dominant ideology (and its proponents) fights to maintain legitimacy against other ideologies (and their proponents). It is a struggle for the right to be perceived as common sense, as a society's defining belief system. All literary texts (and all cultural products) are marked by ideological struggle.

On the face of it, this would seem self-evident. Yet, responses to Johnson's work show just how thoroughly the dominant ideology's conceptions of culture and literature have permeated our available critical vocabulary. Johnson assumes that examining the consensus of public discourse upon which political power consolidates itself has to start somewhere, and so he takes a scalpel to these mechanisms, probing and cutting through the world he knows best. This can be a scary proposition, making some squirm as they recognize friends, enemies, and poets of "reputation." Precisely because Johnson names names (each epigram bears a poet's name), we as readers are called upon to judge our own responses to his mix of invective, humor, and admiration. As the late poet Ed Dorn wrote on an early batch of these epigrams: "It's about time for something of the sort, what with the ass licking that rules the day." One of the keys to Johnson's power is the scalpel he brings to bear upon his own person, implicating himself as clearly and cruelly as anyone. In an article on Johnson's *Lyric Poetry After Auschwitz* and the controversy surrounding Johnson's response to prominent poet Charles Bernstein, poet and visual artist David-Baptiste Chirot writes:

Johnson isn't restricting his interrogating to others, but very much includes himself as well. By using both parts of the Yeatsian dictum that the quarrel with others is politics, and the quarrel with oneself poetry, Johnson opens up his poems to a rawness and vulnerability that's at brutal and black humor odds with the smooth surfaces of "radical artifice" Bernstein advocates. While advocating the use of "skepticism," Bernstein's interrogations are restricted to language and aesthetics and attempt to close themselves off from being questioned by either himself or others. Johnson on the other hand submits himself to his own self-interrogations and those of the reader's.

This debate confronts us with the crucial issue of how style, tone, linguistic register, and format serve to control and contain the possibilities of actual free speech, or speech that might make people uncomfortable. In another essay called "Raw War," Chirot puts these issues in the context of changing trends and resistances developing in American poetry:

After Olson, American poetry has lost a lot of interest in the kinds of speeds Olson wrote of—those of perception, breath, human nerves, actions, awarenesses as a kind of continual training for writing poetry and for being in the world… In her introduction to Manifesto: A Century of Isms, *Mary Ann Caws notes that the energy level of the "postmodernist" manifestoes is largely undone by their "dryness." In contrast to the speed of Olson's vision, there is the static quality of some of the*

final entries in the book, including those of American
L=A=N=G=U=A=G=E poetry.

In "Why American Poetry is Boring, Again," Amiri Baraka
writes that in the current situation, a poetry of "the outdoors,"
of the actual, is being eschewed. Instead there is a desire for
belonging, safety, all the comforts of Homeland Security, with
the streets kept clear of protestors, potential tearerists and ter-
rorists, looters and the like. Baraka writes of the poets' "desire
to be in the social diarrheic of society's value and meaning."
The "blunt consideration" of playing it safe, of not "saying
something," to protect one's career, creates a pervasive dull-
ness, an entropy of the speeds of poetries involved with an
actual which includes war, being part of it or opposed to it.

At the height of the war in Vietnam, poets Robert
Duncan and Denise Levertov charted out other paths
through their friendship and correspondence. While
Levertov worked in public opposition, Duncan, in going
"underground," struck at the heart of complicity: "We want
peace because we are agonized to realize how much we are
involved with and subject to the will of murderous and
conceited men; but the Vietnamese who are fighting for the
truth do not want peace at the sacrifice of their vision of
the good—we, not they, are the ones who need immediate
surrender of the war for the good of our human souls."
Duncan's thoughts immediately became part of a further
conversation with Levertov's husband, Mitch Goodman,
also a prominent anti-war activist. Thus, in a society largely
held in check through various forms of psychological warfare, where "communication," in Christopher Simpson's

definition "meant little more than a form of transmission into which virtually any type of message could be plugged (once one had mastered the appropriate techniques) to achieve ideological, political, or military goals," it is of paramount importance to examine and trace precisely along which lines messages travel. For Duncan, as well, it became important *not* to publish during this period, and he made a pledge in 1968 to not bring out a book length collection for fifteen years. What emerged in 1984, *Ground Work: Before the War*, summons every possible force to find forms commensurate to the cataclysmic events that had taken place during the interim. Duncan's presence of mind in deciding to keep his readership small during that period yields, outside some of the poetry written by veterans of the war, the most powerful poetic document of the time.

Finding alternative forms of trustworthy communication and places to gather has always been a major factor in the formation of new cultural and political possibilities. If one looks at decisive moments in post Second World War American culture, certainly Black Mountain College is a significant point of intersection, particularly as we trace the trajectory of Olson's sphere of communication. After the official breakup of Black Mountain in 1957, Olson spent the next five years in Gloucester, all the while maintaining a voluminous correspondence with dozens of people. In 1963, an opportunity presented itself for him to teach at the State University of New York in Buffalo and Olson went but also invited a whole entourage to come along, whether they were "academically" sanctioned or not. This configuration has often been referred to as Black Mountain II. What hasn't been emphasized enough is that at a deci-

sive point in between the dissolution of Black Mountain
and the influx to Buffalo, Diane di Prima, with LeRoi Jones/
Amiri Baraka, began a newsletter called *The Floating Bear.*
One of *The Bear*'s primary objectives was to speed up communication. As di Prima put it:

*Apart from getting hold of out-of-the way work and unpub-
lished poets, our other major concern, at least for the first year
or so, was speed: getting the new, exciting work into the hands
of other writers as quickly as possible. I remember that the
last time I saw Charles Olson in Gloucester, one of the things
he talked about was how valuable the* Bear *had been to him
in its early years because of the fact that he could get new
work out that fast. He was very involved in speed, in communication. We got manuscripts from him pretty regularly in the
early days of the* Bear, *and we'd usually get them into the
very next issue. That meant that his work, his thoughts,
would be in the hands of a few hundred writers within two or
three weeks.*

The fact that 17 issues of *The Bear* came out in its first year,
1961, was almost inconceivable to poets unused to immediate contact, separated from one another by geography and
poverty. When one looks at the early years of Levertov and
Duncan's voluminous correspondence, from the mid to late
1950s, much of it centers on the exchange of carbon copied
poems or manuscripts. Michael Rumaker, for instance,
describes being a student at Black Mountain College and
the sheer excitement of having Olson read a poem that had
just arrived in a letter from Duncan that day. The idea that
new work could circulate so quickly was truly revolutionary

and certainly may have been one of the factors in making such places of congregation as Buffalo possible. Di Prima would utilize these same principles of speed and immediacy in the later 1960s with her *Revolutionary Letters*, many of which were syndicated to over 200 underground newspapers by Liberation News Service. Here we can trace an important form of lineage: a direct line leading from an initiative like *The Floating Bear* to the underground press, breaking through the Cold War policy of communication as propaganda to the counterculture's call for communication as empowerment, exploration, and kinship. Likewise, one can look at the explosion of work produced by African-American writers centered around an initially small enterprise, Dudley Randall's Detroit-based Broadside Press. While only thirty-five books of poetry were published by African-American poets from 1945 to 1965 by presses with national distribution, Broadside published eighty-one books from 1966 to 1975, putting 500,000 copies into circulation, with print runs on popular poetry titles running from 5,000 to 10,000.

These many years later, when the terms of debate and the scale of protest or response have become all too predictable, where it is almost impossible *not* to be affiliated with the corporate body of the nation, when complicity seems to pervade the core of our being, it is, indeed, telling that some of the most vital questioning takes place in a largely self-contained communication loop, far removed from nodes of specific political activity and places of human gathering. Yet, when controversy breaks out of a self-contained loop and into the public sphere, we are given a crystal-clear indication of just how important the containment of poetry, literature, and cultural activities are in maintaining very well policed boundaries. In the introduction to *Lyric Poetry After Auschwitz*, presented as a letter to the neo-conservative organization Campus Watch, Kent Johnson refers to a "diatribe on the poet and activist Ammiel Alcalay, published in the *American Thinker*" in 2005.

This diatribe, "Poetry, terror and political narcissism," penned by Alyssa A. Lappen, did, indeed, appear, and focused on various activities at different public cultural and academic venues. Most tellingly, the attack chose to focus on my activities just at the point I was putting more and more energy into working in American institutions and not places associated with the Middle East or the Balkans. While I was the ostensible subject of the piece, the underlying target had to do with funding, both of public cultural spaces and cultural institutions, as well as public education. Given that I work at the City University of New York, the country's largest urban public university system, this is quite significant. Even though the article was potentially libelous, it actually proved, ironically, to be one of the most comprehensive validations of the work I had been engaged in for many years. After all, these watchdogs were employed to keep their sights on precisely the kinds of cultural shifts I was promoting and, at least according to the vehemence of this report, I seemed to be having some success. For example, Lappen writes: "Alcalay urged others to use literary events to invite Arabs to present the Arab and pro-Arab point of view." Or, after naming a long list of institutions I have been involved in, as well as their funding sources, Lappen writes: "Is this really the kind of education that public, taxpayer-funded universities and parents should have to pay for?" Naturally, such statements put in stark relief the stakes involved in such economic and ideological warfare. To begin with, we can see the extent to which we have been robbed of an awareness of our own powers and ability to effectively act in the world on matters that have direct political and economic consequence. And this, in turn, reveals just how powerful the sphere of culture actually is, and how disconnected so many apparently progressive forces are from understanding the political role of cultural consciousness.

3

The British scholar and translator Gordon Brotherston, in his masterful *Book of the Fourth World*, writes of this continent's "thorough dispossession" of its native peoples, cultures, and languages. He also writes that "the prime function of classical texts is to construct political space and anchor historical continuity—this is truer still when these classics are understood to consecrate belief, say in our origins as humans, or our debt to the earth." One of the most traumatic moments in that dispossession is described by Ed Dorn, as he characterized the 1890 Massacre at Wounded Knee, and the end of the Ghost Dance movement, as "another small installment in the spiritual death of America."

The late Egyptian film director Yusef Chahine has spoken of "memory as a confrontation, a confrontation with oneself. You must first confront yourself before confronting other people, or a whole country… That's the political context of memory as you look back at yourself…" Certainly this political context of memory is an area largely cleansed from

North American public cultural consciousness. While one can see it at work in so many of the writers discussed in this book, as well as many more not touched on, these writers largely remain outside a general curriculum. One example of a writer that, to some extent, has forced his way into public consciousness through the enormity of his achievement in so many areas is Amiri Baraka. Close friend, associate of, and correspondent for many years with Ed Dorn, Baraka has resisted the spiritual or cosmic death Dorn wrote of by offering creative and political evidence to the contrary. Critical theory and literary history cannot un-categorize Baraka, nor will they place him at the forefront of our living culture. Drawing sustenance from a wide array of American, African-American, and international examples, from W.E.B. Dubois, Langston Hughes, and Charles Olson to Aimé Césaire, Frantz Fanon, and Amilcar Cabral, Baraka has reached back behind the Cold War and its aftermath, to a period in the American culture of the 1930s when radical politics presumed radical innovation. His disruptive and politically contingent practice refuses to conform to style or manner, allowing imagination to roam between the placard and the eulogy, between eyewitness reports stating facts and cosmic journeys reinstating the kinship of souls. His extraordinarily active public engagement with writing and the world spans a half-century. He has both been "anchoring historical continuity" and redrawing the political boundaries of time and space, first in Newark, New Jersey, then in New Ark, out and gone, an otherworldly place through which he channels radio shows, movies, street banter, diatribe, drama, scholarly study, fable, fiction, science fiction, investigative poetics, calculated public rhetoric, and on-the-spot reporting. He is a fantastic witness both to the astonishing un-reality of the daily real and an example of what can be done to answer it.

There are few American writers able to traverse the traditional trio of poetry, prose, and drama, then move into the realm of essays, autobiography, and scholarly study, making a significant mark in each form. While thought of primarily as a poet and a playwright, from his earliest stories like the 1958 classic "Suppose Sorrow Was A Time Machine," to *The System of Dante's Hell*, *Tales*, *6 Persons*, and his most recent *Tales of the Out and Gone*, Baraka's prose has shown the way through the dead-ends and infernal regions of our gimmick-oriented, categorizing, identity based forms of control, modes that confirm and do not resist our spiritual death. He has constantly exposed himself and his ideas to public scrutiny, even attack, opening a window into participation in the amalgamation of selves and ideas that form the creative, political subject. Baraka's example has served as a constant reminder that such selves, ideas, forms, even communities, are won through struggle and confrontation. They are not cheaply packaged and exchangeable things to pick up or drop for personal gain or according to dictates of fashion. Finally, though, this clarity of purpose rests in a stance, a position, a place one has to come to in consciousness and over which there can be no negotiation. The visibility of such a stance, bound to a tangible historical context, is itself a call to action, to activate that part of one's own consciousness that can meet such a challenge in commensurate terms. In recent years, Baraka has been quite explicit about the need to carry on this transmission, continually emphasizing how so many important figures have been covered up. Just as importantly, he has again exposed some parts of his prior selves in order to help us understand the relation of lived experience to knowledge, consciousness, and action.

What was the Black Arts Movement," Baraka asks. "It was some black kids who'd been down with white people in the Village who knew nothing about Harlem but pretended they did 'cause they were black, and then found out when they got up there they didn't know anything about it at all."

Baraka is leading us through the process of understanding how we know what we know, in Laura (Riding) Jackson's terms, how one constructs oneself "out of the wreckage of reality." Willingly or not we participate in the creation of this wreckage. As Baraka writes, "we might go back to a particular tradition that upholds a Rexroth, or a Ken Patchen, or a Langston Hughes, or a Henry Dumas, we might understand who a Zora Neale Hurston is, or a Gertrude Stein, but that is not what America is being advertised as around the world. You're being advertised as the good manners of vampires— so, you don't kill, you write poems. You don't bring democracy to Iraq by blowing it up, by killing the children and starving them. You're the good manners of vampires. You will bite me in the neck, in a poem." Such stinging indictments of the double face of culture brings us to the heart of the matter, and Brotherston's point about the dispossession of nativity. The classical thrust in Baraka's work also has to do with the possession of one's own experience as well as an awareness that what is now considered a classic was once the basis of a culture, and part of a common currency.

We can bookend yet another installment in this spiritual death by visualizing a demonstration whose most dramatic extant record, to my knowledge, is a less than four-minute clip captured by Roz Payne's Newsreel Films, depicting veterans of the wars in Southeast Asia stripping themselves of medals bestowed upon them for bravery and hurling them at the White House. Referred to by participants as a "limited incursion into the country of Congress," and named after two short U.S. led invasions of Laos, this action was the culmination of events that took place over the course of six days, from April 18th to April 23rd, 1971.

About 1,100 veterans, some on crutches or in wheelchairs, led by mothers who had lost their sons in the war, began a march from the Lincoln Memorial to Arlington Cemetery where a ceremony for the dead was held at the Tomb of the Unknown Soldier and the grave of President John F. Kennedy. As the march reached the Capitol steps, a member of the executive committee of Vietnam Veterans Against the War formally presented sixteen demands to Congress. While most veterans marched to the Mall to establish a campground, others went directly into the halls of Congress to lobby for their demands as the Washington District Court of Appeals lifted an injunction requested by the Justice Department that would have barred the veterans from camping on the Mall. On Tuesday the 20th, about 200 veterans attended hearings by the Senate Foreign Relations Committee to end the war. Another contingent of about 200 veterans marched single file across the Lincoln Memorial Bridge and back to Arlington Cemetery, appalled at a previous incident in which some of the contingent had been barred from entrance. Meanwhile, guerilla theater performances take place on the Capitol steps. At the same time, Chief Justice Warren Burger reverses the decision of the Court of Appeals and the veterans are given until 4:30 the next day to break camp.

While lobbying in Congress and guerilla theater (now at the Justice Department), continues on the next day, a group of 50 veterans march to the Pentagon and attempt to turn themselves in as war criminals. With the Supreme Court meeting in special session, a decision comes at 5:30 giving the veterans the option to stay on the Mall and not sleep or sleep and face arrest. The Washington Park Police announce they have no intention of inspecting the campsite that night. The cast of the musical *Hair* comes to entertain the veterans and, at midnight, Senator Edward Kennedy visits. On Thursday the 22nd of April, a large group of veterans marches to the Supreme Court asking why it has not ruled on the constitutionality of the war; they sing "God Bless America" and a hundred and ten are arrested for disturbing the peace. In the meantime, John Kerry testifies for two hours before a special session of the Foreign Relations Committee. Lobbying continues all day and, at nightfall, veterans stage a candle-light march around the White House carrying a huge American flag upside down, as a signal of distress. Finally, on Friday, veterans gather in front of the White House, obstructed by a fence, and cast their medals and ribbons over it, each one declaiming what it is they are dispossessing themselves of. While the images of these veterans are some of the most powerful depictions of dignity and defiance in American history, they remain almost unknown. At the same time, their continuing power can be attested to by the massive efforts that went into defeating the Kerry Presidential campaign in 2004 through attacking his war record, and maligning another veteran, former Senator Max Cleland, a key Kerry supporter, who had lost both legs and part of his right arm in an incident near Khe Sanh in 1968.

By 1969, Ed Dorn had already pronounced the death of a character called "I" in Book II of his extraordinary book-length poem *Gunslinger*. As the stench of putrefaction begins to rise from the corpse of I, we soon learn that "I is dead," after which the Slinger reminisces, saying "it makes me sad / to see I go, he was / I mean I was so perplexed…" When queried in an interview about the death of "I", Dorn refers to a line in which I becomes "the container of the thing it contains." Far from some metaphysical meditation, Dorn goes on to explain this as a reference to "using our returning dead as containers. Back then the CIA was sewing kilos of heroin inside the thorax of the cadavers of our returning dead from Vietnam, sewing it back up, and shipping the body back to Long Beach, San Francisco, and Chicago. These were the first containers of heroin. This was Air America. This was the first big off-the-books money." Just as Olson had insisted on the body as a site of resistance opening into a new era in his 1946 poem "La Préface," the first American poem to refer to the death camps in Europe ("My name is NO RACE   address / Buchenwald…" and later in the poem: "We are born not of the buried but these unburied dead"), Dorn focused all his quite substantial capacity for clarity, at the end of an era, upon the body as well.

The sacrilegious nature of such acts perpetrated upon the bodies of American servicemen exposed the double-sided guerilla nature of the war in Vietnam as an instrument to not only bludgeon the Vietnamese but the American people as well. Were this not evident during the intensity of the urban uprisings in over 125 U.S. cities in 1967 and 1968, it became more so through deeper suppression of civic political movements, the curtailment of public space, the increase in surveillance and incarceration, and the absolutely fierce economic downsizing and outsourcing of American labor and manufacturing that came to characterize the years immediately following the end of the war. John Wieners, a poet who had consistently thrown his lot in with the outcasts of society, in "Children of the Working Class," a 1972 poem written while incarcerated in Taunton State Hospital, wrote: "I am witness / not to Whitman's vision, but instead the / poorhouses, the mad city asylums and re- / lief worklines. Yes, I am witness not to / God's goodness, but his better or less scorn."

The publication, though, of *Winning Hearts and Minds: War Poems by Vietnam Veterans*, marks a significant but almost forgotten episode in the power of the word during this period. Edited by veterans Larry Rottmann, Jan Barry, and Basil T. Paquet, and coming out from 1st Casualty Press in Brooklyn in 1972, the book followed by just a year the Winter Soldier Investigations and the dramatic actions of Dewey Canyon III. This collection was followed by the equally remarkable *Free Fire Zone: Short Stories by Vietnam Veterans* (edited by Paquet and Rottmann, along with novelist Wayne Karlin, also published by 1st Casualty, in 1973). Finally, in 1976, *Demilitarized Zones: Veterans After Vietnam*, edited by Jan Barry and W. D. Ehrhart came out. Even though a number of the writers included in these anthologies have gone on to become quite well known, the anthologies themselves—and most, if not all the lesser-known writers in them—have disappeared from the literary and cultural history of the period. Through their writing, these citizen soldiers take the collective burden of the nation on within and upon their very damaged bodies. What then happens to that burden? To complete Dorn's thought regarding the Ghost Dance, in a remarkable insight surely related to his later indignation at the use of cadavers to smuggle drugs, Dorn wrote, in his 1966 book *The Shoshoneans*: "Some people, that same day, hacked men and women and children to pieces. They, the killers, agents of a national lust, died too. The death the killers died was not psychological and we should be careful to imagine it was not theoretical. December 29, 1890, at Wounded Knee, South Dakota—the massacre marked the end of the Ghost Dance. It also registered another small installment in the spiritual death of America."

4

Significantly, Ed Dorn spent some formative years in England, adding even further to the remarkably honed critical perspective he had on all aspects of life in the Americas. It was there he began working closely with Gordon Brotherston on a number of important translation projects (*Our Word: Guerilla Poems From Latin America*, 1969; *José Emilio Pacheco, Tree Between Two Walls*, 1976; *Selected Poems of César Vallejo*, 1976; *Image of the New World*, 1979, an earlier version of what would become *Book of the Fourth World*; and *Sun Unwound: Original Texts from Occupied America*, 1999). It isn't surprising, then, to find such dramatic clarity of thought about American culture from another English writer, D.H. Lawrence, in his *Studies in Classic American Literature*, a groundbreaking book first published in 1923. In his introduction, Lawrence writes:

One wonders what the proper high-brow Romans of the third and fourth or later centuries read into the strange utterances of Lucretius or Apuleius or Tertullian, Augustine or Athanasius. The uncanny voice of Iberian Spain, the weirdness of old Carthage, the passion of Libya and North Africa; you may bet the proper old Romans never heard these at all. They read old Latin inference over the top of it, as we read old European inference over the top of Poe or Hawthorne.

It is hard to hear a new voice, as hard as it is to listen to an unknown language. We just don't listen. There is a new voice in the old American classics. The world has declined to hear it, and has babbled about children's stories.

Why?—Out of fear. The world fears a new experience more than it fears anything. Because a new experience displaces so many old experiences. And it is like trying to use muscles that have perhaps never been used, or that have been going stiff for ages. It hurts horribly.

The world doesn't fear a new idea. It can pigeon-hole any idea. But it can't pigeon-hole a real new experience. It can only dodge. The world is a great dodger, and the Americans the greatest. Because they dodge their own very selves.

In Dorn's 1981 Olson Lectures, given in Buffalo, he discusses a review of William Carlos Williams's *In the American Grain* written by Lawrence. This comes in an in-depth survey of one of Olson's key texts, *A Bibliography on America for Ed Dorn* which was, in fact, a long-term program of study that Olson prepared for his then student. Dorn notices that Olson assimilates *In the American Grain* into the context of work by other scholars such as geographer Carl Sauer whom Dorn says are "on the ground," and disagrees with that use or possibility of a book which, Dorn says, his temperament would prepare him to dislike but which, nevertheless, he, Dorn, likes. *In the American Grain* was published in 1925, just two years after Lawrence's book, and Dorn notices—despite Lawrence's admiration for Williams—an underlying critique. As Dorn says, "he notices Williams's modernist style, like the snappy talk of the 20s" which interferes with the objects and events at hand. In this context, it is crucial to remember that Olson's most useful critique of both Ezra Pound and Williams's approaches to history are written while he was in the Yucatan, finding out for himself by exploring the sites and living manifestations of Mayan culture. It was this definition of "history," *istorin*, to find out for oneself, that Olson had gleaned from the Greek historian Herodotus, and held close throughout his life. In one of his letters from the Yucatan to Robert Creeley, Olson was looking for a history and a reality that is "wholly formal without loss of intimate spaces, with the ball still snarled, yet, with a light (and not stars) and a heat (not androgyne) which declares, the persistence of both organism and will (human)…" Despite recent critiques that would see Olson as the imperial outsider projecting the white world's fantasy upon non-white peoples, it is well nigh impossible to assimilate such readings into either his lacerating critiques of North American imperial domination or his own actions in decidedly removing himself from access to power structures that were available to him.

In the same lecture, Dorn tries to characterize precisely what Olson's death meant, or what might have passed along with him:

I'm going to, like, backtrack and try to bring forward a certain kind of statement and estimation that I really respect which led up to the 80s and which I'm going to claim to a certain extent died *in January 1970. Whether it died forever is always an open question, but for our time it died. And it has very much to do with the exhortation to "not forget the past," as set forth in Olson's last—what I call the "Last Will and Testament"—but which is called, undoubtedly more rightly, the* Last Lectures.

Don't forget the past. Accept the new illiteracy as a foregone conclusion and a condition that now cannot be overcome and probably shouldn't be. Accept it as a fact of the present. But don't forget the past. It's always been kind of assumed that literacy and the past were connected, somehow—and the hope would then be, could be expressed, that the new illiteracy will have to fashion a means for remembering the past.

Following the cataclysmic events of WWII, writers and artists around the world understood even more deeply, in varying ways, the lessons of the First World War. Civilization was no antidote to barbarity; it might, in fact, be part of its cause. The materials of the past were not to be lamented or gathered in nostalgic fragments to shore up the present, an intention partially animating T.S. Eliot's "The Wasteland," for example. The materials of the past, rather, had to be considered in and for the present. The ancientness of the world, the pastness of the past, formed vivid markers for people growing up in the new, 20th century. The musician Sun Ra followed the discoveries of King Tut's tomb avidly as a child growing up in the 1920s in Birmingham, Alabama, just as a young Olson followed the discoveries of ancient America through the excavations establishing the existence of Folsom Man, dating back to 10,000 BC. These discoveries would profoundly inform their respective and radical notions of time, as well as artistic form and function, as Olson and Sun Ra went on to become two of the century's most important artistic innovators.

Our position in relation to the past, and what literacy of that past might mean—as Dorn emphasizes—has been radically altered. The assault, for example, on Iraq, cannot possibly only be geo-political, opportunistic, and happenstance, but must also have something to do with unprecedented efforts to shift the tides of human motion in relation to our known past and all means of recording and preserving that past. Olson was on to this, in a big way, and Dorn is one of the few who capture the deeper significance of this, as he recites a text that he says "is an oral work, actually, and from shortly after that time, actually 1971," and is a quote from another lecture on Olson, by British poet Jeremy Prynne:

Maximus looks out to sea. He looks through the sea, down into the sea, out into the cosmos, we have the whole of Okeanos, we have the whole of the void, we have the whole of

the circular curve. We have the whole of the condition of
space. The circular curve is an important condition of the
lyric, because the cosmos, in his [Olson's] sense, comprises the
rearward time vector, back to the past, and all the space vec-
tors extended until they go circular, that is to say, until you
reach the ultimate curvature of the whole, so that they solve
themselves as myth. That circular, the curving rhythm, the
condition which you can finally reach to, is the condition of
the cosmos where the cosmos becomes myth. That's true about
the scientific condition as well—that there's no doubt at all
that the limits of space and the limits, for example, of absolute
temperatures, the curvature to which they attain, are all very
closely isomorphic. So that at once the curvature is reached,
the lyric concludes, what takes over is the condition of myth.

This condition of myth has everything to do with what
Olson wrote to Ruth Benedict, back in 1946: "I think that
the record of fact is become of first importance for us lost
in a sea of question… I think if you burn the facts long and
hard enough in yourself as crucible you'll come to the few
facts that matter, And then fact can be fable again." How
does one come to the facts that matter, and how can they
best be recorded? Dorn, again:

In Olson's time, and I take it really that 1970 was a—without
making such a large claim for an actual transaction for a year,
but, say, taking its significance from the actual significance of
his death (which was terminal to all the energy he had to give
to argue sanity, rationality, morality, and excitement, all at
the same time)—if indeed, that did end the greatest speaker
for that condition (a favorite word of his), then January 1970

*in fact did end something with his death. Which was beyond
his mere death, obviously. I mean, everybody dies.*

*The kind of vast and beautiful nostalgia which runs through
most of the books of Maximus is a kind of—a definition of a
really dangerous demand on attentiveness. Like the idea that
if you're not attentive, you're dead. The great poems, for
instance, which speak of the lost fishermen as a class, and the
throwing of the flowers on the water. The great kind of fune-
real exhortations to relate with human motion—not particular individuals. All fishermen were very particular. But the
way we remember them is like their common tragedy, and
their common use. And the precise movement of property
along the public property rolls: where the houses were. Who
owned them. Where they moved to. In other words, a kind of
local record, which possessed almost no inflation at all. No
inflation at all—it was all attention, that kind of local, the
public record, must be what to be a* skald *means. That's the
exhortation to be beyond your poetry, to write poetry, not
your own poetry, nobody could ever care about that.*

*That's about the last time that was said. As we know, the rush
of one's own poetry in the 1970s in one sense could be likened
to an extremely long rapid of all whitewater—which is called,
"your own poetry." You couldn't actually put a canoe in it,
because the reason why it's whitewater is because it would like
break the bottom out of you. That's the reason why a lot of
poetry has been supra-terrain—which simply means: above
the earth. In other words, that was a time when, as anyone
who has even had reports on Olson's behavior would know,
that to look into someone's eyes, was to look through their*

eyes. It was identification with the object, such as we've almost
never seen. That's why "Through the Eyes of Juan de la Cosa"
is actually a masterpiece. Because it defines an entire way of
looking for modern people. Presumably, in his time, everybody
knew that. Because that's what Juan de la Cosa's eyes were for,
that's why he made a map. And of course—to get off laboring
this, the fear of telling you what you already know—that's
why Olson made maps of poems.

If one goes back to Brotherston's definition of a classical
text, "to construct political space and anchor historical continuity," we can begin clearing the cobwebs blocking our
vision, start to declassify our more recent cultural legacy,
and begin understanding what makes our texts classical and
how we might begin mapping this terrain. As Diane di
Prima writes:

> *history is a living weapon in yr hand*
> *& you have imagined it, it is thus that you*
> *"find out for yourself"*

5

Interpreting American poetry through an ideological framework—to actually discern what a poet emphasizes, values,
or ignores—has become a lost art. As complex as Olson's
Maximus Poems are, for example, we can grasp a lot by
always keeping in mind one of its central, very simple messages: work worth doing entails risk, and such work should

be honored and celebrated. Fishing, in this regard, doesn't stand for something else, is not a metaphor, but a figure and a fact, the embodiment of this idea. In a society where art has been reduced to "self-expression," and propaganda has reduced our ability to imagine anything outside of a few big figures presented in a narrow spectrum (modeled on white and black, communism and anti-communism, electoral politics, or educational testing formats), our ability to interpret has become crippled. Whatever is imputed to an author becomes the framework for consideration, without taking into account a writer's own motive force, whether emotional, formal, political, cosmological or all of the above. As we have seen, this works very much like propaganda, using the same viral mechanism of innuendo and insinuation, relying not on the authority of poetic evidence but using the authoritarian critical voice as a means to select, subjugate, colonize and contain the past. As codification has gone into high gear—with the rigid historicization of schools, subsets of schools, racial, ethnic, and gendered categories—the need to decode is an essential survival tool, a way of forcing materials that disrupt and overcome these codes back into circulation in the body and poetic politic.

In a lecture on the American poet H.D., for example, Diane di Prima questions purportedly "feminist" readings of H.D.'s late poems that would abbreviate and categorize passionate feelings in old age as potentially "shameful," in need of some rubric under which they can be placed. Di Prima writes: "In reading a poem we can do no better than follow the oft-repeated axiom of one of my teachers to 'stay with the feeling.' Else we are likely to lose the artist in a thicket of ideologies not her own." In choosing to publish some of di Prima's lectures in *Lost & Found: The CUNY Poetics Document Initiative*, a project I founded in 2009, we wanted to begin making available work that has been largely inaccessible but which forms a bedrock source for that combination of research and poetics characterizing the thought of North American poetry in the 20th, and now 21st centuries. While some might see this project as a further codification of "known" writers, the purpose in publishing correspondence, lectures, journals, and other archived or unavailable materials is to map new relationships over terrain that, despite what we think we might know, actually remains largely unexplored. It is to move from the poetry that Dorn reminds us is largely supra-terrain, above ground, to the subterranean.

The explosion of creative output during the second half of the 20th century is comparable to any great, sanctioned period in cultural history, from western textbook examples like the Elizabethans or the Romantics, to other notable times and places, like the height of the Abbasid period in Iraq or the T'ang dynasty in China. Yet there is no cohesive cultural history of this period that takes into account precisely what was, and still is, at stake. In fact, despite more academic and specialized scholarship on the period, we seem to be getting farther and farther from both the spirit of the age and the very formidable obstacles the people living in it were up against. For each "major" writer, huge blocks of work remains archived or out of circulation; the plight of "minor" writers who might actually be "major" is even more skewed, usually with only a small percentage of their actual work available or known.

Were it generally accepted, for example, that, to paraphrase Robert Duncan, while many thought we were in the age of Auden, we were actually living in the age of Olson, very different histories would get written; it would mean a consideration not only of "poetry" but work in the world: the creation of institutions, of a network of ideas, perspectives, forms, relationships and energies that circulate far beyond the person. Nor should such designations be seen as a wrestling match between boys but a fundamental lens through which our whole cultural, political, and imaginative landscape would suddenly shift and begin looking radically different than it now does, providing a perspective that would certainly engage (even in an adversarial way), writing by women and people whose humanity and access to full expression has been severely abbreviated. At the same time, positing such a perspective should not be put forth as any kind of triumph, as in "our side wins," but as a richer, more historically viable nexus of relations from which to explore, since one might also conclude it to be the age of Langston Hughes or Muriel Rukeyser, for example, or the age of many and not one.

Di Prima's position in this realm is almost unique—as heir and participant to what has been most important and vibrant in our culture during the period following WWII, she has insisted on living with her work as record, document, and palimpsest, without rushing to codify it. This has cast her work in poetry and poetics very much in Robert Duncan's terms, as described in his classic essay, "Man's Fulfillment in Order and Strife":

…in writing I came to be concerned not with poems themselves but with the life of poems as part of the evolving and continuing work of a poetry I could never complete—a poetry

that had begun long before I was born and that extended
beyond my own work in it.

Going against so many of the prevailing shifts in fashion, thought, or ideology, di Prima has steadfastly refused to relinquish possession over the mysteries, over openness to interpretation, and over the paradoxical complexities of plain language. One cannot overstate the importance of her insistence on these principles, since we have become so adept at approaching complex work through critical subjugation and specialized terminologies that attempt to control things that might defy control. Di Prima's method, on the other hand, emphasizes and exercises continual layered readings over time: here the text becomes not a mirror but a well that can always be drawn from. By digging deep into this well—poetry, mythology, sacred texts—di Prima has enacted a bulwark against the technocracy of materialist reductions of human intention and will, particularly in relation to works of art.

Di Prima's adherence to an interpretive practice that does not subsume the range of a writer's own intent is a most unfashionable position, one that clashes head on into every imaginable contemporary orthodoxy, whether aesthetic, poetic, theoretical, or political, and one that has certainly made her work that much more difficult to subjugate to one doctrine or another. Continually revisiting the sometimes problematic nature of the classic texts she has engaged with, rather than labeling them in order to place them in some form of administrative detention or "protective" custody, is an enormous service. And this service is a weight, a burden di Prima carries on our behalf—in the act of writing, thinking, teaching—in order to enact and demonstrate the commitment necessary in performing the rites of poetic passage. Encountering di Prima's lectures, one feels very much in the midst of primary forces, as if one is finally native to the world in which the writer and the reader's engagement with a text actually exist. This, in itself, is a remarkable achievement, since the whole thrust of life in the modern state has been to sever common sense and experience from the often draconian demands the state would exact from us. Though performed with great subtlety, this radical shift changes the nature of both the kind of knowledge brought to bear upon her investigation and the knowledge one, as a reader, can glean from such an encounter. It is still up to each one of us to make something of that knowledge and that encounter.

This echoes one of Muriel Rukeyser's central and most important insights in *The Life of Poetry*, one that fully grasps the relentlessly dichotomous methods of propaganda and psychological warfare:

Everywhere we are told that our human resources are all to be used, *that our civilization itself means the uses of everything it has—the inventions, the histories, every scrap of fact. But there is one kind of knowledge—infinitely precious, time-resistant more than monuments, here to be passed between the generations in any way it may be: never to be used. And that is poetry… It seems to me that we cut ourselves off, that we impoverish ourselves, just here. I think that we are ruling out one source of power, one that is precisely what we need.*

She then goes on to talk about the resistance to poetry as

"an active force in American life." This "resistance" ultimately becomes a form of containment, setting up a contradiction that cuts to the root of our deepest inherited traits of expression: sound, pattern, rhythm, imitation, all key elements of poetry. We are left with power on the one hand, in the form of the state and mechanisms of propaganda, and powerlessness on the other, in the form of poetry. Thus, poetry's historical and very species specific role has been reduced to something one doesn't participate in but is a spectator of, something one doesn't live but "appreciates," something that "makes nothing happen," as opposed to what is actually happening.

6

If one is going to use the tools of dialectical materialism (as so many current critical theorists purport to do), then it would make sense not to simply succumb to a formula (the relentless forces of consumer culture, for example), but to ask why certain things are turned into commodities or given certain critical/theoretical labels. Take what has come to be classified as the Beat movement, for example. While many bemoan the pervasive branding of it or point to problematic general aspects like male domination, or particular issues like the latent "racism" or move to the "right" of a Jack Kerouac, or the publicity hunger of an Allen Ginsberg, few stop to ask—beyond the obvious rationale of a larger profit margin available from the dead—why so much effort has been made to contain the Beats, even posthumously. This containment takes place both through the myopic and ahistorical practice of such labeling, under the guise of multicultural representation and political correctness, and through the commercial branding of imagery, clothes, attitudes, and personalities. Could it be (as both American polymath Kenneth Rexroth and Italian artist, filmmaker, and political thinker Pier Paolo Pasolini realized), because the Beats had tapped into such deep sources of the power of poetry, and because there was an undeniable subversive force to the Beat movement, one that, given the right circumstances, still might rear its head? Even as sober and established a poet and critic as Karl Shapiro understood the implications:

For many years I have been trying to loosen the hold of the academic or "colonial" mind over poetry. It encourages a poetry as well as an entire literature of reference… In a sense it is a useless battle; attacking the Establishment only tends to strengthen it. It would be better to ignore the existence of the literature of reference and to create whatever we think valid than to go on tilting at windmills. This is what the Beat writers did; they were successful because they refused to take part in the academic dialogue.

In the case of the Beats, we can go directly to Lawrence's distinction, in the introduction to his *Studies in Classic American Literature*, between the fear of an idea and the fear of an experience, discussed in more detail further on. As Jed Rasula points out, "the Beat mystique never faded away, but has percolated on through the decades in high schools and on the fringes of college campuses, becoming in the process a semiofficial subaltern anti-intellectualism… The value of that core of original Beats… remains undimmed because they recognized, in [poet Gary] Snyder's words, that Beat 'was a particular state of mind… and I was in that mind for a while.'" Like in the construction of allegorical Cold War Biblical epic films or the uses of imagery at Abu Ghraib referred to earlier, the point of propaganda is to take up space with the largest figures, to crowd everything else out of the picture and guarantee that we look no further. Thus, when all we can see, as poet Michael McClure (one of the participants in the legendary Six Gallery reading in San Francisco in 1955, where Allen Ginsberg first publicly read *Howl*), are "three or four guys in New York City who sort of held hands and hugged each other and had deep and profound literary thoughts for their generation," we lose sight of so much. To begin with, we lose sight of the fact that one of the organizers of the reading at the Six Gallery (formerly the King Ubu Gallery, founded by Jess, Robert Duncan, and painter Harry Jacobus), was Wally Hedrick, husband of the painter Jay DeFeo who went on to paint her monumental masterpiece, *The Rose*, a painting that occupied her for eight years (1958–1966), and may have been the partial cause of her death. Hedrick, an important artist himself, had been an infantryman in Korea and began, in 1957, a series of black paintings protesting the war in Vietnam, years before official American involvement. While people like Hedrick, Jay DeFeo, Jess, and Robert Duncan are rarely associated with the "Beats" or are even seen as somewhat hostile, the context of this momentous occasion remains more complex than the iconic snapshots disguised as history would indicate.

We also lose sight of the Venice Beats in Los Angeles, we lose sight of "outlaw poetry" and all the writers who fall completely outside the purview of academia, those that poet Jack Hirschman calls the Street Generation (writers like Herbert Huncke, Bob Kaufman, Stuart Perkoff, Jack Micheline, Janine Pomy-Vega, and so many others). We lose sight of the countless individuals all across the United States who found in *Howl*, *On the Road*, and so many other manifestations of Beat culture some resonance that validated and affirmed their feelings about the journey of life, experience, education, identity, and creative self-expression, whether in or out of school (in many bookstores, the Beats are shelved by the register, since they are stolen so often). We lose sight of the enormous global impact of the Beats, at various times and in various places. When the whole world is divided into dichotomous zones, and only certain kinds of margins are sanctioned, we lose sight of the fact, as geographer Carl Sauer pointed out in his complex definition of a "culture area" that "Boundaries rather than centers of a physical region are likely to be centers of culture areas." Most importantly, in Rukeyser's terms, we lose sight of the fact that we might be looking for our own powers in all the wrong places.

The pedagogy of distrust in our own common sense, in the witness of our intuition, emotions, and consciousness, begins early. As Rukeyser wrote: "The fear that cuts off poetry is profound: it plunges us deep. Far back to the edge of childhood… Little children do not have this fear, they trust their emotions. But on the threshold of adolescence the walls are built… Against the assaults of puberty, and in those silvery delicate seasons when all feeling casts about for confirmation. Then for the first time, you wonder 'What should I be feeling?' instead of the true 'What do you feel?'" Rukeyser goes on to speak about "repressive codes" that strike "deep at our emotional life." The preoccupation and projection of "security," already pervasive when Rukeyser gathered the materials in *Life of Poetry* in 1949, has moved into overdrive, and her insistence on the contradiction between overarching conceptual policy structures and the taught insecurity of our inner life is more true now than ever, and harder to uncover and get at. Herein, also, lies the power of the Beats: the structures they faced head-on were new, and had not yet become fully internalized. Again, Michael McClure's perspective is illuminating: "We were locked in the Cold War and the first Asian debacle—the Korean War. My self-image of those years was of finding myself—young, high, a little crazed, needing a haircut, in an elevator with burly, crew-cutted, square-jawed eminences, staring at me like I was misplaced cannon fodder. We hated the war and the inhumanity and the coldness. The country had the feeling of martial law." But after the collective experience undergone through the public reading of *Howl*, McClure writes of "knowing at the deepest level that a barrier had been broken, that a human voice and body had been hurled against the harsh wall of America and its supporting armies and navies and academies and institutions and ownership systems and power-support bases."

The idea that a method of interpretation might necessitate living with or through a work immediately puts us in the realm of the "classic," but not necessarily in the terms in which we've been taught to think about the "classics." The alternative is to remove a work or an author from their own life cycle, to label and categorize as a means of placing them into the kind of administrative detention our literary life is largely confined to. In an elaborate and encyclopedic argument, Jed Rasula posits the function of the museum as a place of sponsored incarceration: "the prized objects emerge purified by an isolation that detaches them from the confusing heterogeneity of their natal states… The precondition for this new beginning is an act of violent separation, an act of plunder and excision." He goes on to describe "the objects in the museum" which "appear like migrants or survivors of a natural catastrophe. Their neighbors didn't survive the flood—such is the implication—but they did, and need a new home, a metropolitan hub."

Rasula then creates the American Poetry Wax Museum, a place where objects related to poetry—poems, anthologies, and even poets themselves—can be held. It is in this museum, and through the display of poetry, that pervasive ideological work takes place: "The paramount requirement of the nation form is the conscription of individuals as agents whose (rational or irrational) self-interest reiterates that of the state as it simulates on a grand scale 'the continuity of a subject.' In other words, individual subjects must ceaselessly re-inscribe the pattern of continuity as they constitute a holo-movement of individuation… Little wonder, then, that what is canonized is not so much particular poets, but rather the construction of subjectivity as such, particularly a subjectivity exemplifying an upward and outward spiral of manifest destiny." But what happens when something violently disrupts such transmitted forms of identity and expectation? It is this sense that Tom Hawkins conveys, one of the veterans included in Jan Barry and W.D. Ehrhart's poetry anthology *Demilitarized Zones: Veterans After Vietnam*, when he wrote of "the unprecedented magnitude of betrayal—the common disowning and dissociation of responsibility." This sense of betrayal and dissociation has, indeed, become the thing we hold most in common as citizens of this republic, the "domestic abyss" whose "ransoms have been perfected," to paraphrase David Matlin.

We do know, as Nathaniel Mackey so acutely grasps, that a central tenet of Olson's poetics assumes that imperialism, as Olson put it, gives "a language the international power / poets take advantage of." The absence of awareness of this fact in all facets of U.S. culture, but particularly in the literary realm, is striking. One of the prime targets of strategic power is communication, at all levels. As Christopher Simpson writes in *The Science of Coercion*:

At heart modern psychological warfare has been a tool for managing empire, not for settling conflicts in any fundamental sense. It has operated largely as a means to ensure that indigenous democratic initiatives in the Third World and Europe did not go 'too far' from the standpoint of U.S. security agencies. Its primary utility has been its ability to suppress or distort unauthorized communication among subject peoples, including domestic U.S. dissenters who challenged the wisdom or morality of imperial policies.

In this climate, it is crucial we seek out people active in spheres of our passions and learn what distances might seperate us before assuming some common purpose. Participation must infuse our involvement, along with an awareness of poetry's value as a form that can survive the "wreckage of reality."

Is it any wonder, then, that poetry can be a language not only of survival but of sustenance for those brutally robbed of all the defining structures of social and historical cohesion? In his landmark anthology, *The Vietnam War in American*

Stories, Songs, and Poems, scholar and anthologist H. Bruce Franklin writes:

When Jan Barry, one of the earliest of these veteran poets and a leading figure in promulgating veteran poetry, speaks to students in Vietnam courses, he describes his working-class youth in upstate New York when "the last thing I would ever think of being was a poet." What he wanted to be was a career man in the U.S. Army, and as for poetry, that was something just for "sissies." But what he, along with many others, discovered in Vietnam was that "poetry saved my life."

In this context, the function of poetry—first and foremost—is to reopen lines of recognition to oneself, and then to form the basis of resistance. As poet Duncan McNaughton puts it:

Let's say there is a resistance which knows that on behalf of which it exists and goes about its business accordingly. And let's say the country or the territory of its business is besieged, contested. It's not a question of betrayal that compromises everything—betrayal is built into the epistemology; in fact, it's what makes a real epistemology possible, disagreeable as that may appear to be. What's really up is the fact of collaborators. Which is a, or the, decisive failure to acquire the complete ability to interpret—because only the complete ability to interpret can yield the knowledge of that on behalf of which one is working... The resistance is not a conceit. It is literally the meaning of being's responsibility to the soul.

In wielding this language that is American English—with all the implications and uses to which it has been put—

resistance includes revealing ourselves as we might be seen, as in this devastating poem by W.D. Ehrhart, a former U.S. Marine who served in Vietnam. Here, all the poet can offer is the fact of his own realization, that he comes not to bear culture or civilization but to wreak havoc, wanton destruction, and death:

Do they think of me now
in those strange Asian villages
where nothing ever seemed
quite human
but myself
and my few grim friends
moving through them
hunched
in lines?
When they tell stories to their children
of the evil
that awaits misbehavior,
is it me they conjure?

By displacing himself into the spectres of fear projected at children whose parents or grandparents he once tried to kill, Ehrhart is displacing the power he once wielded, and handing it in trust to the emotional imagination of children who recognize in him an enemy. In this act, Ehrhart refuses "the continuity of a subject" so amply put on display at the American Poetry Wax Museum, while also engaging "the fear that cuts off poetry," and the "repressive codes" that Rukeyser writes strike "deep at our emotional life." The courage of this transposition is a triumph of imagination. In some sense, it is finally ourselves that we must imagine and imagine away, since, as Diane di Prima writes,

the war that matters is the war against the imagination
all other wars are subsumed in it.

"THE DISTANCES"

1

—for Vincent Ferrini, 1913–2007

In July 2003, my brother and I took the old drive from
Boston over the Mystic River Bridge, now called the Tobin,
toward Gloucester, for Vincent's 90th birthday celebration.
We got there around six and headed for the Legion Hall,
by the statue of Joan of Arc. We spotted Vince coming in,
and he grabbed us immediately, enthusiastic as always, dis-
playing us to whomever he was with. By midnight, we
were sitting on the sidewalk, panting. Vince was still out
on the dance floor, rocking the night away.

Vincent was my first correspondent in poetry—according to the letters I have, and I think I have all of them, I
began sending him things in 1969. Olson was still alive,
but Kerouac had died. I was thirteen. School was just a
nuisance of some kind, a backdrop to the things that really
mattered—demonstrations against the war in Vietnam,
talking to kids selling the Black Panther Party paper in
Cambridge, movies, the pool hall, hanging out at the
Grolier Bookshop, letters from Vincent in Gloucester:

> your handwriting's like your carriage!
> liked the two poems, Emily, / and Jay, who didn't
> live long,

Jay Murphy, son of Lynn and Valerie: dead in a rural car
crash. I remember when Lynn picked me and my friend
Paul up hitch-hiking, heading toward the cliffs, and he
mentioned Jay, his stare a million miles away, unfath-
omable. And Jay's older brother Dana, it was he who came
for us, when he was a cop, after we turned end over end

three times on the beach road in the Pinto.

      I told you your sculpture is pure poetry,
                                    aim high,
      get the best gallery in new york, Kramer
will review it,
      you will make fame internationally and it
will be a sell out,

      i, orpheus, predict it.

Vincent, the child of immigrants who'd toughed it out at the GE plant in Lynn, Massachusetts, knew that Kramer and the whole New York art establishment were blind as bats, so he made my teenage poetry sculpture and played Orpheus himself, to confound the system, from his frame shop in Gloucester.

    Always attentive: listening—1970:

glad to have heard Dylan, 2 sides, so far, two great poems, the October one and DEATH SHALL HAVE NO DOMINION, am convinced his voice is too good for most of his poems, he belongs to Shakespeare!

    Chain letters:

on the 8000 bucks, write your name on the second page following the other, just on one sheet, and mail out 20 of the two sheets to friends who need $8,000!

    And at the end of the letter, just to make sure I was paying attention:

LIFE has a page on WISHES, LIES AND
DREAMS this week.

   Closing that cycle of letters, I find this, from March, 1970:

         read prose to get closer to reality, the poets
are
fucking you
up,
         or the song writers,
                        I don't know
                                 perhaps you are
way ahead of
us all,

         i should send you my stuff, instead of
the other way around,
anyway,
            give them to your printer friends,

                        me I am no teacher,
and I can only respond how I feel, how that will
help I do not know,
and I DO NOT WANT EVER TO DISCOURAGE
YOU,

stack them up!
then after a year look at them,
                        you/have different
eyes
                              will

And when I despaired over most of Kerouac's work being out of print, Vincent suggested I write to Allen Ginsberg, which I did, and got a response. When Vince gave me some issues of *Floating Bear*, and I wanted to know where I could get more, he gave me Diane di Prima's address and told me to write her, which I did, and also got a response. The next big run of letters came five years later, in 1975. Again, Vincent, glued to the world:

What am I reading? First the GLOUCESTER DAILY TIMES, THE BOSTON GLOBE, THE NEW YORK TIMES ON SUNDAY. Glanced at Collected Poems of John Beecher, at ALLEN VERBATIM, the Bible once in a while, ARCHETYPAL PATTERNS IN POETRY, and I must get into NABAKOV, they tell me he's the greatest, like just Muhammad,

AND to have gotten the ABC's under your belt is the master stroke, for that I will grant you summa cum laude! Right from this frame shop, so you'll know its really authentic.

If you want to know what recently has grabbed me and held me still? Marshall Berman's review of Eric Erickson's new book in yesterday's NEW YORK TIMES BK REVIEW!!!!!!!

Wherever I was, I would check in. 1978, while I was in Jerusalem, Vincent still gave me the news:

last night saw Pasolini's TEORE-MA, and was pummeled by the lunatic MOON, a shattering experience.

Vincent moved from Pasolini to the union organizer
and artist Ralph Fassanella featured in an exhibit on the
city of Lawrence, the tough mill town where the famous
"Bread and Roses" strike took place—it was all of a piece.

        Last sunday saw Lawrence's
125th year celebrated with paintings by the primitive Union organizer Fassanella, three murals
gave me the chills, mostly about the factory conditions before the Unions had the strength to
deal with the bosses. Knopf published a book of
his paintings and a short biography, 1912 the
great strikes of Lawrence and the works and conditions is all over the place, wonder is that they
were hung there, someone called him an anarchist and when he told me he laughed like any
guffaw you hear in Italy! It must be seen to be
believed, a very sophisticated primitive, the three
murals have a depth that stays in the head.

Always taking the boss's language and turning it over and
over, feet firmly planted on the ground, all senses alive:

        Gloucester is catering to the
tourists, all the big guns are going full blast, a
sickening sign. A backlash against the conserva-
tion 'obstructionists', especially by one Mueller
who hates us for defeating his dream of mam-
moth condominium on the Back Shore. Corruption and pollution shall drag us to the End, but

we'll give them a headache on the way, and perhaps take away all their power, that, or humanity
will have to start from scratch again.

For Vincent, the stakes were always high, even cosmic.
His influence on Charles Olson has been as unremarked as
his own body of work encompassing more than 60 years. *No
Smoke*, his first book and an American classic, came out in
1941. More than thirty-five books followed *No Smoke*, in-
cluding *Blood of the Tenement* (1945); *In the Arriving* (1954);
Selected Poems and *I Have the World* (both in 1967); the
Know Fish series (from 1979 to 1991); and *The Whole Song:
Selected Poems* (edited by Kenneth A. Warren and Fred
Whitehead, 2004), the first recognition Ferrini received from
academia, following years of publication with small presses.
The fact Ferrini's *Selected Poems* appeared in a series edited
by Cary Nelson, a scholar instrumental in recuperating
American poets who have fallen through the cracks due to
suppression and imposed narratives, particularly from the
1930s and 1950s, is significant. The work of Warren and
Whitehead, on Nelson's imprint, has been matched by new
attention to Ferrini's crucial corespondence with Olson, in
Olson's *Selected Letters*, edited by Ralph Maud, and *Charles
Olson: Letters Home 1949–1969*, edited by David Rich.
Ferrini was the subject of nephew Henry Ferrini's award-
winning documentary, *Poem in Action: Ferrini's Vision*.
Vincent Ferrini has been put back into the picture. His
repeated appearances at Beyond Baroque in Los Angeles,
including a full tribute given to him before his death, were
the only national appearances at a major public literary
venue Ferrini was given. In each case, these were initiated
and carried out by Fred Dewey. My awareness of these

events served as a connecting tissue to Fred and a growing sense of the national import of his activities, eventually leading to numerous collaborative projects and concerted efforts to think through Olson's work.

Walter Lowenfels once called Ferrini "the last surviving Proletarian Poet." The web site dedicated to the archives of his friend Charles Olson at the University of Connecticut points out Vincent "may be the only American poet to have participated in both the WPA program of the 1930s and the CETA program of the 1970s, the chief federally sponsored efforts to provide meaningful work for the nation's unemployed artists." As an autodidact starved for knowledge, Vincent poured the contents of the Lynn Public Library into his head and heart, creating a home-made and rooted place of value and practice. Declining relationship to any literary establishment beyond Gloucester gave Vincent the freedom of a tagger, zapping subway cars and the walls of our conceptual vacant lots. Banished from the terms subjugating art to spectacle and criticism, bureaucracy and administration, Vincent lived his poetry with all the fervor, conviction, and intransigence of someone anchored to one spot for dear life. Like a villager rooted to his olive trees, Vincent remained steadfast, holding on for us all.

2

The man held the boy up to the window. All the boy could see through the grates over the sidewalk past the garbage was the bottom half of the tires. The man let him down slow, gently, without a sound. Raising his brows, he put his hand quickly in front of the boy's mouth before the boy had a chance to say a word, and led him quietly down the hall by the shoulder. The boy could see his mother as she sat at her table and read, the light behind her from the small lamp leaving her in shadow, the book she held bright, alive with the light. The man took a jacket from its hook and put his hand against the pocket so the keys and change it contained stayed quiet. He pushed the boy ahead of him, wincing as he heard one of the linoleum tiles the boy's sneaker caught slap back against the floor.

Idemo, he said, with his head already down the hall.

The boy waited outside. Cement and bricks, all the way around. He stretched his neck way up, to a black fence somewhere up above. Words filtered through the clear air that covered him. A blanket of blue enveloped him. Somewhere, out of the box, up the steps, over the fence, he heard the lazy swish of full branches as they swayed in the breeze. Not long before they fell, before leaves filled the sidewalks, before they'd be swept into piles and burned. He would be back in school before they burned the leaves and wouldn't get to see the leaves that burned between eight and two. After supper, he could see the leaves that burned after supper. The smoke curled and drifted into the deep colors of the autumn sky, black drifted into red, purple soon faded back to a slow, stubborn black. The words soft, through the screen.

Blizu? his mother asked.

Some words he got but it was harder when he couldn't see.
Daleko, dalje.

Dobro.

That was one he knew and he was already up the steps and halfway around the car when his father's head topped the sidewalk. His father took the keys out of his pocket and opened the trunk. Half the morning had been spent cleaning out junk. He shut it, left his hand on the handle, shook it and with his other hand let his finger lead a trail around the tight solid fit. With both hands he grabbed the bumper, shaking and tearing at it.

Go on, kick, go ahead.

The boy retreated a few steps and ran towards it. He reared his right foot back and gave the thing a solid hit, smarting as he smashed it.

His father clapped him on the back. With both hands out to embrace the car, he shrugged. Key in, radio on, he leaned past the boy to open the glove compartment. The door stuck but he hit it right and it sprang open. The boy climbed into the back, opening and closing the ashtrays and trying the windows. The man started the motor, revving it up before he let it idle. He pulled out of the space and up the steep hill to the top of the street. As the light changed, the little car got into traffic on the wide boulevard and headed downtown. A few blocks before the Public Gardens, the man slowed down in front of a building.

Fourth floor, that one, he said, pointing.

The boy looked the building up and down, top to bottom, side to side. The stairs, halls, doors, none of the rooms, nothing. Only one image of the place remained from a picture he had seen of himself. It was taken across the street from the building in the wide strip of grass, trees and benches that divided one side of the avenue from the other. He knew it was winter since he was bundled from head to toe, his ears covered with flaps from a small visored cap. A strap ran down from behind his ear across past his chin. He looked up, one arm in front of the other, as if he knew that if he didn't hurry to get to the woman who stood slightly bent awaiting him he would topple over. She was dressed in a long gray coat with a scarf wrapped around her neck. The scarf was long and dangled down to drape across her arms that stood stretched to receive the child. She was hatless, straight nose, thin lips open slightly to show her straight teeth. He wasn't sure whether he'd fallen before he got to her nor could he remember if he'd ever climbed the steps of that building or if she'd carried him.

The old city passed, with its little streets and alleys winding around to the top of the hill where the golden dome shone, before ending in angles, the sun slicing a line across the cobblestones. The car went up the ramp to the bridge alone before merging at the top with other lanes. The tires grated against the meshed iron work. A conglomeration of derricks and cranes hung above the ships on the water. Men ran across the decks like white specks, in and out of the crane cabs. A small sign pointed to the Constitution. A high barbed wire fence surrounded the yard leading to the dock the ship was moored at. The boy saw men on scaffolds lost in the endless grey. Up and down their arms went as they dipped back into the paint cans that hung off small hooks on the cables of their scaffolds. Below them near the water marks other men worked with black shields on their faces. They kept the tip of a small blue flame in one hand and a rod of metal in the other as they worked at the seams.

Shadows played across the hood, through the windshield and over the dashboard, like in that movie his grandfather had taken him to, where the guy dies at the beginning in a motorcycle accident. Past the toll booth the water stopped. To the left a monument stuck straight up on a small hill. Grey and tall it came to a point at the top. Houses surrounded the small circle of green at the base of it and the few gleaming black cannon that sat there. Then the monument stopped. On both sides of the bridge the backs of houses hugged the squat green rail at the edge of the roadway, wooden three and four deckers sandwiched together. Clotheslines ran across from one porch to another. Some of the lines were anchored to the rail on the roadway. The paint on many of the houses was dry and cracked, the clapboards hung warped and slapped back against the frames of the houses. Fences with missing posts sagged and laundry hung from the lines, like white flags or curtains for the women who kicked open their screen doors to shake brooms against the rails, sometimes pushing their way through to look across the roadway at other houses. A billboard whose faded letters advertised marble and granite memorials, cut-rate burials and limousine service, hung crooked, paint curled at the edges. The shadows stopped and the bridge emptied out to a wider, more open road that headed straight for some hills. In front of the hills were groups of new houses clumped together, simple structures with lawns in front, green, pink and yellow. At the point the cars would have pulled into their driveways, the road curved wide closer to the hills then narrowed and went straight.

The boy knew they were close when the trees stopped and the sides of the road turned to jagged granite. He knew someone must have chopped all the rock up between his side of the road and the other and he thought he saw an Indian crest the hill of rock. The Indian must have looked quickly at the highway and told his horse to turn for no sooner did he think he saw him than the Indian disappeared. The rock stopped and the highway emptied into a small rotary. Water began and he could see the docks through telephone poles and scattered buildings. Around the rotary the houses came close together and ran crooked up a narrow steep street. Telephone poles stuck up at odd angles. Some leaned almost to the windows, their thick wires swaying close to thin, white curtains. The street wound, curved, got closer to the water and soon ran right alongside it. Small shacks and houses stood on stilts over the water surrounded by docks and boats, the other side of the road was filled with small shops and bigger houses. Further along, warehouses—their shingles and wood burnt brown and scorched—covered the street from both sides, leaving cars and walkers engulfed in their singed shadows. Now and then a crack between two buildings spread a shaft of light across the street. Closer to the main harbor warehouses gave way to stilted shacks and bigger wharves. They went to the end of the road past the small boatyards to the big one on the point. A few hundred yards along the bumpy wood, the boy's father stopped in front of a small shack and honked the horn.

A curtain on the single window of the place moved. The door opened and a man appeared. He bent over a bit, stuck his arm out to the boy, made a face, growled and roughed up the boy's hair. They laughed. The man picked the boy up and spun him in the air. The boy's father greeted the other man and they talked in the language the boy didn't get even when he could see. The boy's father displayed the car. The man opened and closed the doors, the trunk and hood as if he had only a few seconds to do so before the car blew up. They grinned and shrugged at each other and talked a lot with their hands.

Toro seduto, said the man as he put his arm on the boy's shoulder.

He withdrew it, leapt back a step, reached his right hand across to his left side and from somewhere below his pocket drew his sword out of its scabbard. The boy withdrew his and their tightened fists at the end of their outstretched right arms cut and swung through the air. They pinned each other to the spiles, each threatening the other to pierce the heart and let the loser drop to the water. The one against the spile would slip out from under or motion to the air to heed an oncoming falcon or eagle and slither away to open space. From one end of the wharf to the other they challenged each other. They leapt from the spiles to the creaking sea-washed slats, against the side of the shack and around to the car, as the man jumped to the bumper and across the trunk, running behind his shack and up a plank that led to a boat lying on its side. The mast stuck straight out past the rotten hull as seagulls dove in and out of the pilot house. The boy ran under and back up the plank, chasing the man around the boat. They slipped and slid as the man tight-rope walked the mast and jumped back to the dock before the boy finally pinned him to the door of the shack. The man grimaced in the heat, looking to the heavens. The boy kept his feet firmly planted, his fist clenched. The man cried out, letting his fist open. His arm went forward, as if to stick the sword into the wood. Putting his hands together, he bowed humbly.

Ah, toro seduto. Dio mio! Esecuzione. Arrivederci!

The boy let his fist open, went back a step, drew his empy hand through the air and bowed. They walked back to the car and the boy's father leaning against it.

Forse possiamo mangiare qualche cosa?

Si, andiamo.

They walked down the wharf past the fence to the street. The boy walked between them, looking from one to the other as they talked. A waiter stood out in the sun in front of an open doorway. He adjusted the towel he had draped across his forearm, bringing it across his brow. The boy and his father led the way in as the man followed the waiter, saying *Domani, domani*, with his hand outstretched and fingers together.

The waiter turned and laughed, saying *Basta!*

They walked past the bar to a table in back. As they ate the boy looked at the fish mounted on the wall behind the bar. Murky blue light came across the mirrors from under the rows of bottles. Nets hung down off a deeply stained rich colored moulding that ran the length of the bar about a foot from the ceiling. Soft red light filtered down from the top of the moulding. Different kinds of shells were caught in or tied to the nets. A man behind the bar whistled as he straightened bottles and bent every now and then to stick something in the sink or rummage through the ice. On the way back to the boatyard, the man and the boy took a meager stab at a new duel but were slow to move. They said goodbye and the man watched the boy and his father back out and drive away before he turned and went into his shack.

They drove to the other side of the harbor, past fish packing plants and truck terminals. On the point was a small neighborhood of old wooden houses. The women worked in the plants filleting fish or shucking scallops and the men fished for one thing or another. Kids sat on the hoods of dented cars. Their smaller brothers and sisters ran through the small streets, the pavement broken up in places, a burnt out building here and there.

Same old Charlie, said the boy as he pointed at the old Chevrolet station wagon parked on the street. The wagon was covered with mud, dried dirt and pigeon shit. Two of the tires were flat and a blanket was draped over the hood. They parked right behind it. The boy went to the car and carefully picked a corner of the blanket to peek under. The boy's father surveyed it, ran his fingers across the cracked back window and shook his head: *Poveraccio.*

They walked past the car to stone steps that led to a small backyard. The steps were part of a stone wall that ran the length of five or six houses and curved around the point. The boy's father called for his friend up the back steps and began to climb them. The boy looked under the stairs. He knelt in the weeds to get a closer look at an old figurehead that leaned against the basement wall. Its wood was still solid and a faint glimmer of the paint she was once adorned with still remained. Her face was full with sharp eyes, pulled back at the corners, and thick lips. Her hair ran straight down the back of her head, coming back behind her ear to fall across her neck, barely covering a medallion. Past her against a pile of bricks leaned a white statue of a woman praying. She wore a long white robe. He heard steps on the landing above, then Charlie's voice.

Better come up and get your candy before I finish it.

The boy turned and darted up the steps. Charlie crouched on one knee. He held both his hands out at his sides with his fists closed. The boy picked the right. Empty.

Go ahead, Charlie said.

The boy picked the left. Nothing.

Come on, it's inside.

Charlie got up and the boy craned his neck as the man got bigger and bigger until he was standing straight up. The boy followed the huge man through the doorway as he ducked to get under it. The boy's father was already inside, sitting at a table cluttered with books and papers. The place was filled with books. Maps and pictures were pinned to the walls. Charlie went to a small chest of drawers and took out a long, thin paper bag.

I went all the way to the General Store you know, I don't know whether you're worth it.

Charlie held the bag at a distance. The boy tugged at his pocket. He took the brown paper off, and handed the boy a package of peppermint sticks. The boy wandered around the apartment then stood at a window in the bedroom and look- ed out to sea. A few trawlers could be seen in the distance. Packs of circling gulls followed the boats. They hung near the masts but every now and then dove towards the water or the nets as they were being dragged in.

What's in those buildings Charlie? The boy called to the other room.

Not much.

Can I look?

Ask your old man.

Go ahead.

The boy went down the steps through the yard to the street. He cleared some dirt off the driver's door window of the Chevy and looked inside. The dashboard was moldy and had dead bugs stuck to it. He tried the door. After a kick and a jolt it came open. He got in the driver's seat and looked around. The boy soon tired of the car. When he couldn't get the window open to let some of the smell out he opened the door to let himself out. He walked across the street, stepped through the rusty pipe fence and, hanging on with one arm, made his way along the base of the cement roof of one of the warehouses until he was close enough to jump. He landed well, with a thud. Something crumbled and fell loose below him. He ran across the empty black space to the farthest edge that hung over the water. The building had slid and begun to fall into the sea. Water came up over it, swamping the loading dock as pieces of timber slapped and swung against each other, bobbing up and down. He went down on his stomach, stuck his head over the edge, got up and looked around till he found a small sharp stick by the stack pipe. Back on the edge he dug the stick through the rotten tarpaper and wood, getting his hand in and clearing a space big enough to see through. There was a loft above where the boats used to unload and he got up and walked across the roof slowly, stamping his sneakers every few feet as he moved boards and boxes around to look underneath. Past the pipe, towards the edge, under a pile of old net and broken glass, he found the hatch. He swept it off and pried open the long stuck door with the stick he'd found. The hatch came off in one piece so he pushed it aside and leaned over the hole. From the sea side a shaft of light came through the cracks in narrow beams. He got a long heavy board and struggled to get it over the opening, sliding it onto the loft and poking around at the floor to make sure the boards would hold. He let the plank fall flat across the opening and sat with his legs in the hole, slowly lowering himself. With his arms wrapped around the plank, he dangled there a minute before he let go to fall the last four or five feet. Wood cracked. He stumbled, fell flat towards the floor and rolled to his shoulder before coming to a stop. The plank his foot had broken stuck straight up on both sides, forming a perfect V. On all fours he crawled toward the light at the far end. Boxes got in the way, and other things he couldn't quite see. As he got to the light he turned his back on it, watching the beam shoot back the other way. Many of the timbers above were covered in charcoal and hung lopsided to the floor. To the right, a long frame housed some windows. All the glass was broken and glittered where it lay. Water lapped against the spiles that ran up from the foundation, and planks banged against other planks. When the wind blew, wood creaked as if it was about to snap. The boy made his way toward the glass. There behind the glass brokers had once dealt for the best prices. Boats had tied up below as fishermen hoisted tubs up to the lumpers who bent to the tubs to pull scup, fluke, halibut, cod, mackerel or whatever it was that ran and lay them out in wooden boxes. The boxes went down the belt past the ice chute and ice filled the box to the top before another man hammered the top of the box on and carried it to a dolly that was wheeled to the loading dock. When the truck filled and fresh slime mixed with ice water ran out the holes on the floor of the truck the driver corked the holes and waited for the broker to tell him where the fish went.

The boy stuck his head through the frame. He took out a box of matches that he had in his pocket and lit one. He walked back towards the opening, grabbed the board, hoisted himself up and tore a piece of tarpaper off the edge of the hatch cover. He took another stick and wrapped some of the tarpaper around it along with a piece of net that he'd cut with the stick. Then he put more tarpaper around the net, found a nail, and used it to secure the end of the tarpaper as he descended again and walked back towards the office. Stopping in front of the beam of light, he lit his torch and watched it flare before burning steady. Now and then the net caught and flared. He brought more boxes over to the broken windows and climbed through. Wires dangled above. In the corner nailed cockeyed to the wall hung a melted plastic trophy of some kind that housed the remnants of a thermometer. Empty liquor bottles and beer cans sat on every available beam and on what was left of an old desk. Open charred drawers hung unevenly off their tracks. The boy bent to the floor, looking through a hole at the water below as it washed over a rusted diamond plate bolted to a long piece of timber. The torch flickered and he watched it go out before it hit the water. He pried open another hatch behind him and examined the rotten ladder that led below before going back out of the office to find a long plank that he manuevered through the window frames and down the hatch. With his hands gripped around the plank he let himself slide. Something sailed past his head and he turned with a start when he heard a sudden slap as a piece of wood crashed down behind him, skidded off the diamond plate and fell in the water. He scurried for cover behind one of the spiles. Water washed over his sneakers and he shivered. A voice came from the back of the building, out of the blackness.

What are you doing here?

The boy looked deeper.

This is my fort.

The voice was closer.

I just wanted to look.

Another boy emerged from the shadows, somewhat bigger.

Who are you? asked the bigger boy.

I just wanted to look. If I knew it was your fort you should have said something.

The bigger boy looked at the intruder, then to his feet immersed in water.

It's alright, I guess.

What's the idea of throwing that board at me?

It is my fort.

So what.

I've got to protect it, don't I?

I guess.

Anyways, I didn't aim.

They stood looking at each other a minute when the bigger boy said, Want to see something?

He nodded and followed the bigger boy into the shadows. At the back wall a small door opened to a passageway, a chute only as big as the door. They crawled through the chute, then suddenly slid down part of it into an old freezer room. Some boards nailed to the tops of stacked boxes served as a table on which three or four candles sat, supported by their own melted wax. As chairs the boy used three boxes he had wrapped and tacked bits of old cloth and cushion to. A few pictures and newspaper clippings hung on the walls. A clipping above the table read: *Blind Man Falls, Hits Head, Regains Sight.* There was a picture of the man to the right, Eugene W. Phillips, an old man, a cowboy, wearing a ten-gallon hat and a face filled with lines, a black patch over his left eye. Under the picture and the man's name, the caption read: *Praises the Lord.* The bigger boy eagerly looked at his guest.

What do you think of that, huh?

I guess he liked his dog a lot.

Well, wouldn't you?

Below that was a photograph, framed, of a man leaning against the cockpit of a fighter plane. The collar of his flyer's jacket braced up against his neck, flying forward at the sides as if a strong wind came from his back or another plane was taxiing down the runway behind him. He smiled, holding his

crash helmet in his right hand. The left sleeve of his jacket
hung loosely at his side. The smaller boy edged over the
desk for a closer look but found no arm.

How did he do that?

Oh, he could do anything.

Who is he?

He's dead now.

I mean how could he fly like that?

He could do anything. My brother could do anything.
I've got his medals.

Did he get a lot of them?

Enough.

The smaller boy turned from the wall behind the desk
and looked around at the rest of the place. Flames danced
across the walls. Most of the surfaces were rusty but the
bigger boy had begun to work on the sheetmetal and some
areas had a shine.

You're not from around here.

No.

The bigger boy took a pack of cigarettes out from a
small box under the table.

Want one?

Okay.

They lit them from the candles, sat on the chairs
and smoked.

How long have you had this?

One of my brothers ran the ice. When it burned he told
me about it. He said that no one that never worked here
would ever find me.

I guess not.

I know they wouldn't.

They finished the cigarettes and the bigger boy handed

the other boy a can with the top cut off to put the butt in.

Gotta keep the place clean.

The boy nodded.

Why'd you come in?

Just to see what it was about.

You know the guy who's got the wagon?

Yeah.

I saw you get in.

What were you looking for?

Just looking.

You live around here?

Couple of streets over.

Oh.

They looked at the flames on the walls. The shadows crept up, dancing above and around them on the ceiling.

You fish around here?

My old man's got a boat. Maybe he's out there now. Sometimes I fish with him.

How long do you go?

Long time.

The bigger boy looked at the far wall.

I gotta drill a hole in here somewhere so I can see what's going on, so I can put my spyglass through.

You got a spyglass?

My old man said my brother stole it from a pirate.

Yeah?

Maybe. He doesn't live with my mother so sometimes I'm not supposed to go. Sometimes he meets me here with the boat. Sometimes he flashes the lights and we go all night. How old are you anyways?

Just about twelve, he lied.

That's okay, the way you came in.

Yeah? What about you?

I'll be fourteen.

How many brothers you have anyways?

Six or so, I don't know, maybe there's some no one ever told me about.

Any sisters?

A couple.

How far do you think you'd see if you put your spyglass through that hole?

Probably pretty far. Maybe it'd be farther than boats or birds or water.

That's pretty far.

I guess.

They used to think if you went far enough you'd fall off, like a table.

I know that.

I just thought I'd say so, I figured you knew anyways.

That's okay. My old man had a guy that didn't want to go past Georges. Same reason, I guess. He was a cannibal or something. We left him in Halifax.

Halifax. Where's that?

Nova Scotia.

What's it like there?

It's okay, I guess.

The bigger boy got off the box, crawled under the desk, pulled a piece of floorboard out and fumbled with something. He took the box he had gotten the pack of cigarettes from, put something in it, and shoved the box all the way to the wall. His hand dipped in to his pocket then came out. He put the floorboard back in place, got up, and began to scrape some of the wax off the desk. He scraped a few minutes then went to his chair, shoving it along the floor, under the desk, and neatly squaring it against one of the legs. The younger boy watched the candles, and the thin flame flickering off the dirty glass in front of the pilot.

After leaving the fort, he checked the Chevy but didn't go in. He'd left the warehouse through another easier way the other boy had shown him. A series of ladders through another hatch at the top of the freezer led to a rope that hung off the pipe fence. Most of the ladders had been made with scraps of wood, some pieces were simple footholds nailed to the side of the building. He walked past the Chevy and followed the stone wall around the corner. The street led down a slight hill. At the bottom of it, the sun caught the window of an open door. The window was glossy black but the sun made it gold.

Four or five men sat in the dim amber light the bar threw on them. A few looked out the door over the water towards the sea. The song that had been on, *Give Me 40 Acres*, ended in silence. The bartender sat closest to the door on a stool behind the bar. With his elbow propped on it, he surveyed the newspaper, making a pencil mark every now and then. Another song came on. The record skipped, *If Jesus was alive he'd drive a Peterbilt, Jesus a Peterbilt, Jesus*. The bartender got up and hit a switch to turn it off. He pulled the stool over and got up on it to turn the radio on. Fourth race from Suffolk. A few of the men propped up, edging their elbows closer in on the bar. Seven furlongs. Fast track. High Society led. At the halfway mark One Eyed Jacks came neck and neck. In the stretch Buttered Fluke nosed them both. Buttered Fluke. One Eyed Jacks. High Society. A man at the end of the bar stood with his feet wrapped around the foot hold of his stool. He swayed a bit, then let out a cheer.

What the hell did I tell you. Buttered Fluke.

He cheered again. The men next to him turned, amused. The bartender flicked the radio off and, before turning the song back on, faced the cheering man and told him to shut the hell up.

Don't get so hot about it.

If you're in here at all I sure as hell don't want to have to listen to you.

The man swayed on his perch and let out another louder cheer that rose above the music. The bartender reached up for his collar and drilled him to his seat pushing him once, then again, before letting go. The man sprawled back off his seat and landed on the floor as the others turned to look.

Damnit. Godamnit. Can't a guy just. He stopped, slumped back to the floor, turned over with his nose to the ground, looked at it a minute, then pushed himself up by his arms and walked out the door. He stumbled past the boy to the middle of the street. A few kids ran by chasing each other and almost knocked him over. The man walked to the fence and sat on it. The boy started to walk away but the man saw him, and called out after him. The boy approached cautiously, standing a few feet in front of him.

Buttered Fluke, the man said, and laughed. I gave it to him this morning. Couldn't miss.

The boy nodded. They looked at each other. The boy shrugged. A dog trotted up the hill, a brown mutt. His head hung low with his tongue down and wet. He stopped in front of the boy and the man. The man turned from the boy to the dog.

So the shit finally shows up.

The dog shoved his head against the inside of the man's leg. Rubbing his jowls, he put his paws up to the man's hands. The man lifted the dog up to his knees. The boy reached his hand across the dog's back, stroking his coat. The dog turned his face, cocked a bit to one side, looking at the boy with his mouth open and tongue drooping.

Is he old?

You'd never believe me if I told you where I got him.

Maybe I would.

You wouldn't.

The man hoisted the rope that hung off his belt and opened the knife tied to the end of it. He started to carve something on a post then let the knife drop. He turned to look down the rocks and past them to the water before getting off the fence, straightening his shirt out, and stuffing the knife back into his pocket. He pulled the string on it straight, then adjusted and smoothed out the lump it left in his pants.

Beat, he said, I'm beat, and looked down the road towards the docks.

The boy pet the dog, gently slapping his snout from side to side. The man walked down the hill. Halfway down he let out a sharp whistle. The dog turned from the boy and trotted away. The boy watched them turn the corner and go out of sight. He walked on the water side, letting his hand bounce off the upright posts of the fence. Crossing to where the Chevy was, he looked in again, kicking the flat tires and shaking his head. He went up the stone steps, through the yard and up the steep wooden steps to the landing. Charlie and his father still sat at the table.

What did you find? asked Charlie as the boy came through the screen door.

Not much, they're all burnt down.

Clean up, you're a mess, said his father.

Charlie got up and went to the bedroom.

Catch.

The boy grabbed the towel out of the air and went to the bathroom. He closed the door and hoisted himself up on the edge of the bathtub to get to the cracked mirror the tall man used. He looked down his arms and turned to see the backs of them and his elbows, smudged with tar, grease, dirt, and charcoal. He brushed them off, then brushed off his shirt and pants before turning the water on and scrubbing his face, arms and hands. He got back up on the tub and checked himself in the mirror. Here and there he used the towel to rub a spot clean. He hopped down and wiped the dirt his feet had left at the edge of the tub before hanging the towel on a nail that stuck out from the back of the door. When he walked back out they were still sitting at the table. He looked at them for a minute then went to the bedroom. Out the window he watched the boats as they got closer before the setting sun.

author's note, works used, & bios

AUTHOR'S NOTE

There is a long history—both productive and contentious
—to the final form taken by *a little history*. While working
with Fred Dewey on the materials accompanying *from the
warring factions*, sometime in 2000, he proposed a new book
encompassing a range of the concerns we were discussing
centered on and filtered through the thought of Charles
Olson. As then director of a significant cultural institution,
Beyond Baroque in Los Angeles, and a veteran and co-initiator
of the local neighborhood council movement, Dewey had
been in the process of creating a unique situation: a public
performance arts and workshop space, with an archive and
small press integrated within it, all to generate work outside
the confines of coterie and social-network publishing. And
this in the belly of the beast, the city of Los Angeles, that
has always served as both the manufacturer of our representations and a hotbed of a true alternative cultural politics the rest of the country, particularly New York, the East
Coast, and even San Francisco, could conveniently ignore.
Other projects were in the works: a reprint of Olson's key
text *A Special View of History* (in conjunction with Ann
Charters, the original editor), and work emerging from the
Middle East, most notably a collective translation I was involved with of the former Syrian political prisoner and poet
Faraj Bayrakdar, with an introduction by noted Lebanese
novelist Elias Khoury. The kernel of the work on Bayrakdar
took place between the events of September 11, 2001, and the
initial "shock and awe" assault on Baghdad in March of
2003. The sense of possibility that Dewey's model presented
was palpable and unlike anything on the current scene. By
its very nature and structure, it posed a threat, no matter

how seemingly "small" an abode it was housed in. This was the atmosphere in which *a little history* was initiated.

At the same time, in addition to the war being waged against Iraq, the domestic backlash against the cultural and political openings provided in the aftermath of 9/11 gained momentum. The neo-conservative grasp of the crucial importance of culture flawlessly insinuated itself into liberal discourse, ghettoizing and relegating cultural activities to the sphere of special interests and money-making, creating more false debates to mask a concerted economic and conceptual assault on public space and public education. As a vocal and long-time advocate for both, Dewey, from the late-'90s, began to run into serious headwinds. By the middle of the next decade, he was fighting a battle to maintain the viability and integrity of the institution. He eventually secured a 25-year municipal lease for the building but the conceptual activity-generating model he had put in place, attempting to forge a national and international role from a particular location with a particular history, had indeed been noticed. Many of the classic features of control and suppression went into effect: threat, innuendo, the looming potential of the press to smear and distort, local, regional, and national political tilts, withdrawal of funding, loss of autonomy, and above all, silence over what was being achieved culturally, and so of debate over its contribution. With Dewey's effectively forced departure as director after securing the lease, the model he had envisioned of a cohesive unit—an institution fostering live presentation, discussions, workshops, tributes, and festivals, with an archive, magazine, and publishing venture— was fragmented and blocked. While this breakdown and suppression might seem marginal, taking place at the outskirts of an alternative cultural realm, it is indicative of the deep political processes *a little history* addresses, and it is a story that deserves to be told in greater detail. This was the contentious climate in which work on *a little history* advanced in fits and starts, and was held back.

As far as the editing of the book itself goes, while political and structural forces can determine the options available, as Olson so acutely put it, "man lives among public fact as among private fact" and "either is solely a face of the double of the real." Books are made by people, and collaborative projects can demand a price from those engaging in them that cannot be calculated ahead of time. To begin with, entering into such a process entails commitment and risk, since one is no longer simply following one's own trajectory. Of course, small press editor/publishers not only commit themselves intellectually, creatively and, in this case, politically, but with resources as well, giving extensive time and money to an endeavor that is under assault from all sides: from the dearth of venues to review books or the intricacies of getting books to readers, to much more.

The complexities of this project, and the constraints that it ran up against, turned this into a drawn out process that taxed spontaneity in every way. To begin with, the materials themselves were disparate, particularly the two core lectures centered on Olson. Transforming lectures projected at specific audiences at different times into a coherent conceptual narrative was no mean feat. Attaching different moving parts to this only made things more complicated, some of these elicited and suggested by Dewey, others by me. Throughout, his commitment to following trails of detail and theme to extract the goods and turn thought into meaning has been uncompromising, with insights gained in one part reflected and reiterated in another, a process demanding intelligence, attention to implication and detail, and stamina all around. Dewey's core conception of the book as a dynamic object comprised of many material and related parts presents a truly unconventional and subversive model that can translate into useful political and aesthetic terms, even given the fact this model has now been detached from public space as an originary site. The biggest problem, however, was that, in retrospect, much of the editing process and the extensive delays around it, for various reasons, ran against my ways of working. This contributed to not being able to detach myself from past work and set off on new trajectories. Dewey's tenacity was both a blessing and a curse. At various points in the process I was more than ready to publish the book as a collection of texts, and let them stand as such for the record. In the age-old tension between collecting, writing, and editing, I generally have sided with the collection and presentation of materials for the record, as a precise reflection of times, places, situations, and contexts. Editing by another can work against this. In many ways, this was the significance of Donald Allen's approach in his essential *Writing* series, where one is simply given materials, in an almost archival manner. His series remains a storehouse of treasures from those writers associated with the New American Poetry, the name of the landmark anthology he himself edited. Clearly, Dewey's editing model presents something radically different: namely, commitment to a journey of discovery in which the materials at hand are subjected to an exhaustive and relentless questioning, to see what else they can yield. I have no doubt that he is the strongest representative of this model I have yet encountered. I also have no doubt that, in my own case, despite the length of time involved and the accompanying frustrations, the yield has been rich. But time can also be an impediment. I wonder what new paths I could *not* embark on, feeling stuck, as I was, in the recirculation and further articulation of ideas that had, in some sense, already served their initial function for me. Perhaps that is the point of editing, in which case editors are indeed at odds with writers, and editors kept from proper resources particularly so. This raises a number of crucial questions. How should writers and editors proceed, together and separately, and what are their different interests? Does the artist need to be "autonomous," if that is even possible? How does a writer remain true to the nuanced particularities of vision, syntax, and meaning when working with an editor? Are there times when we're better off without editing? Under what conditions can editors advance creative work and useful reflection? Is a compilation of materials more accurate than older work edited by a person who didn't initiate them? Is an edited text too little or too much? Given the crucial role of editing as a form of censorship under the national security state—and the residue of that legacy permeates our literary culture—how can editing reassert its crucial function as both creative initiator and instigator of more fulfilled work? These are vexing and difficult questions that get to the heart of the nature and relationship of cultural politics and political representation, but they are questions that, in this case, can only be left open to readers and a time when I also become a reader of this work.

—Ammiel Alcalay,
August 2012

Thanks, of course, to Fred Dewey, for the work, support, and for seeing this through on all levels, from concept to editing and design, and to Volker Schartner for meticulous attention to the details of preparing the design for print. Sincere thanks to Robert Booras and Zohra Saed for their patience, and for taking on the concept of the book. Thanks to the many editors, inviters, and interlocutors along the way: Bruce Andrews, Amiri Baraka, Anselm Berrigan, Lee Briccetti, Kathleen Cleaver, Diane di Prima, Kristen Gallagher, E. Tracy Grinnell, Viktor Ivančić, Erica Kaufman, Michael Kelleher, Steve Kurtz, Igor Lasić, Brendan Lorber, Ivan Lovrenović, Scott Malcomson, Ralph Maud, Semezdin Mehmedinović, Albert Mobilio, William Sandoe, Ramsey Scott, Robert Sharrard, Hani Shukrallah, and Lenora Todaro. Thanks to so many at the CUNY Graduate Center, first and foremost and always, to the students. And with particular thanks to the late Neil Smith at the Center for Place, Culture, and Politics, to Aoibheann Sweeney (Executive Director of the Center for the Humanities), and to Omar Dahbour and John Collins, leaders of a seminar I participated in where some of these materials were first aired. Thanks as well to Patrick Lannan and Jo Chapman at the Lannan Foundation, to Mark McMorris and Penn Szittya who kindly initiated the process to have me be the first holder of the Lannan Chair in Poetics at Georgetown University where a crucial stage of synthesis took place. Special thanks to Barry Maxwell who invited me to speak at Cornell, and then to Jane Sprague who chose to transcribe my lecture there and initiate Palm Press with a publication of her transcription. Many thanks to Mikayla Zagoria-Moffet for her invaluable assistance on the index, to Maryam Parhizkar for further help on the index, and to Maryam, Kyle Waugh, and Bradley Lubin for their scrupulous proofreading.

This book developed from a broad range of materials written or spoken in a wide variety of circumstances. Below is a list of forms and versions that went into the mix, in roughly chronological order:

"A Fading Poetry," *The New York Times* and *International Herald Tribune*, April 4 and 6, 2001

"Disaster Areas: Jalal Toufic's Hybrid Poetics," *Voice Literary Supplement*, April, 2001

"Guided Missives: *Selected Letters of Charles Olson*," *Bookforum*, Fall, 2001

"a little history," in *The Form of Our Uncertainty*, a tribute to Gil Ott, edited by Kristen Gallagher (Buffalo & Tucson: Chax Press/Handwritten Press, 2001)

"Sunday Drive: A Memoir of Charles Olson," *Minutes of the Charles Olson Society*, #45, April, 2002

Poetry, Politics and Translation: American Isolation & the Middle East (Ithaca: Palm Press, 2003); edited by Jane Sprague, with her transcription of a lecture given in the Critical Perspectives on the War on Terror series, sponsored by the Cornell Forum for Justice and Peace, Cornell University, November 7, 2002

"Politics & Imagination: After the Fall of Baghdad," *Al-Ahram Weekly*, July 3–9, 2003

"Creative Activism," *Al-Ahram Weekly*, August 14–20, 2003

"Writing the Body Collective: Abdellatif Laabi's Visionary Poetics," forward to *The World's Embrace: Selected Poems* by Abdellatif Laabi (San Francisco: City Lights, 2003)

"Many Happy Returns," on Vincent Ferrini, *Beyond Baroque*, Vol. 26, No. 2, ed. Fred Dewey, 2004

"Passwords: On Charles Olson," presented at Poets House, February 18, 2004

"Battle Lines: The Letters of Robert Duncan & Denise Levertov," in *Bookforum*, March, 2004

"Academic Freedom In America—Postcript: A Conversation with the Critical Art Ensemble," Center for the Humanities at the CUNY Graduate Center; February 18, 2005; another version of this also appeared in the *Cold River Review*, volume 3, No. 1, Spring, 2008

"Introduction to Adonis; delivered at An Evening with Adonis" (with Pierre Joris, Mark McMorris, and Anne Waldman), part of the Arab Cultural Festival and Beautiful November Poetry Conference, CUNY Graduate Center, November 4, 2005

"On the Limits of Translation," an interview with Ramsey Scott (www.loggernaut.org/interviews/ammielalcalay, 2005)

"Olson Now" with Michael Kelleher, *The Poetry Project Newsletter*, October/December 2005

"OlsonNow: A Conference of Working Groups on Charles

Olson," organized with Mike Kelleher and Fred Dewey, The Poetry Project at St. Marks Church, co-sponsored by Fred Dewey & Beyond Baroque, December 3, 2005

"notes for Bruce Andrews," *New Yipes Reader* (edited by Bruce Andrews), no. 5, January, 2006

"Sadder than Water," by Samih al-Qasim, *The Poetry Project Newsletter* #210; February–March, 2007

"Kent Johnson: By Way of Introduction," appeared as "Kent Johnson: umjesto uvoda," in a Bosnian collection of Kent Johnson's, *Lirska Poezijia Nakon Auschwitza* (Sarajevo/Zagreb: Ajfelov most, 2007)

"Introduction to Keynote Address Delivered by Amiri Baraka" at "Let Freedom Ring: Art and Democracy in the King Years," a Lannan Literary Symposium, Georgetown University, April 17, 2008

OlsonNow: A blog on the poetry and poetics of Charles Olson, edited by Michael Kelleher and Ammiel Alcalay (http://olsonnow.blogspot.com)

"Afterword" to Diane di Prima, *R.D.'s H.D, Lost & Found,* 2.3 (New York: Center for the Humanities, 2011)

"What to Whom," *Aufgabe* #11, 2012

WORKS USED

Adonis. *An Introduction to Arab Poetics*, trans. from Arabic by Catherine Cobham (London: Saqi Books, 2003)

_____. *A Time Between Ashes and Roses*, trans. from Arabic by Shawkat M. Tourawa (Syracuse University, 2005)

Alcalay, Ammiel. *from the warring factions*, ed. Fred Dewey. Preface by Diane di Prima, disc. with Benjamin Hollander (Los Angeles & New York: Re: public / UpSet, 2012, new edition; original edition, Beyond Baroque 2002)

_____. *"neither wit nor gold" (from then)* (Brooklyn: Ugly Duckling, 2011)

_____. *Islanders* (San Francisco: City Lights, 2010)

_____, Kate Tarlow Morgan. "The Body Is A House," *The Worcester Review*, Vol. XXXI, # 1 & 2 (2010)

_____. *Scrapmetal* (New York: Factory School, 2007)

_____. *Memories of Our Future: Selected Essays 1982–1999* (San Francisco: City Lights, 1999)

_____, ed. and trans. *Keys to the Garden* (San Francisco: City Lights, 1996)

_____. *After Jews and Arabs: Remaking Levantine Culture* (Minneapolis: University of Minnesota, 1993)

Alleg, Henri. *The Question*, trans. from French by John Calder, intro. by Jean-Paul Sartre (New York: George Braziller, 1958)

_____. *The Question*, with new afterword by the author (Lincoln: University of Nebraska, 2006)

Allen, Donald, Warren Tallman. *The Poetics of the New American Poetry* (New York: Grove, 1973)

Allison, Robert J. *The Crescent Obscured: The United States and Muslim World, 1776–1815* (University of Chicago, 2000)

Anderson, Perry. "Force and Consent," *New Left Review* 25 (http://www.newleftreview.net/NLR25101.shtml)

Apess, William. *A Son of the Forest*, ed. B. O'Connell
(Amherst: University of Massachusetts, 1997)

Ayler, Albert. *Holy Ghost: rare and unissued recordings
(1962–70) 9 CD Spirit Box* (Austin: Revenant, 2005)

Baker, Nicholson. *Double Fold* (New York: Vintage, 2001)

Baker, Raymond W., Shereen T. Ismael, Tareq Y. Ismael, eds.
Cultural Cleansing in Iraq (London: Pluto, 2010)

Baldwin, James. *The Evidence of Things Not Seen* (New York:
Henry Holt, 1985)

Baraka, Amiri. *Tales of the Out & The Gone* (New York:
Akashic Books, 2007)

_____. *Somebody Blew Up America & Other Poems*
(Philipsburg: House of Nehesi, 2003)

_____. *The Fiction of LeRoi Jones/Amiri Baraka* (Chicago:
Lawrence Hill Books, 2000)

_____. [Jones, LeRoi] *Blues People: Negro Music in White
America* (William Morrow, 1999)

_____. *Daggers and Javelins: Essays 1974–1979* (New York:
William Morrow and Company, Inc. 1984)

_____. *The Autobiography of LeRoi Jones/Amiri Baraka* (New
York: Freundlich Books, 1984)

_____, ed. *African Congress: A Documentary of the First
Modern Pan-African Congress* (New York: William
Morrow and Company, Inc., 1972)

_____. *Raise, Race, Rays, Raze: Essays Since 1965* (New York:
Random House, 1972)

_____. *Black Magic: Poetry 1961–1967* (Indianapolis and
New York: Bobbs-Merrill, 1969)

_____, Edward Dorn. *Selections from the Collected Letters:
1959–1960*. ed. Claudia Moreno Pisano. *Lost & Found*,
1.1 (New York: Center for the Humanities, 2009)

Barry, Jan, W.D. Ehrhart, eds. *Demilitarized Zones: Veterans
After Vietnam* (Perkasie: East River Anthology, 1976)

Basso, Keith H. *Wisdom Sits In Places: Landscape and Language Among the Western Apache* (Albuquerque: University of New Mexico, 1996)

Bertholf, Robert J., Albert Gelpi, eds. *The Letters of Robert Duncan and Denise Levertov* (Berkeley: University of California, 2004)

Boughedir, Ferid, director. *Caméra Arabe*. Documentary, VHS (1984)

Bourdieu, Pierre. *The Algerians*, trans. from the French by Alan C.M. Ross, preface Raymond Aron (Boston: Beacon Press, 1962)

Boyle, Richard. *Flower of the Dragon: The Breakdown of the U.S. Army in Vietnam* (San Francisco: Ramparts, 1972)

Bragdon, Kathleen J. *Native People of Southern New England, 1500–1650* (Norman: University of Oklahoma, 1996)

Brandt, Daniel. "Multiculturalism and the Ruling Elite," *NewBase NewsLine* No. 3, October–December 1993 (http://www.namebase.org/news03.html)

Brotherston, Gordon, *Book of the Fourth World* (Cambridge University, 1992)

Bruner, Edward. *Cold War Poetry* (Urbana and Chicago: University of Illinois, 2001)

Butler, Smedley D. *War Is a Racket* (Los Angeles: Feral House, 2003)

Byrd, Don. *The Poetics of the Common Knowledge* (Albany: State University of New York, 1994)

_____. *Charles Olson's Maximus* (Urbana: University of Illinois, 1980)

Cabral, Amilcar. *Return to the Source: Selected Speeches* (New York: Monthly Review, 1974)

Cassady, Carolyn. *Off the Road* (Woodstock & New York: Overlook Press, 2008)

Cassady, Neal. *Collected Letters, 1944–1967*, ed. Dave Moore (New York: Penguin, 2004)

Césaire, Aimé. *Discourse on Colonialism*, trans. from French by Joan Pinkham, intro. Robin D. G. Kelley (New York: Monthly Review, 2001)

Churchill, Ward, Jim Vander Wall. *The COINTELPRO Papers: Documents from the FBI's Secret Wars Against Dissent in the United States* (Cambridge: South End, 2002)

_____. *Agents of Repression: The FBI's Secret Wars Against the Black Panther Party and the American Indian Movement* (Cambridge: South End, 2002)

Clarke, John. *In the Analogy* (Toronto/Buffalo: shuffaloff, 1997)

_____. *From Feathers to Iron: A Concourse of World Poetics* (San Francisco: Tombouctou/Convivio, 1987)

Clay, Steven, Rodney Phillips. *A Secret Location on the Lower East Side: Adventures in Writing, 1960–1980* (New York: Granary Books, 1998)

Coen, Joel and Ethan. *The Big Lebowski.* DVD (Polygram, 1998)

Coleman, Wanda. *The Riot Inside Me* (Boston: David R. Godine, 2005)

Collins, Jess. *Jess: A Grand Collage 1951–1993*, ed. Michael Auping (Buffalo: Albright-Knox, 1993)

Creeley, Robert. *The 1963 Vancouver Poetry Conference / Robert Creeley's Contexts of Poetry with Daphne Marlatt's Journal Entries*, ed. Ammiel Alcalay. *Lost & Found, 1.5* (New York: Center for the Humanities, 2009)

Critical Art Ensemble. *The Molecular Invasion* (New York: Autonomedia, 2002)

_____. *Digital Resistance* (New York: Autonomedia, 2001)

Cronon, William. *Changes in the Land: Indians, Colonists, and the Ecology of New England* (New York: Hill & Wang, 2003)

Darwish, Mahmoud. *In the Presence of Absence*, trans. from Arabic by Sinan Antoon (Brooklyn: Archipelago, 2011)

_____. *Journal of an Ordinary Grief*, trans. from Arabic by Ibrahim Muhawi (Brooklyn: Archipelago, 2010)

_____. *Memory for Forgetfulness,* trans. from Arabic by Ibrahim Muhawi (Berkeley: University of California, 1995)

de Beauvoir, Simone, Gisele Halimi. *Djamila Boupacha,* trans. from French by Peter Green (New York: Macmillan, 1962)

Derounian-Stodola, Kathryn Zabelle. *Women's Indian Captivity Narratives* (Penguin, 1998)

Dewey, Fred. "The Muse Revisited, Or Simone Forti's Non-Fictional Imagination," afterword to Simone Forti *Oh, Tongue,* ed. by Fred Dewey (Los Angeles: re: public, 2013)

_____. *A Polis For New Conditions* (Los Angeles: FRDewey Projects 2010); reprinted *Zen Monster,* Vol. 1, No. 3, 2011

di Prima, Diane. *The Mysteries of Vision: Some Notes on H.D.,* ed. Ana Božičević. *Lost & Found,* 2.2 (New York: Center for the Humanities, 2011)

_____. *R.D.'S H.D.,* ed. Ammiel Alcalay. *Lost & Found, 2.3* (New York: Center for the Humanities, 2011)

_____. *Charles Olson Memorial Lecture,* eds. Ammiel Alcalay and Ana Božičević. *Lost & Found, 3.4* (New York: Center for the Humanities, 2012)

_____. *Recollections of My Life as a Woman* (New York: Penguin, 2001)

_____. *Revolutionary Letters* (San Francisco: Last Gasp, 2007

Dorn, Edward. *Charles Olson Memorial Lectures,* ed. Lindsey Freer. *Lost & Found, 3.5* (New York: Center for the Humanities, 2012)

_____. *Ed Dorn Live: Lectures, Interviews, and Outakes,* ed. Joseph Richey (Ann Arbor: University of Michigan, 2007)

_____. *Way More West,* ed. Michael Rothenberg (New York: Penguin, 2007)

_____. "Edward Dorn: American Heretic," *Chicago Review* 49:3/4 & 50:1 (Summer 2004)

_____. *Way West: Stories, Essays & Verse Accounts: 1963–1993* (Black Sparrow, 1993)

_____. *The Collected Poems* (Bolinas: Four Seasons, 1975)

_____, photographs by Leroy Lucas. *The Shoshoneans* (New York: William Morrow, 1966)

Duncan, Robert. *Charles Olson Memorial Lecture,* eds. Ammiel Alcalay, Meira Levinson, Bradley Lubin, Megan Paslawski, Kyle Waugh, and Rachael Wilson. *Lost & Found,* 2.4 (New York: Center for the Humanities, 2011)

_____. *The H.D. Book* (Berkeley: University of California, 2011)

_____. *Fictive Certainties* (New York: New Directions, 1985)

_____. *Ground Work: Before the War* (New York: New Directions, 1984)

_____. *Bending the Bow* (New York: New Directions, 1969)

_____. *NET Outtakes* 11.2.1965. VHS (The American Poetry Archive; Poetry Center, San Francisco State University)

_____. *The Opening of the Field* (New York: Grove, 1960)

Durham, Jimmie. *A Certain Lack of Coherence: Writings on Art and Cultural Politics* (London: Kala, 1993)

Ehrhart, W.D. *Beautiful Wreckage: New & Selected Poems* (Easthampton: Adastra, 1999)

_____. *In the Shadow of Vietnam: Essays, 1977–1991* (McFarland & Company, 1991)

_____, ed. *Carrying the Darkness: Poetry of the Vietnam War* (New York: Avon, 1985)

Eshleman, Clayton. *Juniper Fuse: Upper Paleolithic Imagination & the Construction of the Underworld* (Hanover: Wesleyan/University Press of New England, 2003)

Fanon, Frantz. *The Wretched of the Earth,* trans. from French by Constance Farrington. preface by Jean-Paul Sartre (New York: Grove, 1965)

Fass, Ekbert. *Young Robert Duncan: Portrait of the Poet as Homosexual in Society* (Santa Barbara: Black Sparrow, 1983)

Ferrini, Henry. *Polis is This: Charles Olson and the Persistence of Place.* (http://www.polisisthis.com)

Ferrini, Vincent. *The Whole Song: Selected Poems,* eds. Kenneth Warren, Fred Whitehead (Urbana & Chicago: University of Illinois, 2004)

_____. *No Smoke* (Gloucester: Curious Traveller, 1999) (reprint of 1941 edition)

Fetzer, Jim, Four Arrows (Don Trent Jacobs). *American Assassination: The Strange Death of Senator Paul Wellstone* (Brooklyn: Vox Pop, 2004)

Forbes, Jack D. *Africans and Native Americans: The Language of Race and the Evolution of Red-Black Peoples* (Urbana & Chicago: University of Illinois, 1993)

Franklin, H. Bruce. *Vietnam and Other American Fantasies* (Amherst: University of Massachusetts, 2000)

Gazecki, William. *Waco: The Rules of Engagement.* DVD (New Yorker Films, 2003)

Ginsberg, Allen. *Spontaneous Mind: Selected Interviews 1958–1996* (New York: Harper Collins, 2001)

George, Alan. *Syria: Neither Bread Nor Freedom* (London: Zed Books, 2003)

Terry Golway, ed. *American Political Speeches* (New York: Penguin, 2012)

González, Roberto J. *American Counterinsurgency: Human Science and the Human Terrain* (Chicago: Prickly Paradigm, 2009)

Grace, Nancy M., Ronna C. Johnson. *Breaking the Rule of Cool: Interviewing and Reading Women Beat Writers* (Jackson: University Press of Mississippi, 2004)

Graeber, David. *Toward An Anthropological Theory of Value:* (New York: Palgrave, 2001)

_____. *Fragments of an Anarchist Anthropology* (Chicago: Prickly Paradigm, 2004)

Griffin, David Ray. *The New Pearl Harbor* (Northampton: Olive Branch, 2004)

_____. *The 9/11 Commission Report: Omissions and Distortions* (Northampton: Olive Branch, 2005)

Hare, Nathan. "Algiers 1969: A Report on the Pan-African Cultural Festival," in *New Black Voices*, ed. Abraham Chapman (New York: New American Library, 1972)

Harris, Wilson. *Selected Essays* (London and New York: Routledge, 1999)

Havelock, Eric A. *Preface to Plato* (New York: Grosset & Dunlap, 1963)

Henderson, David. *'Scuse Me While I Kiss the Sky: The Life of Jimi Hendrix: Voodoo Child*, revised edition (New York: Atria, 2008)

Hodgson, Marshall G.S. *Rethinking World History: Essays on Europe, Islam and World History* (Cambridge: Cambridge University, 1993)

_____. *The Venture of Islam* (Chicago: University of Chicago, 1974), 3 volumes.

Hollander, Benjamin. *Vigilance,* afterword by Murat Nemet-Nejat (Los Angeles: Beyond Baroque, 2005)

Howe, Susan, *The Birth-mark: unsettling the wilderness in American literary history* (Hanover: Wesleyan/University Press of New England, 1993)

_____. *My Emily Dickinson* (North Atlantic, 1985)

Hukanović, Rezak. *The Tenth Circle of Hell*, ed. Ammiel Alcalay, trans. from Bosnian by Colleen London and Midhat Ridjanović (New York: Basic Books, 1996)

Hurston, Zora Neale. *Folklore, Memoirs, and Other Writings* (New York: Library of America, 1995)

Johnson, Chalmers. *Dismantling the Empire: America's Last Best Hope* (New York: Metropolitan Books, 2011)

_____. *Nemesis: The Last Days of the American Republic* (New York: Metropolitan Books, 2007)

_____. "The Smash of Civilizations," *The Crisis of the American Republic* (New York: Metropolitan Books, 2006)

_____. *The Sorrows of Empire: Militarism, Secrecy, & the End of the Republic* (New York: Metropolitan Books, 2004)

Julien, Isaac. Director, *Baadasssss Cinema*. DVD (Docurama, 2002)

Kaufman, Bob. *Cranial Guitar: Selected Poems* (Minneapolis: Coffee House, 1996)

Kerouac, Jack. *Windblown World: The Journals of Jack Kerouac 1947–1954,* ed. Douglas Brinkley (New York: Penguin, 2004)

_____. *Selected Letters 1957–1969*, ed. Ann Charters (New York: Penguin, 1999)

_____ and Ginsberg, Allen. *The Letters,* eds. Bill Morgan and David Stanford (New York: Penguin, 2010)

Kerry, John and Vietnam Veterans Against the War. *The New Soldier* (New York: Collier Books, 1971) and at http://freekerrybook.com

Klein, Joe. *Woody Guthrie: A Life* (New York: Dell, 1980)

Kubler, George. *The Shape of Time* (New Haven: Yale University, 1962)

Kyger, Joanne. *Letters To & From*, eds. Ammiel Alcalay and Joanne Kyger. *Lost & Found: 3.7* (New York: Center for the Humanities, 2012)

Laabi, Abdellatif. *World's Embrace: Selected Poems*, ed., intro. by Victor Reinking, trans. Anne George et al, foreword Ammiel Alcalay (San Francisco: City Lights, 2003)

_____. *Rue de Retour,* trans. from French by Jacqueline Kaye, foreword by Breyton Breytenbach (London: Readers International, 1989)

_____, ed. *Souffles* (http://clicnet.swarthmore.edu/souffles/sommaire.html)

Laroui, Abdallah. *The Crisis of the Arab Intellectual,* trans. from French by Diarmid Cammell (Berkeley: University of California, 1977)

Lawrence, D.H. *Studies in Classic American Literature* (New York: Viking, 1964)

Lepore, Jill. *Name of War: King Philip's War & Origins of American Identity* (New York: Vintage, 1999)

Le Sueur, James D. *Uncivil War: Intellectuals and Identity Politics During the Decolonization of Algeria* (Philadelphia: University of Pennsylvania, 2001)

London Review of Books (http://www.lrb.co.uk/v23/n20/letters.html)

Macey, David. *Frantz Fanon: A Biography* (New York: Picador, 2000)

Mamdani, Mahmood. *When Victims Become Killers: Colonialism, Nativism, and the Genocide in Rwanda* (Princeton University, 2001)

Matlin, David. *Prisons: Inside the New America From Vernooykill Creek to Abu Ghraib* (Berkeley: North Atlantic Books, 2005)

Marlatt, Daphne. *Selected Writing,* intro. by Fred Wah, (Vancouver: Talonbooks, 1980)

Maud, Ralph. *Charles Olson at the Harbor* (Vancouver: Talonbooks, 2008)

_____. ed. *Minutes of the Charles Olson Society,* Vancouver (issues 7; 8; 10; 38; 46)

_____, ed. *A Charles Olson Reader* (Manchester: Carcanet, 2005)

_____. *What Does Not Change: The Significance of Charles Olson's "The Kingfishers"* (Madison, NJ: Farleigh Dickinson University, 1998)

_____. *Charles Olson's Reading: A Biography* (Carbondale and Edwardsville: Southern Illinois University, 1996)

McAlister, Melani. *Epic Encounters: Culture, Media, and U.S. Interests in the Middle East, 1945–2000* (Berkeley: University of California, 2001)

McClure, Michael. *Scratching the Beat Surface* (New York: Penguin, 1982)

McCoy, Alfred W. *A Question of Torture: CIA Interrogation from the Cold War to the War on Terror* (New York: Metropolitan Books, 2006)

_____. *The Politcs of Heroin: CIA Complicity in the Drug Trade* (Chicago: Lawrence Hill Books, 2003)

McNaughton, Duncan. *Capricci* (Bolinas: Blue Millennium, 2003)

Mehmedinović, Semezdin. *Nine Alexandrias*, trans. from Bosnian, preface by Ammiel Alcalay (City Lights, 2003)

_____. *Sarajevo Blues*, trans. from Bosnian & preface, Ammiel Alcalay (San Francisco: City Lights, 1998)

Melhem, D. H. *Heroism in the New Black Poetry* (Lexington: University Press of Kentucky, 1990)

Morgan, Kate Tarlow. *Circles & Boundaries*, afterword by Ammiel Alcalay (Queens, New York: Factory School, 2010)

_____, Ammiel Alcalay. "The Body Is A House," *The Worcester Review*, Volume XXXI, Nos. 1 & 2 (2010)

Naquet, Pierre Vidal. *Torture: Cancer of Democracy, France and Algeria 1954–1962*, trans. from French by Barry Richard (Hammondsworth: Penguin, 1963)

Neilson, Jim. *Warring Fictions: Cultural Politics and the Vietnam War Narrative* (Jackson: University Press of Mississippi, 1998)

Nelson, Cary. *Revolutionary Memory: Recovering Poetry of the American Left* (London and New York: Routledge, 2001)

_____. *Repression and Recovery: Modern American Poetry and the Politics of Cultural Memory, 1910–1945* (Madison: University of Wisconsin, 1989)

Nicosia, Gerald. *Home to War: A History of the Vietnam Veterans' Movement* (New York: Three Rivers, 2001)

Nielsen, Aldon Lynn. *Integral Music: Languages of African American Innovation* (Tuscaloosa: University of Alabama, 2004)

Notley, Alice. *The Descent of Alette* (New York: Penguin, 1992)

_____, Douglas Oliver. *The Scarlet Compendium* (New York: Scarlet Editions, 1992)

Olson, Charles. *Muthologos: Lectures and Interviews*, revised 2nd edition, ed. Ralph Maud (Vancouver: Talonbooks, 2010)

_____. *Letters Home, 1949–1969*, ed. David Rich, preface by Peter Anastas (Gloucester: Cape Ann Museum, 2010)

_____. *OlsonNow*, archived materials from Olson Now events (http://www.OlsonNow.blogspot.com)

_____. *Selected Letters*, ed. Ralph Maud (Berkeley: University of California, 2000)

_____. *Charles Olson and Frances Boldereff: A Modern Correspondence*, eds. Ralph Maud, Sharon Thesen (Hanover and London: Wesleyan/University Press of New England, 1999)

_____. *Collected Prose*, eds. Donald Allen, Benjamin Friedlander (Berkeley: University of California, 1997)

_____. *Maximus to Gloucester: The Letters and Poems of Charles Olson to the Editor of the Gloucester Daily Times 1962–1969*, ed. Peter Anastas (Gloucester: Ten Pound Island Book Company, 1992)

_____. *Charles Olson & Robert Creeley: The Complete Correspondence*, vol. 1-10 (Santa Barbara: Black Sparrow, 1980–1990)

_____. *Letters for Origin*, ed. Albert Glover (New York: Paragon House, 1988)

_____. *Collected Poems*, ed. George F. Butterick (Berkeley: University of California, 1987)

_____. *The Maximus Poems*, ed. George F. Butterick (Berkeley: University of California, 1983)

_____. *Muthologos: The Collected Lectures and Interviews*, ed. George Butterick (Bolinas: Four Seasons Foundation, 1978)

_____. *Charles Olson & Ezra Pound: An Encounter at St. Elizabeths*, ed. Catherine Seelye (New York: Grossman, 1975)

_____. *Charles Olson in Connecticut: Last Lectures*. As heard by John Cech, Oliver Ford, Peter Rittner (Iowa City: The Windhover Press, 1974)

_____. *NET Outtakes*. VHS (The American Poetry Archive; Poetry Center, San Francisco State University, 3.12.1966)

Park, Milbury and Angela M.H. Schuster. *The Looting of the Iraq Museum, Baghdad* (New York: Harry N. Abrams, 2005)

Parker, Edie Kerouac. *You'll Be Okay: My Life With Jack Kerouac* (San Francisco: City Lights, 2007)

Pontecorvo, Gillo. *The Battle Of Algiers*. DVD (Criterion Collection, 2004)

Pound, Ezra. *The Pisan Cantos*, ed. Richard Sieburth (New York: New Directions, 2003)

al-Qasim, Samih. *Sadder The Water,* trans. from Arabic by Nazih Kassis, intro. Adina Hoffman (Jerusalem: Ibis Editions, 2006)

Rasula, Jed. *The American Poetry Wax Museum: Reality Effects, 1940–1990* (Urbana: National Council of Teachers of English, 1996)

Rights in Conflict: "The Chicago Police Riot": The Official Report to the National Commission on the Causes and Prevention of Violence (New York: Signet, 1968)

Rothenberg, Jerome, Pierre Joris, eds. *Poems for the Millenium, Volume Two: From Postwar to Millenium* (Berkeley: University of California, 1998)

_____, Diane Rothenberg, eds. *Symposium of the Whole* (Berkeley: University of California, 1983)

Rottman, Larry, Jan Barry, Basil T. Paquet, eds. *Winning Hearts and Minds: War Poems by Vietnam Veterans* (New York: 1st Casualty, 1972)

Rumaker, Michael. *Black Mountain Days* (Asheville: Black Mountain Press, 2003), new edition (New York: Triton, 2012)

_____. *Robert Duncan in San Francisco* (San Francisco: Grey Fox, 1996), new edition, eds. Ammiel Alcalay and Megan Paslawski. (San Francisco: City Lights, 2012)

_____. *Selected Letters*, ed. Megan Paslawski *Lost & Found* 3.6 (New York: Center for the Humanities, 2012)

Rukeyser, Muriel. *The Collected Poems of Muriel Rukeyser* (University of Pittsburgh, 2005)

_____. *Willard Gibbs* (Woodbridge: Ox Bow Press, 1988)

_____. *Out of Silence: Selected Poems* (Evanston: Triquarterly Books, 1997)

_____. *The Life of Poetry* (Ashfield: Paris Press, 1996)

Ruppert, Michael C. *Crossing the Rubicon: The Decline of the American Empire at the End of the Age of Oil* (Gabriola Island, BC: New Society, 2004)

Sanders, Ed. *Investigative Poetry* (San Francisco: City Lights, 1976)

Sauer, Carl O. *Selected Essays 1963–1975* (Berkeley: Turtle Island Foundation, 1981)

_____. *Land & Life: A Selection of Writings* (Berkeley: University of California, 1963)

_____. "Forward to Historical Geography" (http://www.color ado.edu/geography/giw/sauerco/1941_fhg/1941_fhg.html)

Schotz, E. Martin. *History Will Not Absolve Us: Orwellian control, public denial, and the murder of President Kennedy* (Brookline: Kurtz, Ulmer, & DeLucia, 1996)

Scorsese, Martin. *No Direction Home: Bob Dylan.* DVD
    (Paramount, 2005)

Scott, Peter Dale. *Deep Politics and the Death of JFK*
    (Berkeley: University of California, 1993)

Scully, James. *Line Break: poetry as social practice*
    (Willimantic: Curbstone, 2005)

Serfaty, Abraham. *Écrits de prison sur la Palestine* (Paris:
    Éditions Arcantère, 1992)

Shepp, Archie. *Live at the Pan-African Festival* CD (Fuel
    2000 Records)

Silkin, Jon, ed. *The Penguin Book of First World War Poetry*
    (New York: Penguin, 1996)

Simpson, Christopher. *Blowback: America's Recruitment of
    Nazis and Its Effect on the Cold War* (New York: Collier
    Books, 1988)

_____. *Science of Coercion: Communication Research &
    Psychological Warfare 1945–1960* (New York: Oxford
    University, 1994)

Silber, Glenn and Barry Alexander. *The War At Home.* VHS /
    DVD (First Run Features, 1979)

Sinclair, John. *The John and Leni Sinclair Papers at the Bentley
    Historical Library* (http://www.umich.edu/~bhl/bhl/ref
    home/jls/John.htm)

Slymovics, Susan. *The Performance of Human Rights
    in Morocco* (Philadelphia: University of Pennsylvania,
    2005)

Sloan, Mary Margaret, ed. *Moving Borders: Three Decades of
    Innovative Writing by Women* (Jersey City: Talisman
    House, 1998)

Smith, Richard Cándida. *Utopia and Dissent: Art, Poetry,
    and Politics in California* (Berkeley: University of
    California, 1995)

Spears, André. "Warlords of Atlantis: Chasing the Demon of Analogy in the America(s) of Lawrence, Artaud and Olson," *Canadian Review of Comparative Literature*, June–Sept. 2001

Spicer, Jack. *Jack Spicer's Beowulf Parts I & II*, eds. David Hadbawnik, Sean Reynolds. *Lost & Found* 2.5 (New York: Center for the Humanities, 2011)

_____. *The House that Jack Built: The Collected Lectures of Jack Spicer*, ed. Peter Gizzi (Hanover and London: Wesleyan/University Press of New England, 1998)

Stein, Charles. *The Secret of the Black Chrysanthemum* (Barrytown: Station Hill, 1987)

Szwed, John F. *Space is the Place: The Lives and Times of Sun Ra* (Da Capo, 1998)

Talisman (Jersey City: Talisman House), Issues 1, 6, 17

Tedlock, Dennis. *Finding the Center* (Lincoln: University of Nebraska, 1978)

The Challenge of Crime in a Free Society: A Report by the President's Commission on Law Enforcement and Administration of Justice (New York: Avon, 1968)

The Kerner Report of the National Advisory Commission on Civil Disorders (New York: Bantam, 1968)

The 9/11 Commission Report: Final Report of the National Commission on Terrorist Attacks Upon the United States (New York: W.W. Norton & Company, no date; New York Times/St. Martins, 2004)

Thompson, Paul. *The Terror Timelines: Year By Year, Day By Day, Minute By Minute* (New York: Harper Collins, 2004)

Tillion, Germaine. *France & Algeria: Complementary Enemies*, trans. from French by Richard Howard (New York: Alfred A. Knopf, 1961)

_____. *Algeria: The Realities*, trans. from French by Ronald Matthews (New York: Alfred A. Knopf, 1958)

Toufic, Jalal. *Forthcoming* (Berkeley: Atelos, 2001)

Tyler, Royall. *The Algerine Captive* (New York: Modern Library, 2002)

Tyson, Timothy B. *Radio Free Dixie: Robert F. Williams and the Roots of Black Power* (Chapel Hill: University of North Carolina)

Valentine, Douglas. *The Phoenix Program* (New York: Avon, 1990)

Van De Mieroop, Marc. *Cuneiform Texts and the Writing of History* (Routledge: London & New York, 1999)

Wakoski, Diane. *Toward A New Poetry* (Ann Arbor: University of Michigan, 1980)

Waldman, Anne, Laura Wright, eds. *Beats at Naropa: An Anthology* (Minneapolis: Coffee House, 2009)

_____. *Vow to Poetry: Essays, Interviews & Manifestos* (Minneapolis: Coffee House, 2001)

_____, Marilyn Webb, eds. *Talking Poetics From Naropa Institute, Volumes One and Two* (Boulder & London: Shambala, 1978–79)

Warren Commission Report: Report of the President's Commission on the Assassination of President John F. Kennedy (New York: St. Martin's, 1992, reissue)

Weaver, Helen. *The Awakener: A Memoir of Kerouac and the Fifties* (San Francisco: City Lights, 2009)

Whalen, Philip. *Selections from the Journals 1957–1977. Parts I & II*, ed. Brian Unger. *Lost & Found* 1.4 (New York: Center for the Humanities, 2009)

_____. *The Collected Poems of Philip Whalen*, ed. Michael Rothenberg (Hanover: Wesleyan/University Press of New England, 2007)

_____. *On Bear's Head* (New York: Harcourt, Brace & World/Coyote, 1969)

Wieners, John. *The Journal of John Wieners Is To Be Called 707 Scott Street* (Los Angeles: Sun & Moon, 1996)

_____. *Cultural Affairs in Boston,* ed. Raymond Foye (Santa Rosa: Black Sparrow, 1988)

_____. *Selected Poems 1958–1984,* ed. Raymond Foye (Santa Barbara: Black Sparrow, 1986)

_____, Charles Olson. *Selected Correspondence,* ed. Michael Seth Stewart. *Lost & Found* 3.3 (New York: Center for the Humanities, 2012)

Williams, Robert F. *Negroes with Guns* (New York: Masrzani and Munsell, 1962)

Winter Soldier (Milliarium Zero, Winter Films, and Vietnam Veterans Against the War/New Yorker Video, 2006)

Wood, Nancy. *Germaine Tillion, une femme-mémoire* (Paris: Éditions Autrement, 2003)

Zieger, David, dir. *Sir! No Sir!* (Docurama, Displaced Films, 2005)

Poet, novelist, translator, editor, critic, and scholar, AMMIEL ALCALAY grew up in Boston, Massachusetts and spent time in nearby Gloucester, where family friends included Charles Olson and Vincent Ferrini. High school, from 1969 to 1973, particularly when not in attendance, proved instructive. Through the Grolier and Temple Bar Bookshops in Cambridge, he befriended many poets, including John Wieners. Writing came early and remained present despite many different kinds of work, studies at City College, years abroad (living in Jerusalem and sojourning in former Yugoslavia), and completion of a doctorate in Comparative Literature, under the tutelage of the late Allen Mandelbaum. Alcalay is Deputy Chair of the PhD Program in English at the CUNY Graduate Center, and former chair of Classical, Middle Eastern & Asian Languages & Cultures at Queens College. Areas of academic involvement include American Studies, Comparative Literature, Medieval Studies, and Middle Eastern Studies. He was the first holder of the Lannan Visiting Chair in Poetics at Georgetown University and was a visiting professor at Stanford University.

His books include *from the warring factions* (re:public / UpSet, 2012, New Edition), *"neither wit nor gold"(from then)* (Ugly Duckling, 2011), *Islanders* (City Lights, 2010), *Scrapmetal: work in progress* (Factory School, 2007), *Memories of Our Future: Selected Essays, 1982–1999* (City Lights, 1999), and *After Jews and Arabs: Remaking Levantine Culture* (University of Minnesota Press, 1993). One of the only translators working from Bosnia during the war in ex-Yugoslavia, he was largely responsible for the appearance of accounts by Bosnians, including books by journalist Zlatko Dizdarević and camp survivor

Rezak Hukanović. Other translations include *Sarajevo Blues* (City Lights, 1998) and *Nine Alexandrias* (City Lights, 2003) both by Bosnian poet Semezdin Mehmedinović, *Keys to the Garden: New Israeli Writing* (City Lights, 1996), and the co-translation (with Oz Shelach) of *Outcast* by Shimon Ballas (City Lights, 2007). With Megan Paslawski, he co-edited Michael Rumaker's *Robert Duncan in San Francisco* (City Lights, 2012). Along with Anne Waldman, Alcalay was one of the initiators of the Poetry Is News Coalition, and organized, with Mike Kelleher and Fred Dewey, the Olson-Now project. He is the founder and general editor, under the auspices of the PhD program in English and the Center for the Humanities at the CUNY Graduate Center, of *Lost & Found: The CUNY Poetics Document Initiative* (http://center forthehumanities.org/lost-and-found).

*

Writer, editor, teacher, and activist FRED DEWEY's writings have been published internationally, including in the *New Statesman, LA Times,* and *Metropolis.* His publications include the pamphlet *A Polis for New Conditions* (reprinted in *Zen Monster*) and contributions to the anthologies *The Lowndes County Idea, The Architecture of Fear* (Princeton Architecture), *Most Art Sucks* (Smart Art), and *Cork Caucus.* He directed Beyond Baroque Literary/Arts Center in Los Angeles from 1995–2010, building the Center's archive and founding, editing, designing, and publishing a new imprint for the Center featuring first versions of Simone Forti's *Oh, Tongue* and Ammiel Alcalay's *from the warring factions,* as well as seventeen other books and anthologies featuring work by Jean-Luc Godard, Diane di Prima, Abdellatif

Laabi, Daniel Berrigan, and others. Dewey curated the poets monument on the Venice, CA boardwalk and helped place neighborhood councils in LA's city charter. More recently, he conducted a working group on the writings of Hannah Arendt at General Public in Berlin from 2011 to 2012. His forthcoming book is *The School of Public Life* (doormats).

INDEX

S

V

W

UPSET PRESS

Theater of War: The Plot Against the American Mind
Nicholas Powers, 2005

The Comeback's Exoskeleton Matthew Rotando, 2008

Born Palestinian, Born Black & The Gaza Suite
Suheir Hammad, 2010

Halal Pork & Other Stories Cihan Kaan, 2011

Vocalises Jenny Husk, 2012

The Blond Texts & The Age of Embers Nadia Tueni
(translated by Amir Parsa), 2012

RE: PUBLIC / UPSET

from the warring factions Ammiel Alcalay. New edition
with an introduction by Diane di Prima and conversation
with Benjamin Hollander. Edited by Fred Dewey, 2012

a little history Ammiel Alcalay. Edited with a preface
by Fred Dewey, 2012

RE: PUBLIC

Oh, Tongue Simone Forti. New edition with post-script by
Jackson Mac Low. Edited with an afterword by Fred Dewey.
Forthcoming, 2013

All UpSet Press titles can be ordered from upsetpress.org
or from its distributor the University of Arkansas Press.